Text Type and Texture

Functional Linguistics
Series Editor: Robin P. Fawcett, Cardiff University

This series publishes monographs that seek to understand the nature of language by exploring one or other of various cognitive models or in terms of the communicative use of language. It concentrates on studies that are in, or on the borders of, various functional theories of language.

Published:

Functional Dimensions of Ape-Human Discourse
Edited by James D. Benson and William S. Greaves

System and Corpus: Exploring Connections
Edited by Geoff Thompson and Susan Hunston

Meaningful Arrangement: Exploring the Syntactic Description of Texts
Edward McDonald

Systemic Functional Perspectives of Japanese: Descriptions and Applications
Edited by Elizabeth Thomson and William Armour

Explorations in Stylistics
Andrew Goatly

From Language to Multimodality: New Developments in the Study of Ideational Meaning
Edited by Carys Jones and Eija Ventola

Forthcoming:

The Texture of Casual Conversation: A Multidimensional Interpretation
Diana Slade

A Multimodal Approach to Classroom Discourse
Kay O'Halloran

Reading Visual Narratives: Inter-image Analysis of Children's Picture Books
Clare Painter

An Introduction to the Grammar of Old English: A Systemic Functional Approach
Michael Cummings

Morphosyntactic Alternations in English: Functional and Cognitive Perspectives
Edited by Pilar Guerrero Medina

Text Type and Texture

In honour of Flo Davies

Edited by
Gail Forey and
Geoff Thompson

LONDON   OAKVILLE

Published by Equinox Publishing Ltd.
UK: 1 Chelsea Manor Studios, Flood Street, London SW3 5SR
USA: DBBC, 28 Main Street, Oakville, CT 06779

www.equinoxpub.com

First published 2008. This paperback edition published 2010.

British Library Cataloguing-in-Publication Data
A catalogue record for this book is available from the British Library.

ISBN-13   978 1 84553 912 2   (paperback)

Library of Congress Cataloging-in-Publication Data

Text type and texture / edited by Gail Forey and Geoff Thompson
    p. cm. — (Functional linguistics)
Includes bibliographical references and index.
ISBN 978-1-84553-214-7 (hb)
    1. Discourse analysis. 2. Interpersonal communication. I. Forey, Gail, 1961-
II. Thompson, Geoff, 1947-

P302.T3655 2008
401'.41—dc22
                        2007026704

Typeset by S.J.I. Service, New Delhi
Printed and bound in Great Britain by Lightning Source, Milton Keynes, UK.

Contents

Preface

We offer this collection in Florence Davies's honour. Those of us contributing to the volume have all been touched by her infectious enthusiasm to enquire into and challenge issues related to language and meaning. Florence has made valuable contributions in a range of areas: our understanding of Theme and cohesion, the analysis of written text, reading processes, pedagogical applications, and many more. Her generosity of spirit means that many of her insights are found in the work of others: one of her most lovable characteristics has been her willingness to share ideas, and to put as much energy into encouraging and stimulating others as into ensuring that her own work gets published. We hope that this collection will carry forward her influence and will go some way towards repaying that generosity.

Acknowledgements

Permission to reproduce material has been obtained from Hodder Education for extracts from *GCSE Modern World History* (Chapter 9) and from the *Sydney Morning Herald* for 'placeintime bondi beach' (Chapter 12).

List of contributors

Leila Barbara is Professor of Linguistics at the Catholic University in São Paulo; she works in Systemics and in Research Methods in Applied Linguistics. Her main research interests are Discourse Analysis, specifically related to work, business and the professions, including Education and the description of the Portuguese language.

Tony Berber Sardinha is Professor of Applied Linguistics with the Linguistics Department and the Applied Linguistics Graduate Program, the Pontifical Catholic University of São Paulo, Brazil. His main interests are Corpus Linguistics, SFL, Metaphor, Translation, and Language Teaching. He maintains a website with corpus analysis tools at http://www2.lael.pucsp.br/corpora.

Caroline Coffin is a Reader in Applied Linguistics at the Centre for Language and Communication at the Open University, UK. Drawing on Systemic Functional Linguistics, she has conducted research in a wide range of educational contexts and has been responsible for the design and production of undergraduate and postgraduate distance courses in applied linguistics, grammar and discourse analysis. She is currently Co-director of the Educational Dialogue Research Unit

John Corbett is Professor of Applied Language Studies at the University of Glasgow. Amongst his publications are 'Language and Scottish Literature', 'Written in the Language of the Scottish Nation' and 'An Intercultural Approach to English Language Teaching'. He currently edits the journal 'Language and Intercultural Communication' and he directs the Scottish Corpus of Texts and Speech (www.scottishcorpus.ac.uk).

Beverly Derewianka is Professor of Language Education at the University of Wollongong, Australia, where she is Director of the Centre for Research in Language and Literacy. She has worked in the fields of literacy and TESOL for some twenty years. Her research draws on Systemic Functional Linguistics to investigate language development in later childhood and adolescence.

Gail Forey is an Associate Professor and Associate Director for The Research Centre for Professional Communication at the Hong Kong Polytechnic University (PolyU). She has carried out research and published in the areas of written and spoken workplace discourse, language education and teaching development.

Peter H. Fries is Professor Emeritus of English and Linguistics at Central Michigan University. He has taught Systemic Functional Linguistics in China and in Australia. He has been publishing in Systemic Functional Linguistics since 1974. Much of his work has focused on the textual metafunction in discourse.

Hugh Gosden is interested in the application of tools of SFL such as thematic analysis to contexts within English for Academic Purposes. Of particular focus is the experience of young researchers writing their first scientific papers for international publication. Formerly at Tokyo Institute of Technology, he has designed and teaches specialist EAP courses which integrate much of his published work in this area.

Michael Hoey is Baines Professor of English Language at the University of Liverpool since 1993 and was Director of the Applied English Language Studies Unit at the University between 1993 and 2003. He is the author of many articles and books, most recently *Textual Interaction* (2001) and *Lexical Priming – a New Theory of Words and Language* (2005).

Susan Hood is a senior lecturer in the Faculty of Education at the University of Technology, Sydney (UTS), where she teaches discourse analysis and research methods on Masters programs in Applied Linguistics and TESOL. Her PhD thesis from UTS was on evaluation in academic discourse from a Systemic Functional Linguistic perspective.

David Hyatt works in the School of Education, University of Sheffield where he is the Director of three programmes: the MEd in English Language Teaching; the MA in Education Policy and Practice; and Singapore Distance Learning Programme. He is also a tutor on the MA Literacy and Language in Education Programme and a core member of the Literacy Research Centre. He has an MEd TEFL from the University of Bristol and a PhD in critical literacy from the University of Sheffield.

J R Martin is Professor of Linguistics (Personal Chair) at the University of Sydney. His research interests include systemic theory, functional grammar, discourse semantics, register, genre, multimodality and critical discourse analysis, focusing on English and Tagalog – with special reference to the transdisciplinary fields of educational linguistics and social semiotics. He is the author and co-author of a number of recent and influential publications which are frequently used in applied linguistics and education studies. Professor Martin was elected a fellow the Australian Academy of the Humanities in 1998, and awarded a Centenary Medal for his services to Linguistics and Philology in 2003.

Ann Montemayor-Borsinger works at Instituto Balseiro, Cuyo National University, a graduate and postgraduate centre for physicists and engineers in Patagonia, Argentina. She is also Invited Professor at the Institute of Linguistics, University of Buenos Aires. Her research and publications focus on written academic discourse and applications of Systemic Functional Linguistics to Spanish. She has an MEd from the University of Bristol and a PhD from the University of Glasgow.

Geoff Thompson is Senior Lecturer in Applied Linguistics at the University of Liverpool. He currently runs the MA in TESOL, and teaches courses on Functional Grammar and language teaching methodology. He has three main areas of research interests: functional grammar, discourse analysis and teaching materials development. He has published an introductory book on Functional Grammar (second edition 2004), and with Susan Hunston co-edited a volume on evaluation in text (2000) and one on systemic linguistics and corpus linguistics (2006).

Susan Thompson is Director of the English Language Unit at the University of Liverpool (a post held earlier by Flo Davies). She also teaches on the MA and undergraduate programmes. Her main research interests are in spoken discourse, particularly academic presentations, and she has published papers in these areas in journals such as *JEAP* and the *Australian Review of Applied Linguistics*.

Introduction

Gail Forey and Geoff Thompson

This book consists of selected papers from a collection presented to Florence Davies on her 70th birthday by former colleagues and students together with invited contributions from a number of other scholars working in relevant areas. In line with Florence's linguistic areas of interest, the main focus of the volume is on aspects of the textual resources that are used to construct texture, with particular reference to different text types. The broad theoretical framework shared by all the chapters is that of Systemic Functional Linguistics (SFL).

It has long been accepted that texts are not random accumulations of sentences. One key quality which distinguishes a text is that it has texture (Halliday and Hasan 1976): that is, the parts of the text have a unity in their linguistic choices which is perceived by users as appropriate to the socio-cultural and discourse environment that the text inhabits. Unity here does not mean uniformity: rather, it indicates that the multitude of interlocking choices of meaning and wording embodied by the text are recognised as mutually relevant, that each makes sense in the context of the others. Texture in written text arises as the writer attempts to monitor and control the flow of information through the text in a manageable way so that the reader is guided towards the kind of interpretation intended by the writer. Different threads of meaning are interwoven in such ways that readers can (normally) construct coherent interpretations. These threads are realised across the text by a wide range of resources such as grammatical signals of cohesion (Halliday and Hasan 1976), lexical repetitions of various kinds (Hoey 1991), devices for encapsulation and prospection (Sinclair 1992/2004) and for participant tracking (Martin 1992), and – most relevant to many of the contributions in the present volume – patterns of thematic choice.

As the list of texturing resources above suggests, most SFL work on texture has focused on resources within the textual metafunction. Matthiessen (1995: 22) points out that the textual metafunction has a 'special status': 'Specifically, it construes ideational and interpersonal meanings as information that can be shared by speaker and addressee; and it enables this sharing by providing the resources for guiding the exchange of meaning in text'. That is, the textual metafunction comprises the linguistic systems which enable writers and speakers to organise the experiential and interpersonal meanings in their messages coherently in the context within which those messages are located; and it is therefore clearly central to the creation of texture. However, it is increasingly recognised that patterns of interpersonal meanings across texts can also contribute to texture. In particular, the phenomenon of 'evaluative coherence' (Thompson and Zhou 2000: 123) has come to the fore through work within the APPRAISAL model (Martin and White 2005), which has led to a shift from a concentration on individual expressions of stance to an exploration of the cumulative patterns of evaluative orientation across texts. There is also growing interest in exploring the texturing function of particular intersections of interpersonal and textual meanings, such as the presence of evaluation in thematic position, or the interweaving of Subject and Theme across a text.

A further crucial insight, which opens up rich avenues for investigation, is that the ways in which texture is realised are sensitive to context: that is, they vary according to the type of text. To take a very simple example, patterns of thematic choice which would be entirely appropriate to casual conversation would normally appear unacceptably random, repetitive or personal in formal expository writing. Davies (1997) has suggested that certain kinds of selections within the Theme system characterise particular genres; and similar claims can be made for the other texturing resources, although much work is still needed to explore all the ramifications of this. As the title of the present volume indicates, one of the aims is to extend our understanding of the complex interrelations between text type and texture.

The chapters in the present volume fall into four parts. Part I explores one of the major resources for constructing texture: the starting point of Theme. Here some of the controversial and highly debated aspects of Theme are discussed. In Part II the scope widens to include an examination of the deployment of thematic resources in a range of genres: the discussion encompasses academic and popular science texts, political television interviews, and workplace texts. The book then moves on in Part III to outline the way in which patterns of interpersonal choices across text contribute to texture. A supplementary focus of all these chapters is the differences in the texturing resources that are used, and the ways in which they are used, in different text types. In the final part of the book a generalisable method is outlined for investigating texture, with the aim of helping analysts to apply SFL in order to understand the unfolding of meaning in texts.

Part I The current understanding of the concept of Theme

The first two chapters deal with general issues in our understanding of Theme. Fries, a major contributor to the discussion of Theme for many years, provides an account of the effect Theme and New have on our perception of written text. Based on his 30 years study of Theme, Fries summarises the considerable advances that have been made and, synthesizing previous work, proposes a number of key considerations in investigating Theme. The chapter as a whole is thus designed as an attempt to frame an agenda for future research on the structure-assigning aspects of the textual metafunction. Thompson and Thompson also approach the concept of Theme from a theoretical perspective, focusing especially on the criteria for the identification of Theme; and they explore aspects which remain controversial in this area, such as the inclusion of Subject as part of Theme following a marked Theme. Their arguments lead them to adopt a position which partly runs contrary to much current thinking on the analysis of marked Themes (see e.g. Martin and Rose 2003). The dynamic, exploratory and, at times, contentious discussion of Theme in these two chapters both reflects how far our understanding of this texturing resource has developed and contributes to the fruitful ongoing debate concerning the boundaries and interpretation of Theme.

Part II Thematic choices in a range of text types

The six chapters in Part II (Corbett, Gosden, Montemayor-Borsinger, Hyatt, Forey, Hoey) examine thematic choices in a range of text types, discussing the different kinds of meanings appearing in Theme which are particularly significant for each genre, and suggesting how these relate to the broader socio-cultural context. Corbett explores the texturing of comparable ideational matter in two different registers. He focuses on a discussion of Theme choice in popular and academic science texts and shows how the differences in the choice of Theme reflect the different communicative purposes. Gosden is concerned with helping novice research writers to handle more confidently the process of submitting papers for publication in international journals. He argues that it is particularly important for the novice writers to develop a sense of the motivation behind referees' comments in responding to reviews. With a better understanding of the peer review genre, prospective authors may be able to frame their replies to referees' criticisms more effectively. One way of guiding them towards this understanding is through raising awareness of the importance of the thematic content of referees' comments. Gosden demonstrates this approach through an analysis of the Theme choices in a corpus of peer reviews of scientific papers. Montemayor-Borsinger, again focusing on academic scientific texts, provides a longitudinal study of academic writers as they move from apprentice to expert status in publishing in academic journals. She investigates in detail changes in the ways in which they develop the texture of their argument through the choice of Theme as they become accepted members of their academic community. Hyatt tackles the texture of adversarial political interviews. His database of television political interviews, questionnaires and interviews with specialist informants offers an overview of the argumentative meaning making devices exploited by interviewers and interviewees, and how the potential for resistant readings/ hearings of a text may be developed. Forey explores workplace texts, focusing on one particular feature of interpersonal meaning construed by projecting clauses in initial position in a clause or clause complex. She discusses how the choice of Theme in workplace text is related to 'control and power' (Iedema 2003). Hoey ties thematic choices in with other resources which contribute to texturing in written text, including lexical priming (Hoey 2005). Illustrating his discussion with sample analyses of well- and poorly-written texts, he explicitly addresses the implications for improving the writing skills of novice writers. A fundamental assumption of the chapters in Part II, as of much of the work within SFL, is the commitment to understanding the nature of a range of texts and genres that embody different forms of meaning-making in the wider community, in such a way that the insights can be applied in educational contexts at primary, secondary and tertiary level, and beyond. The discussions in all of these chapters have a great deal to offer curricula and pedagogic development. The practical potential for a genre-based curriculum has been exemplified in the work of Martin and Christie 1997, Martin and Rose 2007, and Macken Horarik 2001, to name but a few, and the explorations in this volume are designed to provide information about texts on which educational decisions can be based and, in some cases, specific recommendations for pedagogic application.

Part III Interpersonal patterns and prosodies

The chapters in Part III (Coffin and Derewianka, Hood, Berber Sardinha and Barbara) centre around interpersonal patterns, partly in Theme but also across texts as a whole. Coffin and Derewianka examine the shift from the more linear texturing of a traditional, late 20th century history textbook to the multimodal pastiche of contemporary textbooks. They probe the implications of this shift for the student reader in terms of creating a coherent reading of the text. They focus on issues such as the interpersonal and textual resources that the multimodal text draws on in achieving coherence (or not) and how these differ from those found in traditional linear texts. Returning to the topic of academic texts, Hood discusses the interpersonal prosody and patterning developed through the choice of Theme. Hood focuses on the discourse semantic patterning of interpersonal meaning in her combined analysis of ATTITUDE and GRADUATION evoking ATTITUDE (see Hood 2004; Martin and White 2005) within the thematic choices of research writing. Finally in this part, Berber Sardinha and Barbara take the discussion in a different direction, arguing that the identification of recurrent patterns of textualisation in specific text types can be a way into exploring how stereotypes may emerge. They focus on the use of modality in transcripts of business meetings held in Portuguese in Brazilian and Portuguese business companies, and link the differences that emerge to the different stereotypes that each of the groups has of the other. Thus, Part III particularly throws light on the intermeshing of textual and interpersonal concerns in construing discourse texture. Davies (1988: 174) argues that writers are not only concerned with the content being reported, but 'are also necessarily committed to particular stances or points of view'. These chapters on interpersonal patterns and prosodies provide a clearer understanding of the 'manipulative potential' through which the writer or speaker presents their viewpoint.

Part IV Methodological approach extending the understanding of texture

Martin closes the collection with an overview and illustration of a methodological approach by which our understanding of texturing can be further extended. In his chapter, Martin draws on his extensive experience of discourse analysis to provide a detailed account, which will be illuminating for both the experienced and the novice text analyst, of how to approach a text, and shunt from the text to the context to the ideological meanings constructed. In doing this, he brings together many of the threads of earlier chapters and shows how they can be integrated in a comprehensive analysis of how a text works as a text.

The volume as a whole thus aims to strike a balance between mining a particular aspect of texturing resources (Theme) exhaustively from both the theoretical and applied perspectives, and opening up other important avenues of research. Our overall goal is to set out current views on the complexity of these resources, and map out future lines of enquiry.

References

Christie, F. and Martin J. R. (eds.) (1997) *Genre and Institutions: Social Processes in the Workplace and School.* London: Cassell,

Davies, F. (1988). Reading between the lines: thematic choice as a device for presenting writer viewpoint in academic discourse. *The ESPecialist* 9 (2): 173–200.

———— (1997). Marked Theme as a heuristic for analysing text-type, text and genre. In *Applied Languages: Theory and Practice in* ESP, J. Pique and D. Viera (eds.), 45–71. Valencia: Servei de Publications Universitat de Valencia.

Halliday, M. A. K. and Hasan, R. (1976). *Cohesion in English.* London: Longman.

Hoey, M. (1991). *Patterns of Lexis in Text.* Oxford: Oxford University Press.

———— (2005). *Lexical Priming: A New Theory of Words and Language.* London: Routledge.

Hood, S. (2004). Managing attitude in undergraduate academic writing: a focus on the introductions to research reports. In *Analysing Academic Writing.* L. Ravelli and R. Ellis. (eds.), 24–44. London: Continuum.

Iedema, R. (2003). *Discourse of Post-Bureaucratic Organizations.* Amsterdam: John Benjamins Publishing Company.

Macken-Horarik, M., 2001. "Something to shoot for": a systemic functional approach to teaching genre in secondary school science. In *Genre in the classroom: multiple perspectives,* 17–42, A. M. Johns, (ed.) London: Lawrence Erlbaum Associates.

Martin, J. R. (1992). *English Text: System and Structure.* Amsterdam: John Benjamins.

Martin, J. R. and Rose, D (2007) Designing literacy pedagogy: Scaffolding democracy in the classroom. In *Continuing Discourse on Language.* Volume 1, J. Webster, R. Hasan and C. Matthiessen (eds.) London: Continuum.

Martin, J. R. and Rose, D. (2003). *Working with Discourse.* London: Continuum.

Martin, J. R. and White, P. R. R. (2005). *The Language of Evaluation, Appraisal in English.* London and New York: Palgrave Macmillan,

Matthiessen, C. M. I. M. (1995). THEME as an enabling resource in ideational knowledge construction. In *Thematic Development in English Text,* M. Ghadessy (ed.), 20–54. London: Pinter.

Sinclair, J. 1992. Trust the text. In *Advances in Systemic Linguistics: Recent Theory and Practice,* L. Ravelli and M. Davies (eds.), 1–19. London: Pinter. Reprinted 2004 in updated form in *Trust the Text: Language, Corpus and Discourse,* J. Sinclair and R. Carter (eds.), 9–23. London: Routledge.

Thompson, G. and Zhou, J. (2000). Evaluation and organization in text: The structuring role of evaluative disjuncts. In *Evaluation in Text: Authorial Stance and the Construction of Discourse,* S. Hunston and G. Thompson (eds.), 121–141. Oxford: Oxford University Press.

1 The textual metafunction as a site for a discussion of the goals of linguistics and techniques of linguistic analysis

Peter H. Fries

Central Michigan University

1.1 Introduction

I am happy to be included in a volume honouring the work of Flo Davies. I have known her for many years and have appreciated her approach to the study of language, and, in particular, her approach to the study of the functions of Theme. Given her work on Theme in English, I thought it would be appropriate to use my contribution to address some theoretical issues inherent in exploring the textual metafunction. The structure assigning components of the textual metafunction (the thematic system and the information system) have been a part of systemic functional grammar since the initial formulations of the metafunctional model in the 1960s. During the roughly 40 years since that time, a veritable industry has arisen, in which investigators have explored the natures of these two structures and their effects in texts.

Of course, in the time that these concepts have been explored, we should expect considerable variation in conception as to their significance and how they should be explored. In my early work, in which I used textual evidence to establish the relevance and importance of Theme and New information and the relation between these two concepts, I used Daneš's notion of 'thematic progression' and introduced the notions of 'method of development' and 'point' as means of relating the clause level structures of Theme and New to their textual effects. It is flattering to me that these three concepts have been used, adopted and adapted in many following works. But sometimes I worry about how they are treated. For example, method of development is sometimes generalised so greatly that everything in the text can be considered to be relevant to the development of the text. Of course if a concept refers to everything in the text, it is of minimal use. Interestingly, method of development has also at the same time developed in the language of some authors into a term which refers simply to an aspect of form. Thus, in an email discussion one person wrote the sentence in Quotation 1.

[Q1]   Given that Method of Development *means* 'the set of Themes in a text', what use will the concept be if we now say the Method of Development can be in the Rhemes? [my emphasis]

While this wording is extreme, other studies which examine thematic progression and method of development (most recently Crompton 2002, 2004) simply explore whether certain texts exhibit a consistent method of development, but do not explore the sorts of meanings expressed in those texts. The result is that these analyses also effectively treat method of development as if it merely referred to form.

Similarly, thematic progression has sometimes been pursued in a particularly form-oriented manner. Authors such as Bäcklund (1990), Crompton (2002, 2004) and Francis (1989) have investigated thematic progression merely by examining Themes of sequences of successive clauses or sentences, with little regard for the conjunctive or other structural or semantic relations which hold among the clauses.

Finally, several descriptions of the semantic or grammatical properties of Themes in texts (e.g. Francis 1989; Fries 1982, 2002; Love 2004) consider the grammatical properties of the Themes alone. (Exceptions to this trend are Berry 1987, and, following Berry, Fries 1995 and 1996.) The result of such an approach is that we have no evidence that the characteristics discovered in this way are distinctive of Theme in those texts or are merely characteristics of those texts in general. For example, if we find that a text frequently uses spatial location as Theme, does this result from the fact that this text contains many references to spatial location, and we would expect that at least some of them would occur as Theme? Or is it because spatial location is being used in a special way in this text?

Since I am one of the people primarily responsible for the use of the terms *method of development, thematic progression* and *N-Rheme*, I would like to devote this chapter to a discussion of these and related notions. First, I want to describe the larger theoretical and historical context so that you can see my view of where these concepts fit into a larger picture. Then I want to suggest what I see as a way forward, and end with a few examples of ways that these concepts can be usefully explored.

1.2 Personal background

Since the techniques which we use to study something are greatly affected by our goals, I will take a personal tone in this chapter and will begin with some personal history. As many readers may already know, I am the son of Charles C. Fries, a prominent American linguist of the first half of the twentieth century who was interested in the description of English grammar.

In his household, linguistics was very much the focus of daily conversation. Indeed, in the eyes of a young child, it often seemed that life existed primarily to illustrate general linguistic principles. Some lessons were repeated *ad nauseam*. These lessons include statements such as 'All the significant features of language are items in contrast.' 'Functional roles (not physical reality) are most important.' Quotation 2 provides his discussion of the strike in baseball (published in Fries 1952, but repeated very often in conversation) in which he pointed out that the various physical acts that functioned as strike had few features in common.[1] What made them similar, in his view, was their common function in the rules of the game.

[Q2]   It is true that all strikes are the 'same' in baseball. But that 'sameness' is not physical identity; it is not even physical likeness with an area of tolerance. **All strikes are alike in baseball only in the sense that they have the same functional significance.** (Fries 1952: 72. My emphasis)

Finally, and most directly relevant to my discussion here, he felt that what was said in language was of less importance than how the community responded to what was said. He often said that you can say anything. The question that interested him was how listeners will understand what you say. In other words, Fries repeatedly and explicitly rejected the description of patterns in language as a major goal for linguistics. This rejection separated him from most other American linguists of his time. Quotation 3 illustrates the goals of linguistics described by Zellig Harris. The goals he outlines are typical of other American linguists of the time. It is clear that he is primarily interested in discovering patterns which enable him to describe the language efficiently.

[Q3]   Descriptive linguistics ... is a particular field of inquiry which deals not with the whole of speech activities, but with the regularities in certain features of speech. These regularities are in the distributional relations among the features of speech in question, i.e. the occurrence of these features relatively to each other within utterances. (Harris 1951: 5)

Now compare this quotation with Quotations 4 and 5 from Fries. These quotations illustrate that Fries was interested in predicting listener responses to the language that they perceive. More specifically, he wanted to describe the signals within the language that lead listeners to interpret the language the way they do.

[Q4]   It is our task ... not only to describe the items of form and arrangement which constitute the devices that signal structural meanings, but also, and especially, to set forth the contrastive patterns of the system through which these items acquire signalling significance. (Fries 1952: 61)

[Q5]   [structural] grammar aims not at definitions and classifications but at such a description of the formally marked structural units as will make possible a valid prediction of the regular recognition responses that the patterns will elicit in the linguistic community. (Fries's 1967: 668)

I should say that these quotations from Fries were not merely lip-service gestures to some unobtainable goal. Rather, the goal of attempting to account for listener interpretations was a fundamental tenet of the approach to language. It influenced Frie's actions at every level, and was a major feature which distinguished his work from the approaches of most other American structuralists.

Given Fries's influence on my thinking, you can imagine my reaction when I heard Halliday saying things like Quotation 6, particularly the portion emphasised in bold.

[Q6]   In any piece of discourse analysis, there are always two possible levels of achievement to aim at. One is a contribution to the understanding of the text: **the linguistic analysis enables one to show how, and why, the text means what it does.** ... [This] is one that should always be attainable provided the analysis is such as to relate the text to general features of the language — provided it is based on the grammar, in other words. Halliday 1994: xv; my emphasis.[2]

To my way of thinking, this statement was like coming home. Admittedly, there are significant differences between our systemic position and Fries's model of language. Systemicists are not limited to his questions, but we do address them. Also, when we address his questions, the ways we answer the questions differ from his. Though we are like him in that we relate the particulars of language that we find in a text to the system as a whole, our views of the system – in his words, 'the contrastive patterns of the system' – are more abstract than his and address issues which he did not address. Yet, despite the differences, we continue an interest in variants of his question. If I may talk more personally, I should say that it is possible to read everything that I have done in systemic grammar as heavily influenced by the goals described in Quotations 4 and 5.

1.3   Theoretical background: systemic theory

Let me now shift to a second component of the background for this chapter: the systemic model.

Within systemic theory we divide the stream of speech into the three metafunctions: ideational, interpersonal and textual. Further within the textual metafunction we discuss the two structure-assigning systems: the thematic system and the information system. The thematic system assigns the structural elements Theme and Rheme,[3] and the Information system assigns the elements New and Given (see Halliday 1967: 204; 1970: 161; 1994: 36, 298 for basic descriptions of these concepts). Systemicists use these four structural functions as constructs to account for certain aspects of the meanings of utterances in context. Thus the descriptions of the meanings conveyed by these structures is of critical importance to our ability to use them in grammatical descriptions. While these four theoretical constructs are used to account for certain aspects of the meanings of texts, we should remember that they are elements of clause structure, or of the structure of the information unit. They are not directly part of text structure any more than the words *and, but* or *moreover* are directly part of text structure.

As a final comment on the theoretical status of these four concepts (Theme vs. Rheme and Given vs. New) it is worth pointing out that for purposes of counting, most people who deal with these structural functions do so in a rigidly particulate way. (If you are going to count, you need to make a decision: something is either part of the Theme, or it is not part of the Theme.) However, Halliday and others actually see thematic status as a cline. Thus we often see diagrams like Figure 1.1 (Halliday 1994: 337) where these two functions are presented as continua.

Given that thematic and information structure are inherently continuous, it is hardly surprising that systemicists disagree about the

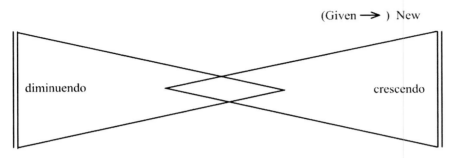

Theme (⟶ Rheme)

Figure 1.1 From Speaker to listener: The wave-like effect of thematic and focal prominence (Halliday 1994: Figure 9-6).

boundary points of what constitutes Theme. Exactly how far into the clause does thematic status extend? While all systemicists take Halliday's lead in including the first constituent of the ideational metafunction as Theme, there is considerable disagreement as to whether the Theme extends even further into the clause. Thus if a Subject which expresses a participant role is preceded by a circumstantial Adjunct, is that Subject also part of the Theme? (See Thompson and Thompson, this volume, for further discussion.)

A second issue concerns how abstractly we should take thematic status. Can understood elements be thematic? For example, suppose we have a branched clause with an elliptical Subject as in Examples 1a and b:

(1)   a. John came in and sat down.

        b. John came in and immediately began talking.

Does the second clause in 1a and in 1b contain a Theme? If so, what is it? In general, a consensus seems to be growing that elliptical Subjects should be considered Theme when no Ideational Adjunct precedes them as in Example 1a. There is less consensus as to the Theme in Example 1b. However even there many people consider the Theme of the second clause to include *immediately* and the missing Subject. There is even less agreement for identifying Themes in non-finite clauses where the Subject is not present and cannot be added, but is clearly understood.

Finally we need to explore the effect of discontinuous groups and phrases on thematic status. For example, how should nominal groups with either pre-posed or post-posed Qualifiers be analysed? The underlined portions of Examples 2a and b illustrate the sorts of constructions I am referring to.

(2)   a. ... a large number of students across the country, including LEP students which account for over 3 million students in the United States. *Of these*

3 million, the majority are concentrated at the lower grade levels, as opposed to the higher grade levels.

b. *Decisions* are being made by local officials in our communities that could drastically affect the quality of our lives.[4]

The underlined portions of these two examples each constitutes a single nominal group (*the majority of these three million* and *decisions that could drastically affect the quality of our lives*). However, because of the non-canonical order of the two nominal groups we can say that in each the Qualifier is separated from the remainder of the group. We are therefore left with a choice. Either we consider the entire nominal group as Theme, in which case we ignore the special order of the constituents. Or we consider only those portions of the nominal groups which are found in first position in the clause to be Theme (printed in italics in 2). In the second analysis, we relax the requirement that the Theme must be a clause-level constituent.

In short, there is general agreement concerning what constitutes a Theme in most cases, but in certain problematic constructions the systemic community has not yet reached total agreement.

A third challenge to people interested in the description of Theme is the degree to which Theme can be seen to be a unified concept. Huddleston (1988) and Fawcett (2003) take the position that the sorts of things that occur initially are so varied that there can be no common semantic thread. Their arguments seem to be based on the following logic. When they examine the local grammar and the semantics of clauses and clause complexes, they identify a great variety of syntactic structures which may function as Theme. This variety may express meanings as varied as participant Themes, circumstantial Themes, textual Themes, interpersonal Themes, etc. They then decide that no such motley lot of meanings could possibly have a single unified function in text and so they either reject the notion of Theme altogether (as Huddleston does) or reject the notion of Theme as a unified structure (as Fawcett does). By contrast, I take my father's notion of the importance of function as a deep lesson. Even though something looks like a varied 'rag-bag' (in Fawcett's term) of different constructions and meanings at the level of clause or sentence, that does not necessarily prevent its having a single function at a higher level. I note for example that even though information that is presented as New exhibits an even greater variety of meanings – sometimes even including only a portion of a word – few linguists have suggested that New is not a single unified function.

Now, the functions assigned by thematic structure and information structure presented quite different sorts of challenges to linguists. One very important difference has been the different rhetorical challenges. While rhetoric is not a theoretical issue, it is an issue which must concern all innovative theoreticians. If we think back to the 1950s and early 1960s, it is clear that all linguists who dealt with the spoken language had used some sort of concepts resembling Given and New. Certainly there was great variation in how each person's concept was defined and used, but still there was general consensus that similar concepts were needed. By contrast, the notion of Theme was quite controversial. It was controversial not because there were many definitions for Theme, but rather many linguists of the time found no need for any such concept at all. Let me use as an example my father's attitude toward Psychological Subject and Logical Subject. These are notions which Halliday (1994) has linked with Theme and Actor respectively. In 1960 my father wrote a letter to me concerning my Ph.D. thesis which I was beginning at that time. As an incidental part of that discussion he wrote what is in Quotation 7. Here he clearly indicates his distrust and confusion concerning psychological subject and logical subject.

[Q7] I'm a bit concerned about this 'logical' subject in distinction from 'grammatical' subject. The Europeans have been especially fond of these problems and have carried [it] to extremes in some instances. It's not too bad when limited to structures with 'it', but when they use their 'psychological' subject we are lost.

For example it has been said as follows:

In such an assertion as 'John <u>shot</u> the bear' John is the 'subject' because he obviously did something to the <u>bear</u>, which is thus the 'object'.

But in 'John <u>saw</u> the bear' <u>John</u> certainly did nothing <u>to</u> the bear, but the light rays and vibrations from the <u>bear</u> acted upon <u>John</u>. And in the following 'John feared the bear', the <u>bear</u> really affects <u>John</u> so here clearly <u>bear</u> is the 'psychological subject'.

It is quite alright to work out things of this sort and understand all the logical implications of the utterances we deal with. The basic matter to remember I believe is Bloomfield's statement '... a language can convey only such meanings as are attached to some formal feature; the speaker can signal only by means of signals.' Whenever there is a meaning that is conveyed, it's our job to try to discover the precise signals of that meaning.[5]

I have included an extended portion of his letter here because the last paragraph articulates an important part of his objection. Specifically, in his opinion, the descriptions of the notions of logical and psychological subjects had not tied them to any expression in form. He needed to see some discussion of the formal signals of these meanings before he would consider them to be useful linguistic constructs.

One of Halliday's innovations, as he developed Systemic Functional linguistics, was to connect the concepts that he derived from 'psychological subject' and 'logical subject' (Theme and Actor) to some sort of formal realisation. That innovation in itself addresses a large portion of Fries's objection to these concepts. But, and this is an issue which still remains with us, the price of connecting the notion of what has come to be termed *Theme* within our theory with a particular formal realisation (initial position in English) is that we need to (a) define as exactly as we can the meaning and nature of Theme and then (b) see if the formal expression consistently relates to that meaning. This issue has been with us as long as the concept has been formulated. We have made progress, but a great deal of work still remains to be done.

As I saw it, when I began to work on Theme, several issues had to be addressed.

1. We needed to establish **that** Thematic position is meaningful (i.e. that Theme signals some sort of meaning), and **if** it is meaningful, what does it mean?

2. We needed to establish that there is some commonality in meaning among the various things that occur within the Themes.

3. We needed to establish some general agreement concerning exactly what constitutes the Theme in individual clauses.

In the case of information presented as New, there was much more solid agreement among systemicists and among linguists in general. Systemicists agreed that:

1. The distinction between New and Given is meaningful.

2. There is a commonality of meaning as to what is presented as New. In short, presenting information as New means roughly 'pay attention to this'.

3. The core of the New information is signaled in the spoken language by the location of the tonic syllable within a tone group. New information at least includes that tonic syllable. It may also extend forward towards or to the beginning of the intonation group. On the other hand it may be restricted to the constituent that includes the tonic syllable only.

In summary, in the late 1960s and early 1970s, we could assume that the audience agreed that some concept such as New information was needed. By contrast, most of the linguistic world found no need for the Theme/ Rheme distinction. Because of this social context, most of my early work focused attention on Theme. You can see this in the title of my 1981 paper: 'On the status of Theme in English: Arguments from discourse'. It is of interest that while I focused my attention on Theme, I found myself forced to address other related concepts as well.

If we bring the discussion up to date, systemicists now generally agree that it is necessary to describe thematic structure and information structure. They generally agree as to what constitutes Theme in individual clauses. And they generally agree that the Themes in the clauses of a text provide some sort of framing or orienting function for the remainder of the message. I believe systemic functional grammarians have agreed for a long time on the general outlines of the information system, including the meanings associated with its functions New and Given.

But, in fact, I need to modify my last statement concerning information structure. It is true that we agree concerning the nature of information structure in the spoken language, and indeed scholars such as Halliday, Greaves, Tench and Elmenoufy have greatly advanced our knowledge of the information system in the spoken language. There is much less work which addresses the information structure of written language. Let me explain what I mean. Given a written text, we can ask either of two questions about the information structure in that text.

1. What information in this text functions as New?

2. What is there in the written record of this text that leads readers to interpret a particular bit of information as New?

Clearly the two questions are not paraphrases and must be answered by different techniques. The first question is merely a question of identification and can be answered, for example, by reading (or getting one or more other person to read) the text aloud, recording the reading, and then analysing the recording. This approach, taken by, among others, Martin Davies (1989) and Michael Halliday (1992), has been used with great success. However, notice that that approach to Question 1 avoids Question 2 – the question my father would have asked. How do you know that this is New information? In effect, the getting-someone-to-read approach makes the readers take the written signal, and figure out what is or is not New. The readers then are obliged to convert their understandings of the written signal into spoken language as best they can, and then the linguist analyses the spoken language. But of course the original signal was not spoken language. We need to address seriously how readers know that certain information is presented as New or Given in the written language.[6]

1.4 Investigating the textual metafunction in written English: past efforts

Those readers who know my work may have noticed that I have not mentioned thematic or rhematic progression. I have omitted N-Rheme and I have ignored method of development, point and topic. I have not mentioned these concepts because I do not consider them to be theoretical constructs within the lexico-grammar. Thematic progression has the closest association to the lexico-grammar since one can discover thematic progression simply by noting the sequence of Themes in successive clauses or sentences of a text and then discovering if these Themes are cohesively connected to information expressed in some preceding sentence, and if yes, where is that sentence, and in which portion of the preceding sentence is that information located? (Of course, interpreting the significance of what one finds this way requires much more information about the text.)

N-Rheme is the term I have used to refer to the last clause-level constituent. This concept has no theoretical status. It is a working tool that I have used in order to address how we know that certain information is presented as New in writing. That is, N-Rheme is to be interpreted as a portion of the answer to my question concerning how we know that certain information is being presented as New. It is a useful working tool because of the unmarked association of New with the end of the clause. Thus placement of information within the N-Rheme constitutes one of about six techniques available to writers to cue readers concerning what is being presented as New information in a written text.[7]

When we come to the third group of terms (*method of development, point* and *topic*), in my opinion, the usefulness of these concepts depends on their not being lexico-grammatical constructs. Rather it is necessary to my agenda that they be understood as meanings.

Let me explain the way I understand these terms by retracing my intellectual history in these matters.

1.4.1 Early work – focus on Theme

Back in the late 1960s when I first encountered Halliday's notion of Theme, I was doubtful of how useful it was as a concept. On the one hand,

Quotation 7 from my father indicates the general attitude of many linguists in the 1960s toward the notions of the distinction between psychological and logical subjects – notions reasonably similar to the notions of Theme and Actor. On the other hand, assigning thematic status to the initial constituent of a clause seemed too simple to work.

However, I was also familiar with the notion of 'end weight' discussed by a number of grammarians at that time and earlier, and I had also recently read several works by Alfred Reszkiewicz (1966a, 1966b), a Polish grammarian who was interested in describing word order in Old and Middle English. He created a scale of grammatical complexity and used this scale as a means to predict that the more grammatically complex constituents would be found towards the end of Old and Middle English clauses. Halliday's notion of the Theme/Rheme and Given/New distinctions was similar enough to Reszkiewicz's ideas that Reszkiewicz's success in accounting for word order in Old and Middle English implied that the concept of Theme was at least sufficiently interesting to be worth serious investigation. The question then arose as to how to investigate this concept.

I paraphrased my father's basic question as: 'What are the signals in the language of a text which lead listeners/readers to interpret it the way that they do?' and began to ask how I could investigate Theme. The question for me became one of how I could relate this putative element of clause structure (Theme) to listener or reader interpretations. Could I, by examining the information that was placed in the Themes of a clause, predict in any way the interpretations which readers/listeners might give to that clause?

Just from considering the nature of Theme and the general types of meanings it was claimed to be tied to, it was clear that trying to gather persuasive evidence based on single isolated sentences or clauses would be difficult, if not impossible. It was obvious that I had to go to texts as my source of data. Preliminary evidence suggested that thematic content might be meaningful. In my reading I found an article by Enkvist (1978) which suggested that two of the thematic progressions described by Daneš (1974) seemed to correlate with different genres. The difference in genres constitutes a difference in meanings (admittedly very crudely considered).

Would it be possible to find any better evidence of the meaningful nature of thematic position? To do that, it was clear that I would need to relate clause Themes with specific interpretations of particular texts. However, if I was to avoid the accusation of circularity, I would have to go to texts that had been analysed by others. That is, someone else had done the interpretation. That way no one could say that my hypotheses concerning Theme had influenced my interpretations. I would only be responsible for the analysis of the language forms. At about the time that

I became interested in Theme, I was reading works on teaching composition, and had happened on the work of Frances Christiansen who had published his analyses of 15 sample passages with the goal of illustrating various types of structures that one could find in paragraphs (Christiansen 1965). I also found a few additional paragraphs which had been analysed by other composition experts in a manner that was reasonably similar to the approach taken by Christiansen. I ultimately ended up with a body of slightly over 20 paragraphs to examine. This body of analysed short texts provided an ideal (though small) place to begin my exploration of the degree to which Theme correlated with the interpretations provided by others.

Of course since I was depending on the interpretations of others, I had to be satisfied with the interpretations that they gave me. It turns out that, at that time, the American tradition in rhetorical work emphasised the relations of coordination and subordination. Further, my sources did not use either the clause or the sentence as the unit of analysis but something that approximated the T-unit as described by Hunt (1965). Hunt defined a T-unit as a complete independent clause plus any other clauses that are dependent on it. The result of my study was that I was satisfied that the content of the T-unit Themes did indeed correlate with the structural interpretations described by the composition experts.

But that study merely established that Theme correlated with the particular structural impressions. It did not address a causal relation between the content of the Themes and the impression conveyed by the texts. This question required a sort of controlled experiment. Could I, by changing the content of the Themes of texts, change the reactions of listeners/readers to those texts? Luckily some of the texts that I had used in my study of the correlation of thematic content with the structural interpretations of texts lent themselves to this type of study. I used Texts 3 and 4 amongst others as examples of this sort of experiment (see Fries 1981/1983 for another example).

(3)   **English Constitution – original version**
      <u>Underline</u> marks T-unit Themes.

      Bold font indicates references to the dominant nominal participant of the paragraph.

      [1]   <u>**The English Constitution – that indescribable entity**</u> – is a living thing, growing with the growth of men, and assuming ever-varying forms in accordance with the subtle and complex laws of human character.

      [2]   <u>**It**</u> is the child of wisdom and chance.

[3a]   The wise men of 1688 moulded it into the shape we know,

[3b]   but the chance that George I could not speak English gave it one of its essential peculiarities – the system of a Cabinet independent of the Crown and subordinate to the Prime Minister.

[4]   The wisdom of Lord Grey saved it from petrification and set it upon the path of democracy.

[5]   Then chance intervened once more.˙

[6a]   A female sovereign happened to marry an able and pertinacious man,

[6b]   and it seemed likely that an element that had been quiescent within it for years – the element of irresponsible administrative power – was about to become its predominant characteristic and change completely the direction of its growth.

[7]   But what chance gave chance took away.˙

[8a]   The Consort perished in his prime,

[8b]   and the English Constitution, dropping the dead limb with hardly a tremor, continued its mysterious life as if he had never been.

* Note that the English Constitution is also strongly implied in sentences 5 and 7

[Strachey 1924: 192]

(4)   **English Constitution – revised version placing all references to English Constitution within the Theme**

[1]   The English Constitution – that indescribable entity – is a living thing, growing with the growth of men, and assuming ever-varying forms in accordance with the subtle and complex laws of human character.

[2]   It is the child of wisdom and chance.

[3a]   It was moulded into the shape we know by the wise men of 1688,

[3b]   but it was given one of its essential peculiarities – the system of a Cabinet independent of the Crown and subordinate to the Prime Minister by the chance that George I could not speak English.

[4]   It was saved from petrification and set upon the path of democracy by the wisdom of Lord Grey.

[5]   Then chance intervened once more.

[6]   Its predominant characteristic almost became an element which had been quiescent within it for years – the element of irresponsible

administrative power, because a female sovereign happened to marry an able and pertinaceous man.

[7]   <u>But what chance gave</u> chance took away.

[8a]   <u>it</u> dropped the dead limb with hardly a tremor, because the Consort perished in his prime,

[8b]   <u>and **the English Constitution**</u> continued its mysterious life as if he had never been.

Text 3 itself seemed to me to constitute a sort of uncontrolled experiment. On reading this passage, I felt that there were three major sorts of notions: references to the English constitution, the opposition between wisdom and chance, and the image of living growing and changing. I also felt that these three ideas played radically different roles in this paragraph. The English Constitution was the topic. The image of living growing and changing was the basic point that the paragraph was trying to present, and that image was developed through the opposition between wisdom and chance. Those different impressions correlate with the placement of those ideas in the T-units of the paragraph. References to wisdom and chance regularly are placed within the Themes; references to living growing and changing are kept out of the Themes; and references to the English constitution (the topic of the passage) are found both inside and outside the Themes.

Of course, while those facts are suggestive, they do not establish thematic content as a factor in signalling the different effects. When we compare Text 4 with Text 3 the evidence is somewhat better. In creating Text 4, I attempted to change readers' reactions to the paragraph by changing the information placed in the Themes. Specifically, I placed all references to the English Constitution within the Themes of their T-units. Most readers agree that Text 3 and Text 4 create quite different effects in spite of the fact that Text 4 is derived from Text 3 merely by reordering the words in each T-unit. Text 3 seems to develop using the opposition between wisdom and chance, while Text 4 develops by talking about what happened to the English Constitution.

At the time that I was exploring these issues, I felt that I had conclusively proved that the content of the Themes was the cause of the difference in impressions produced by these paragraphs. Note that all the reference chains were undisturbed; the entities were brought into the texts in basically the same order; the cohesive harmony in the texts was unaltered by the revisions. Indeed, in many cases the grammar of the component sentences either remained exactly the same or underwent minimal changes such as moving an Adjunct from the beginning of the sentence to the end or vice versa.

Of course, it turns out that not only did I change the content of the Themes, I also changed the content of the Rhemes, and more specifically, I regularly changed the content of what I have come to call the N-Rhemes. This is one reason I have come to believe that one cannot explore the semantic contribution of Theme in the written language separate from the contribution of Rheme and N-Rheme.

Results such as these led me to create the following hypotheses:

H-1 If a text segment is perceived as having a single method of development, then the words which contribute to the expression of that method of development will occur thematically within the T-units of that text segment.

H-2 If a text segment is perceived as expressing a single point, then the words which contribute to the expression of that point will occur within the Rhemes of the component T-units of that text segment.

H-3 The perception of a nominal item as topic of a text segment is unrelated to the thematic or rhematic placement of the references to that item.

As is clear from Hypothesis 3, I found in my earliest work that there was a tenuous relation between paragraph topic and Theme, and since that time I have personally tried to avoid language that connects Theme with either clause or paragraph topic. Downing (1991) and several others have also taken a similar position. Indeed Thompson (2004: 159) has suggested using the term *experiential Theme* instead of *topical Theme*.

The hypotheses above require several comments. First, as I said earlier, it was critical to my agenda that the hypotheses relate form (placement of information inside or outside the Theme) with meaning (method of development, point and topic). Thus, *method of development, point,* and *topic* had to be seen as interpretations of text portions. They are semantic concepts. If I may return to Quotation 1, in which it was said 'Given that Method of Development **means** "the set of Themes in a text"', it should now be understood that that interpretation of my work creates a problem for me. The wording in Quotation 1 changes the concept of 'method of development' from a meaning to a unit of form.[8] Though it makes 'Method of Development' into a well-defined construct, it does so at the price of making my reasoning circular. However, one of the consequences of leaving method of development as a meaning is that it is ill-defined. I do not have a good description of what I mean by this term. So far, I have only succeeded in providing examples.

One consequence of using an ill-defined concept is that others interpret it in various ways. The data that I used in my early work were primarily short paragraphs chosen by composition specialists to illustrate some aspect of the meaning of the passage. The passages were abnormally clear. As I look back over them, they had a heavy concentration of the RST relation of 'elaboration'. Typically the data I worked with had a clear topic sentence which was then followed by some sort of expansion of that topic. It seems to me that that situation is the easiest place to find a clear method of development. (Incidentally, I also note that people like Martin 1992a, Matthiessen 1995 and Thompson 2004 often – but not exclusively – use texts with a high concentration of elaboration to illustrate method of development.) While it is possible to expand the concept of 'method of development' to apply to other rhetorical situations (as in fact I did in the latter part of my 1981 article when I talked about an apology as a method of development), it may be more difficult to see method of development in a range of other clause relations.[9]

Method of development has also been criticised on the grounds that many texts do not demonstrate a simple, clear method of development. In my view, since simple method of development is intended as a meaning, saying that texts exist which do not exhibit a clear method of development is similar to saying that there are texts that do not express cause-effect relations. 'Clear or simple method of development' was never intended on my part to be a textual universal in the sense that all texts must exhibit a clear method of development. Indeed, it is not proposed even as a requirement for all good texts. Rather it is a meaning – perhaps one of several similar potential textual meanings, which need to be explored as part of a larger system of meanings.

I also need to discuss what these hypotheses do not consider. Specifically, when I made them I was very much aware that they ignored the relation of Theme to text structure. This, in my opinion, was a major failing, but I knew of no way to make an understandable hypothesis and at the same time integrate the relevance of text structure. The failing was obvious for the notion of topic where I hypothesised that there was no relation between Theme and topic, yet it was very likely that Themes of certain structurally important sentences would express the topic of the passage. Since in my article I had discussed the relation of Theme to text structure just before I discussed thematic progressions and method of development, I hoped that the relevance of text structure would go without saying. Apparently I was wrong.

Luckily, while some linguists ignored text structure in their exploration of thematic progression and method of development, others (for example

Davies 1988, 1994, 1997; Downing 1991; Martin 1992a, 1992b; Martin and Rose 2003; and Matthiessen 1995) were sensible enough to discuss the relation of thematic content to the structure of texts and/or the context in which the texts were produced. Davies (1994: 176–83), for example, provides an extended discussion of an example text in which she divides the text into several subsections (text units) identified largely on functional grounds but also on several features of form. One focus in this first stage in her analysis is the assignment of each text unit to one of three functions: Interactive, Organisational or Topical. An examination of the Themes within each unit that she identifies in the text shows that many of her units (particularly the ones she assigns to a topical function) exhibit a considerable amount of simple (though not completely uniform) thematic progression and method of development (in my sense of those terms).

Martin takes a different approach to including larger text structure in his analyses. He uses the notions of Macro Theme, Hyper Theme, Macro New and Hyper New to discuss thematic and rhematic content in text segments. While his terms suggest that the text segments used are defined solely in terms of Theme and Rheme, in fact other criteria are also used in identifying segments. (See the use of the term 'phase' of a text in Martin and Rose 2003 for a less misleading term.) In my view (even at the time when I created my hypotheses), the attempts like these to integrate larger text structures and functions into the interpretation of thematic content address a factor that is critical to our understanding of the significance of what is presented as Theme or as New information.

Finally a number of people have commented that more than the Themes contribute to the development of a text. I have already partially agreed with this point when I said that we need to examine the sorts of information that are found in the Rhemes or N-Rhemes of the clauses as well as the Themes. It is indeed difficult to tease out the effects of the Themes from the effects of the N-Rhemes in written language. On the other hand, when some people have suggested that we also need to consider the cohesive ties within Theme, the identity and similarity chains, together with chain interactions (in short, all the components of cohesive harmony), I worry. I worry for two reasons. First, I worry that the notion of development is being taken in a much more general way than I intended. If the notion gets too general, then all texts develop, and all parts of each text contribute to the way it develops. The result of this interpretation is that the notion of method of development applies to everything in the text, and therefore it becomes unusable.

The second reason I worry concerns my early experience with my pseudo experiments. Text 3 above differs from Text 4 only in the order of the words within each sentence. The order of the sentences remains the same. The entities referred to, the cohesive items and chains and cohesive harmony remain the same in the two texts. In so far as we agree that these two texts have different effects on their readers, those different effects are signalled solely by the differences in the order of the words within the sentences. Of course since I changed the word order of entire sentences in these texts, these text pairs do not establish exactly which changes in word order are responsible for which changes in interpretation. However, our theoretical constructs of the distinctions between Theme vs. Rheme and New vs. Given remain plausible explanations for the changes in interpretation, particularly when we remember the association of New with the end of the clause – the N-Rheme.

In light of the discussion so far, the question arises of how can we profitably investigate Theme and New further.

1.5 Investigating the textual metafunction in written English: suggestions for future projects

As a preliminary to a discussion of some specific suggestions for future studies, I would like first to suggest some basic principles to use as we investigate the thematic and information systems. I should point out that as I describe some of these illustrative projects I will present tables which describe results. These tables are suggestive only. In each case I merely engaged in a mini-pilot study to see if the project was feasible and likely to obtain reasonable results.

The goal of these projects is to explore the meaning and function of Theme and the relation between thematic information and New information. Of course we cannot get at New information directly in written language. As a result, I use the association of New information with the ends of clauses and create a working concept which I call N-Rheme to refer to the last constituent of the clause.[10] I therefore divide a clause into three sections as in Table 1.1.

As I explore Theme and N-Rheme, I use the two following hypotheses concerning the roles of Theme and N-Rheme:

> H-4 N-Rhematic information contains the newsworthy information, information which is in focus in that message. As a result the

Table 1.1: Theme and Rheme in a clause

Theme	Rheme	
	Other	N-Rheme
Orienter/framework for the message	Left-over portion	Associated with the unmarked locus of New information
If you	suffer	from poor circulation, pain and swelling, chronic or acute edema,

N-Rhemes are likely to contain information which is directly relevant to the goals of the text or text segment.

H-5 Thematic information serves as orienter for the message which is about to come up. As a result it responds to local issues in the text and is less likely to contain meanings which are directly relevant to the goals and purposes of the text or text segment.

It is worth pointing out that Hypothesis 4 has two relevant readings. On the one hand, it predicts the sorts of meanings which should be found in the N-Rhemes of the clauses of a text. In the other reading it implies the sorts of meanings which normally will not occur in the Themes. That is, not only does Hypothesis 4 state what should be in the N-Rhemes, it also implies a negative correlation between thematic placement and meanings that are related to the goals of the text or text segment.

The general approach that I advocate is to connect the information placed within the Themes and the N-Rhemes (or conversely kept out of the Themes and N-Rhemes) with some aspect of the meaning of texts as a whole. At this point it is useful to describe what I mean by meaning or related to meaning here. Let me begin by saying that I take the statement by Halliday and Hasan (1976: 2) seriously. They describe text as 'best regarded as a SEMANTIC unit; a unit not of form but of meaning'. In addition Halliday (Halliday and Hasan 1985: 38) also describes register as 'a semantic concept'. He continues:

It can be defined as a configuration of meanings that are typically associated with a particular situational configuration of field, mode and tenor.

Field, mode and tenor are the theoretical constructs which we use to describe the social interaction within which the text is to play a role and to construct. As a result, anything that concerns the purposes of the text as a whole or the role of the text in the social interaction can be construed as having consequences for the meanings to be expressed.

In addition, meaning includes the generic structure of the text, as well as the phases it goes through (see Gregory 2002 and the references in his bibliography) or the spectrum of types of information that is expressed in the text (see Longacre 1981, 1989, 1990). In addition meaning also includes relations of subordination or coordination of ideas, as well as relations addressed through RST relations, etc. Certainly genre type is also relevant here. Finally, I would like to include notions such as method of development, point, topic, etc. However, a warning is in order here: the more general or vague the description of the meaning, the less help it will be in exploring Theme and New, because it will provide minimal help in making predictions concerning the meanings that will be expressed. For example, saying that a particular text portion expresses a generalisation is of little help for the purposes here, since such a statement does not provide any information which can be used to predict which specific portions of the clauses and sentences are likely to contain the relevant information.

Given that we are attempting to relate thematic and non-thematic placement to text meanings, we can take either of two major types of approaches to this task; both approaches are needed before we have finished our work. On the one hand, we can look at the text, figure out some important meaning that the text as a whole, or some well-defined portion of the text, is supposed to express, and then examine the language that is used to achieve that purpose. On the other hand, we can use form as our starting point and look for the various ways particular formal constructions are used.

Let me refer to the first approach to this investigation as the 'functional approach'. I will refer to the second approach as the 'formal approach'. I should emphasise that these two labels should not be taken to indicate that I have a preference for one or the other. Indeed both approaches address both form and function. They differ only in their starting points. Both approaches are useful; each one provides information that the other cannot give.

Let me quickly illustrate the two approaches. It has become a commonplace to say that marked circumstantial Themes establish a new framework within a text. For example, a typical task achieved by marked circumstantial Themes in a narrative is to establish a new temporal or locational setting. However, before we accept this claim, we need to explore this statement systematically, both from a functional point of view and from a formal point of view. The functional approach would examine a set of texts, locating every point at which a new setting is established. Then, at each place where a new setting is created, the functional approach would examine what happens in the language that sets that new scene.

This approach would focus of course on the first sentence and its Theme, but it would also consider any other aspect of the text that would seem to be involved with the scene setting function.

A formal approach to the problem would locate all Circumstances in the text, separate those that are thematic from those that play some other role and examine the differences in discourse effect of the two (or more) groups. Are those Circumstances which serve as Theme associated with moving to a new stage in the text in a way that the non-thematic Circumstances are not? We need to explore both aspects of the data exhaustively before we can say that we have finished systematically evaluating the hypothesis concerning the relation between circumstantial adjuncts and the scene setting function.

1.5.1 Illustrative projects: The functional approach

As discussed above, the functional approach should begin by examining places in texts where very specific, known, goals are to be achieved – places where we know a great deal about the text or text portion before we encounter the language.[11] We can then relate what we find in the language to what we know about the text.

Project illustration 1: Placement of expressions of urgency in demands for money

As part of a study of a fund-raising letter (see Fries 2002), it became useful to investigate the wording of the actual request for support from the addressee. The relevant sentence in the letter I was looking at was Example 5:

(5)   Please make a special contribution to Zero Population Growth today.

Was the wording used in this particular letter typical? In particular, I wanted to examine the placement of the word *today*. In order to examine this placement, I needed to examine the purposes of fund-raising letters in general, and the function of the request within such a letter. These letters are often written by executives of some group to members of that group. That is, they are written on behalf of a known organisation to members of that organisation with the purpose of raising funds. It is important to note that the audience has already demonstrated an interest in the cause espoused by the group before the letter is composed. They are already members of that group. The result is that the writer can count on an audience that is generally favourable in principle, and only needs to establish a particular need for money at this time. Of course, one of the tasks which the writer must achieve is to make sure that the readers actually send money at this time. The typical approach to achieve this last goal is to point out that the need is urgent, and to ask people not to delay in sending their contribution. It is well-known in the fund-raising business that readers may be forgetful, and if the readers delay in their response they are likely to give their money to other issues that get their attention. Therefore the writers of these fund-raising appeals typically attempt to stir their readers to immediate action.

Because of the situation just described, most fund-raising letters contain some sentence or sentences which express a direct request for support. This direct request may be realised through an imperative (*send money!*) or the request may be couched more indirectly (*I hope you will send money*). In addition, most of these requests for support will contain some wording to express a sense of urgency (*Send money* **now**, or **today**. *We* **desperately** *need your contribution.*) or the importance of your contribution (*Your help is* **vital** *to our continuing success.*) in order to get their readers to act while they remember to do so. Most of the expressions of urgency involve an Adjunct which expresses some appraisal that involves a temporal concept (*now*, *immediately*, *today*, etc.) or some Adjunct or modifier which appraises the importance of the contribution (*Your help is* **vital** *to our success*). I found 22 fund-raising letters and examined them for sentences which expressed an identifiable request that was worded either as a direct request, or as an indirect request. Of the 22 letters, two contained no sentence which expressed a clear direct or indirect request.[12] Some letters contained more than one request. Indeed two letters contained five identifiable requests each. The resulting corpus of direct requests therefore totalled 37 sentences. Of these 37 requests, 13 requests contained no expression of appraisal of time or urgency. (Seven of these 13 were found in letters where several requests were made, and at least one of the other requests contained expressions of urgency.) Each of the remaining 24 sentences contained at least one appraisal concerning urgency or time. Three sentences contained two such references to time. As a result, the corpus contained 27 appraisals. *Today* (with 16 occurrences) and *now* (with four occurrences) were the most frequently used temporal Adjuncts in the data. Three temporal Adjuncts were neither Theme nor N-Rheme. Of these three, two occurred in clauses in which the N-Rheme also expressed an appraisal regarding the urgency of the contribution, and the third occurred in a sentence which was followed by a sentence devoted expressly to communicating the urgency of the need. Two temporal Adjuncts were placed within the Themes of their clauses, while 22 appraisals indicating urgency occurred in the N-Rhemes of their clauses. These results are summarised in Tables 1.2 and 1.3.

In this small data set, Hypotheses 4 and 5 above are generally confirmed. A very important meaning to be expressed in these requests is the appraisal of urgency. By far the bulk of these appraisals are found in the N-Rhemes of their clauses. Almost all the exceptions are found in special circumstances, such as cases where the N-Rheme already contains an appraisal of urgency, or instances where the next sentence is devoted to such an appraisal. At the same time that we see that these appraisals are typically placed within the N-Rhemes of the clauses, we also see that they are typically not placed within the Themes of these clauses. That is, a negative correlation exists between these appraisals and placement in the Theme.

Project illustration 2: Generic Structure Potential

A second sort of project to investigate Theme and New would be to look at texts in which the generic structure tells us a great deal about what meanings are important. I am thinking of descriptions such as those by Hasan (Chapter 3 in Cloran *et al.* 1996) and by Swales (1990), in which certain parts of the description provide very detailed descriptions of what is important. Let me take the Swales description of the tasks to be achieved in introductions as an illustration. He has created what he calls the CARS (Create a Research Space) model for introductions of academic articles. He describes the structure of introductions as a series of moves, and steps within the moves which are intended to achieve certain goals.

Let me illustrate my point with a discussion of Move 1, 'Establishing a territory'. We are told that there are three optional steps within Move 1

Table 1.2: Clauses which contain appraisals of urgency in requests in fund-raising letters

Fund-raising Letters	Sentences which express a Request	Requests with no appraisals of urgency	Requests which contain at least one appraisal of urgency
22	37	13	24

Table 1.3: Locations of appraisals of urgency in requests in fund-raising letters

Theme	Other	N-Rheme	Total appraisals in 24 requests
2	3	22	27

and these three steps are described with differing degrees of detail. For example, the description of Step 2, 'Make topic generalisations', is quite vague. All that we are told is that there may be some general statement concerning the particular topic that will be addressed in the following paper. While this description does provide us with a general description of the meanings to be expressed, it tells us nothing about which specific meanings are likely to be emphasised, and so it provides us little help as we try to predict which information is likely to be presented as New, and which might be used as Theme.

By contrast, the description of Step 1, 'Claiming centrality', is much more help. In Swales (1990: 143), we are told that:

> Centrality claims are appeals to the discourse community whereby members are asked to accept that the research to be reported is part of a lively, significant or well-established research area.
>
> ...
>
> ... authors of a RA can make a centrality claim at the introduction's outset in a number of ways. They can claim interest, or importance; they can refer to the classic, favorite or central character of the issue; or they can claim that there are many other investigators active in the area.

Clearly, a core goal of Move 1 Step 1 is to articulate a type of appraisal. The question then arises as to whether the placement of these appraisals fits Hypothesis 4 above. This hypothesis predicts that, since expressing these appraisals is a major goal of this section of the RA, the appraisals would typically appear in the N-Rhemes of their clauses and *not* within the Themes of the component clauses.

I examined the 14 examples that Swales provides for his readers (page 144) and also added another 14 examples that I had collected. I also divided the various appraisals into four types: those that expressed temporal currency (*over the past 20 years*), those that dealt with interest (*there has been an increasing interest in ...*), those that directly referred to the quantity of researchers (*many linguists*) and finally those that directly expressed the importance of the issue (*... is vital*). Table 1.4 presents the results.

The data suggest that there may be a general trend for these appraisals to be placed within the N-Rhemes of their clauses. In other words, there is a general trend which confirms Hypothesis 4. But the general trend may result from several distinct patterns. Expressions of temporal currency usually involve expressions using circumstantial adjuncts and these circumstantial adjuncts are very often thematic. The results here suggest

Table 1.4: Locations of four types of appraisals in clauses which enact Swales' Move 1 Step 1

	Theme	*Other*	*N-Rheme*	*Totals*
Temporally current	5	1	3	9
(Increasing) Interest	2	5	10	17
Quantity of researchers	1	0	1	2
Importance of issue	2	1	5	8
Totals	10	7	19	36

that it is worth-while to examine both the general trend and the exceptions to that trend.

Project illustration 3: Texts with matched portions – Problem-Solution texts

It is very useful to examine texts or text portions which illustrate relations which have two closely related parts. I am thinking here, for example, of texts which directly encode a matching relation such as generalisation and elaboration (in which the elaboration provides some example of the generalisation or some detail of the generalisation). Other less obvious instances of matching are to be found in texts in which a problem is described and then a solution to that problem is proposed. In order to be successful, such texts must match the solution to the problem that has been described. That is, one cannot randomly combine some problem with some solution and automatically come up with a successful text. Rather, the solution must be seen to solve the problem which has been described. Since the two sections must match, we should be able to use the description of the problem as a means of predicting meanings that will be emphasised in the presentation of the solution.[13]

Let me illustrate with a quick discussion of Text 6: part of an advertisement for Walk Care. The example provides an analysis of the first six sentences of the advertisement (the portion which expresses the problem–solution relation) with the non-embedded clauses separated and given numbers.

(6)   [1.1] A major advance for those with poor circulation

[2.2] If you suffer FROM POOR CIRCULATION, PAIN AND SWELLING, CHRONIC OR ACUTE EDEMA,

[2.3] [you] plug in THIS CLINICALLY PROVEN FDA-APPROVED AT-HOME THERAPY

[2.4] and [you] feel better FAST.

[3.5] <u>WalkCare™ – a quiet, non-invasive and comfortable treatment –</u> reduces PAIN

[3.6] and <u>[WC]</u> enhances THE BLOOD FLOW IN YOUR LOWER BODY.

[4.7] Just <u>[you]</u> slip on THE FOOTNEST™ SLIPPERS

[4.8] and <u>[you]</u> experience THE POSITIVE EFFECTS OF FOOT COMPRESSION THERAPY.

[5.9] As <u>the four-chambered slippers</u> inflate and deflate SEQUENTIALLY (HEEL TO ARCH TO BALL-OF-FOOT TO TOES),

[5.10] <u>WalkCare</u> simulates A WALKING TYPE MOTION [[THAT SUPPORTS || AND TEMPORARILY ENHANCES BLOOD FLOW FROM THE FOOT UP THE CALF, || STIMULATING THE CALF MUSCLES TO PROPEL BLOOD TOWARD THE HEART, || INCREASING BLOOD CIRCULATION IN LOWER EXTREMITIES.]]

[6.11] IDEAL FOR THOSE WITH LIMITED MOBILITY, CONDITIONS ASSOCIATED WITH DIABETES, EVEN PREGNANT WOMEN.

Small caps indicate N-Rheme. Underline indicates Theme. (Original underlining has been deleted.) Elliptical and understood information has been filled in between square brackets.

In Text 6, clauses 1.1 and 2.2 enter the notion of poor circulation as a problem into the discourse. Clause 2.3 suggests that the reader use the advertised product and 2.4 predicts good results. Then clauses 3.5 through 4.8 describe the general function of the therapy and evaluate it again for certain circulation problems. Clauses 5.9 and 5.10 describe how the product operates and the physical effect it will have on the user. Finally 6.11 evaluates the product and again specifies the audience it is intended to help.

Since clauses 1.1 and 2.2 raise poor circulation and pain as problems, the solution should be seen to have some connection to correcting or mitigating those problems. That is, the proposed solution should be seen to stimulate circulation and reduce pain. Further, since this text comes from an advertisement of a product we can predict that a major goal of the text is that readers will come away from reading the text with a favourable impression of the product. Thus good evaluations of the product are important. Indeed these ideas are repeated several times in the N-Rhemes of the clauses which follow clauses 1.1 and 2.2. Clause 3.5 mentions *reduces pain* as an effect of this therapy with *pain* in the N-Rheme. Clause 3.6 mentions *enhances the blood flow in your lower body* – again referring to *blood flow* in the N-Rheme. Similarly *blood flow* and *blood circulation* are mentioned again in the N-Rheme of 5.10. Finally the last portion of 6.11 can be seen as related to blood flow. Limited mobility is often both the cause and the result of poor circulation. Diabetes is associated with poor circulation, and even pregnancy is associated with poor circulation to the legs.

The remaining N-Rhemes generally provide information concerning the approved nature of the therapy (2.3), or a direct positive evaluation of the therapy (2.4, 4.8). By contrast, most of the Themes of the problem section refer either explicitly or implicitly to *you*—the reader, or to the therapy (Walk Care/slippers). The results of this analysis are summarised in Table 1.5.

Table 1.5 shows that the problem section raises the issue of poor circulation. Then the solution section addresses this issue by regularly placing meanings which are related to poor circulation, pain and edema, or express positive evaluations of the product, or describe how the product works in the N-Rhemes of the clauses. That is, these meanings are expressed in the portions of the clauses which are most likely to be interpreted as expressing New information.[14]

1.5.2 Illustrative projects: Form oriented studies

Finally, let me move to a study which starts from form. I want to use as my foundation an important study by Thompson and Zhou (2000) in which they demonstrate that thematic interpersonal Adjuncts may establish conjunctive relations. In particular, they examined thematic interpersonal Adjuncts in clause relations which expressed hypothetical–real, or concessive clause relations. One of the examples they cite is Example 7.

Table 1.5: Summary of the content of the Themes and N-Rhemes of the clauses in Text 6

Problem Section: Clauses 1.1 and 2.2

Theme			N-Rheme				
you	Product	Product evaluation	you	circulation etc.	Therapy Process	Product evaluation	product
1	0	0	0	2	0	1	0

Solution Section: Clauses 2.3–6.11

you	Product	Product evaluation	you	circulation etc.	Therapy Process	Product evaluation	product
4	3	1	1	3	2	4	1

(7)   Our intelligence was almost always better than that of the British. *Unfortunately* Washington's judgement sometimes disallowed facts.

As they point out, the *unfortunately* 'denies the positive expectation set up by the preceding text' (Thompson and Zhou 2000: 130). They also note that if we were to delete the word *unfortunately*, the coherence of the clause pair would be degraded.

Although they amply establish their point that these interpersonal adjuncts establish conjunctive relations, they explicitly restrict their examination to interpersonal adjuncts that were Themes, and thus they do not set out to establish that thematic status has anything to do with their results. For a full picture, we need to examine all instances of interpersonal adjuncts, whether or not they are placed within the Themes of their clauses, to see how they contribute to the perception of these two clause relations. Is there a difference in interpretation between those that are thematic and those that are not?

I did a mini-pilot study of such a project involving the word *actually*. *Actually* is of interest since Halliday and Hasan (1976) in their classic study of signals of cohesion include *actually* as a signal of conjunction with no comment. On the other hand, the definitions of *actually* in, for example, the Collins COBUILD dictionary all have a decidedly interpersonal flavour, highlighting such functions as signalling surprise or making an utterance more polite. In addition, many tokens of *actually* do not actually signal a relation between clauses. Only some do. Is it possible to use thematic status to tease apart those tokens that do indicate a conjunctive relation from those that do not? In this pilot project I studied 50 instances of *actually*. Twenty-five of these examples occurred thematically in their clauses, and 25 occurred somewhere in the Rheme of their clause. To keep the project simple, I divided the meanings of *actually* into three groups. Group 1 involves cases in which *actually* is contained in a clause that corrects some portion of a previous assertion. Usually the correction is not of a major point. Example 8 presents a typical instance:

(8)   We take it to a community group. We take it to a person who employs students who leave school. **Actually**, probably, we take it to people at the Defense Department which are the largest employer of school graduates immediately upon leaving school ...

The sentence which begins with *actually* corrects the impression that we take it to just any person who employs students. The *actually* clause is clearly not intended as a major point, but is an attempt to be technically accurate. The implication of this use is that a portion of the previous sentence is technically inaccurate. This usage clearly indicates a conjunctive relation between clauses.

The second group of meanings involves meanings that are not specifically correcting. Example 9 is typical.

(9)   ... this morning you sounded like you support the Daschle proposal or the Daschle language. Do you believe that Daschle does – that this *actually* goes further than partial birth abortion legislation that the House passed?

In this example there is no previous sentence which is partially corrected by the *actually* sentence. Rather *actually* in this sentence behaves as a kind of modality. This usage does not indicate a relation between clauses.

The third group consists of cases that were difficult to classify on the basis of the information that I had available; and it also includes one example in which *actually* repeats an occurrence of the same word in the previous context. For the purposes of this small-scale study, I classified these as 'Undecided'.

Table 1.6 presents the results.

While it is dangerous to take the results of such a small study seriously, we can take the results to indicate that a comparison of the role of *actually* when it is Theme and *actually* when it is not Theme is worth serious investigation. It seems that the conjunctive use of *actually* is most prominent when that word occurs as Theme. Further an examination of the examples suggests that the conjunctive function of *actually* is prominent when it is Theme precisely because its status as Theme emphasises an interpersonal environment for the interpretation of the remainder of the message – an environment that is not so emphasized when *actually* occurs in other parts of the clause.

If these results hold, we may have an important extension of the notion of the staging or orienting function of Theme into the interpersonal world.

1.6   Conclusion

Let me summarise what I have said here. I have focused on the ways that choices of Theme and New affect our perception of written texts. I have commented only in passing on issues that concern the clause-internal

Table 1.6: Locations of the corrective and non-corrective uses of *actually*

	Corrective	*Non-corrective*	*Undecided*
Theme	18	0	7
Non-theme	0	23	2

structural nature of Theme – not because these issues are unimportant, but because I did not have adequate time to address them. I would only like to say that the trinocular approach to our concepts implies that one significant factor to consider in deciding exactly how much to consider as included in Theme should involve its function in larger structures such as text.

We have been studying Theme and New for over 30 years and we have learned a great deal. However, we still have a great deal to learn. One particularly important gap in our knowledge is the means by which writers indicate to their readers what functions as New in their texts. A second need is further research on the discourse functions of a greater range of Themes, including interpersonal Themes. A third issue for further work arises out of the trends in the results of the functional studies suggested in sections 5.1.1–5.1.3. The perceptive reader will notice that Hypothesis 4, which concerns the information which is placed within the N-Rheme, seems likely to be supported. On the other hand Hypothesis 5, which concerns the information that will be placed with the Themes, receives only negative support. That is, information that is seen to be relevant to the goals of the text or text segment tends not to be placed within the Themes of that text or text segment. Certainly a negative correlation is a correlation. However, we still need to develop a way in which we can predict with any certainty the nature of the information that is placed within the Themes of a text. That is, we need to determine some positive predictor of the Themes of a text or text segment. Can we develop an approach which uses information about the context in which the text functions to predict thematic content before we actually see the text as we did with the content of the N-Rheme?[15] (By contrast with the functional approach, the formal approach illustrated in section 5.2 has an excellent chance of uncovering a positive effect of thematic status.) These three issues need to be addressed systematically and carefully before we can say we have finished our investigation of the textual metafunction in written English.

As a final comment, let me say that this chapter can be taken as an attempt to frame an agenda for future research on the structure-assigning aspects of the textual metafunction. I have begun with a discussion of basic principles to explain why I frame the agenda as I do. Section 5 of the chapter can be taken as suggesting a number of projects of varying sizes which would explore text-based issues that I see as relevant to developing our knowledge of how the textual metafunction operates. Most of this discussion has focused on Theme. Partially in reaction to a number of works which have taken what seem to me a rather formalistic approach to the investigation of Theme and New, I have tried to suggest ways in which these concepts can be profitably studied in conjunction with their function in texts. These suggestions illustrate several general principles of approach.

1. A fundamental assumption which underlies everything said here is that we can only learn about the effect of choosing Theme and New on the perception of texts by systematically examining these constructs in texts. However, simply looking at Theme or at New in one text or in a group of texts, though helpful, will not truly establish the usefulness of these concepts. We need to do more.

2. We need to link formal characteristics of texts through the grammar of the language to some aspect of their interpretation, and ultimately to reader behaviour.

3. We can approach the investigation of Theme and New from either of two starting points: we can take a functional approach and start with functions within texts, and then ask what sorts of forms fill those functions, or we can take a formal approach and start with the forms and ask what is the range of functions which those forms fill. We need both approaches, and neither approach is sufficient by itself for a systematic, exhaustive study.

4. When we engage in a project which takes a functional approach, we need to examine texts (or text portions) about which we have a great deal of detailed knowledge before we encounter them.

5. Finally, we need to make exhaustive analyses of our corpora. If we start with text functions and interpretations, we need to investigate all examples of those interpretations and functions to discover all the ways that they are cued in our corpus. If we start with forms, we need to examine all examples of the forms we are considering that occur in the texts we are examining.

I believe that using these principles as guides for our research in these areas will help us advance our knowledge of these structures.

Acknowledgements

I would like to thank Agnes He and William Spruiell for their comments on an earlier version of this chapter.

Notes

1. It is instructive to compare Fries's position concerning the strike with the position of other American linguists concerning the phoneme. I take the Bloch and Trager (1942: 38) description as typical of the time:

    > we are able to organize the infinitely many sounds heard in the utterances of a speech community into a limited number of classes ... called PHONEMES. The sounds which constitute a single phoneme are phonetically similar, in the sense of sharing some feature of articulation or some combination of features (resulting in a characteristic auditory effect) absent from the members of all other phonemes.

    For Bloch and Trager, the phoneme is a class of phones which have some physical similarity. For Fries a phoneme is an abstraction which is signalled by some phonetic substance.

2. While Halliday expressed similar sentiments in the early 1970s, I am unable to locate any printed statement from that time.

3. The thematic system in particular is 'lopsided' in that Theme is defined positively while Rheme is defined as everything that is not Theme. As a result of the negative definition of Rheme a number of linguists (e.g. Fawcett 2003) have felt that Rheme is an unnecessary concept. Indeed, Fawcett points out that there is nothing unitary about Rheme and so he does not use that notion.

4. This example has been modified from the original by deleting the Adjunct which originally served as Theme. It seems to me, however, that the modified version is quite possible.

5. It is important to remember that Fries wrote this letter in 1960 – well before Halliday had published his model. Fries never named the nameless 'Europeans' and I never asked him about who he meant. I presume that he was referring to some of the Prague school scholars, but I am not sure.

6. I choose the word *presented* by intent. I make the assumption that not all information which is unfamiliar has the function of New. Therefore the writer needs to do something to tell the reader which information to pay attention to.

7. Clearly the ordering of information within the sentence is only one of several means available to writers. Others include the grammatical constructions used (particularly ones such as the 'cleft' construction which normally are associated with special intonations), punctuation, cohesive relations, rhetorical questions, matching relations and systematic repetition (see Winter 1994), and finally, visual layout, font type, etc. None of these factors provides a totally accurate set of signals. All provide cues that a

sensitive reader can use as a means of determining what functions as New in a particular text.

8. It is worth noting, however, that a slight rewording of this sentence would avoid the problem. If it had read the method of development is *realized* by the set of Themes in a text, or is *signalled* by the set of Themes in the text, I would have no objection since the verbs *realize* and *signal* relate entities of different types.

9. The interaction of Theme with clause relations (e.g. as addressed by RST analysis) is well worth exploring systematically.

10. There is insufficient space to address systematically the question of how we should investigate the signals of New in written English. As a result, I will use the notion of N-Rheme as a sort of place holder for a real investigation of this issue.

11. Notice I am arguing against using randomly chosen texts for this type of study.

12. There was no doubt that these letters were requests for funding. Rather the requests were made very indirectly and extended over several sentences.

13. One must be careful about the notion of prediction in text. In general, given stage *n* in a text, it is not possible to predict with complete accuracy what will occur in stage *n*+1. Rather, stage *n* will provide information which may be used to limit what is likely to occur in stage *n*+1. Once stage *n*+1 has occurred, the analyst can usually figure out what factors were relevant in creating stage *n*+1. I have elsewhere called this 'post-facto' prediction (see also note 15 below).

14. It is worth mentioning that these N-Rhemes are interpreted as New information even though the notions of poor circulation and the problems arising because of it have already been mentioned earlier in the text. I see no reason to consider these references to be contrastive. In other words, the solution section of this text regularly presents as New, information that has been mentioned earlier in the problem section. See Fries (2001: 100–2) for a more careful discussion of this phenomenon in two other advertisements which have a problem-solution structure.

15. Nothing in what I say here should be interpreted to imply that thematic content is unprincipled. Partly the difficulty in predicting Theme relates to predicting local issues in a text in a universal way. At the very least we can engage in what I call 'post-facto' prediction. That is, once we see the content of the Theme of a clause, we can usually relate that content to fairly obvious principles which led to the choice of exactly that information as Theme of the particular clause. Jay Gould has discussed this issue in the context of predicting the evolution of species using the term 'contingent development'.

References

Bäcklund, Ingegerd. (1990). Theme in English telephone conversation. Paper delivered at the 17th International Systemic Congress, Stirling, Scotland. June 1990.

Banks, D. (ed.). (2004). *Text and Texture: Systemic Functional Viewpoints on the Nature and Structure of Texts.* Paris: L'Harmattan.

Berry, M. (1987). The functions of place names. In *Leeds Studies in English New Series XVIII: Studies on Honour of Kenneth Cameron*, T. Turville-Petre and M. Gelling (eds), 71–88. Leeds: School of English, University of Leeds.

Bloch, B. and Trager, G. (1942). *Outline of Linguistic Analysis.* Baltimore, MA: Linguistic Society of America.

Christiansen, F. (1965). A generative rhetoric of the paragraph. *College Composition and Communication* 15: 144–56.

Cloran, C., Butt, D. and Williams, G. (eds) (1996). *Ways of Saying: Ways of Meaning Selected Papers of Ruqaiya Hasan.* London: Cassell.

Crompton, P. (2002). Theme in argumentative texts: an analytical tool applied and appraised. Ph. D. dissertation. Department of Modern English Language and Applied Linguistics, Lancaster University

Crompton, P. (2004). Theme in discourse: 'Thematic progression' and 'method-of-development' re-evaluated. *Functions of Language* 11 (2): 213–49.

Daneš, F. (1974). Functional sentence perspective and the organization of the text. In *Papers on Functional Sentence Perspective*, F. Danes (ed.), 106–28. The Hague: Mouton.

Davies, F. (1988). Reading between the lines: Thematic choice as a device for presenting writer viewpoint in academic discourse. *The ESPecialist* 9 (2): 173–200.

Davies, F. (1994). From writer roles to elements of text: interactive, organisational and topical. In *Reflections on Language Learning*, L. Barbara and M. Scott (eds) 170–83. Clevedon, England: Multilingual Matters.

Davies, F. (1997). Marked Theme as a heuristic for analyzing text-type, text and genre. In *Applied Languages: Theory and Practice in ESP*, J. Piqué and D. J. Viera (eds), 45–79. Valencia: Universitat de Valencia.

Davies, M. (1989). Prosodic and non-prosodic cohesion in speech and writing. *Word* 40: 255–62.

Downing, A. (1991). An alternative approach to Theme: a systemic-functional perspective. *Word* 42: 119–43.

Enkvist, N. E. (1978). Stylistics and text linguistics. In *Current Trends in Text-linguistics*, W. U. Dressler (ed.), 174–190. Berlin: de Gruyter.

Fawcett, R. (2003). The many types of Theme. <www.isfla.org>.

Francis, G. (1989). Thematic selection and distribution in written discourse. *Word* 40: 201–21.

Fries, C. C. (1952). *The Structure of English.* New York: Harcourt, Brace & Co.

Fries, C. C. (1967). Structural linguistics. *Encyclopaedia Britannica*. Chicago, IL: Encyclopaedia Britannica, Inc.

Fries, P. H. (1981). On the status of theme in English: arguments from discourse. *Forum Linguisticum* 6: 1–38. Reprinted, 1983, in revised form in *Micro and Macro Connexity of Texts*, J. S. Petöfi and E. Sözer (eds), 116–52. Hamburg: Helmut Buske.

Fries, P. H. (1982). Charles C. Fries, Signals grammar and the goals of linguistics. *LACUS Forum* 9: 146–58.

Fries, P. H. (1995). Themes, methods of development, and texts. In *On Subject and Theme: From the Perspective of Functions in Discourse*, R. Hasan and P. H. Fries (eds), 317–59. Amsterdam: John Benjamins.

Fries, P. H. (1996). Theme and New in written English. In *Functional Approaches to Written Text: Classroom Applications*, Thomas Miller (ed.). *TESOL France* 3(1): 69–85. Reprinted in *Functional Approaches to Written Text: Classroom Discourse*, Thomas Miller (ed.), 1997. Washington, DC: USIS.

Fries, P. H. (2001). Issues in modeling the textual metafunction: A constructive approach. In *Patterns of Text: In Honour of Michael Hoey*, M. Scott and G. Thompson (eds), 83–107. Amsterdam: John Benjamins.

Fries, P. H. (2002). The flow of information in a written text. In Fries, P. H., Cummings, M., Lockwood, D. and Spruiell. W. (eds) (2002). *Relations and Functions within and around Language*. London: Continuum, 117–55.

Fries, P. H., Cummings, M., Lockwood, D. and Spruiell. W. (eds) (2002). *Relations and Functions within and around Language*. London: Continuum.

Gregory, M. (2002). Phasal analysis within Communication Linguistics: Two contrastive discourses. In Fries, P. H., Cummings, M., Lockwood, D. and Spruiell. W. (eds) (2002). *Relations and Functions within and around Language*. London: Continuum, 316–45.

Halliday, M. A. K. (1967). Notes on transitivity and theme in English Part 2 *Journal of Linguistics* 3.2: 199–244.

Halliday, M. A. K. (1970). Language structure and language function. In *New Horizons in Linguistics*, J. Lyons (ed.), 140–64. Harmondsworth, England: Penguin.

Halliday, M. A. K. (1992). Some lexicogrammatical features of the Zero Population Growth text. In *Discourse Description: Diverse Linguistic Analyses of a Fundraising Text*, William C. Mann and Sandra A. Thompson (eds), 327–58. Amsterdam: Benjamins.

Halliday, M. A. K. 1994. *Introduction to Functional Grammar* (2nd edition). London: Arnold.

Halliday, M. A. K. and Hasan, R. (1976). *Cohesion in English*. London: Longman.

Halliday, M. A. K. and Hasan, R. (1985). *Language, Context and Text: Aspects of language in a social-semiotic perspective* Geelong, Vic.: Deakin University Press. Republished, 1989, by Oxford University Press.

Harris, Zelig (1951) *Methods in Structural Linguistics* Chicago, IL: University of Chicago Press.

Huddleston, Rodney. (1988). Constituency, multi-functionality and grammaticalization in Halliday's functional grammar. *Linguistics* 24: 137–74.

Hunt, K. (1965). *Grammatical Structures Written at Three Grade Levels.* Champaign-Urbana, IL: National Council of Teachers of English.

Longacre, R. E. (1981). A Spectrum and Profile approach to discourse analysis. *Text* 1: 337–59.

Longacre, R. E. (1989). Two hypotheses regarding text generation and analysis. *Discourse Processes* 12: 413–60.

Longacre, R. E. (1990). Storyline concerns and word order typology in East and West Africa. University of Texas at Arlington. Mimeo.

Love, A. (2004). Drawing on (a lot of) Given: One aspect of Theme choice in newspaper editorials. In Banks, D. (ed.). *Text and Texture: Systemic Functional Viewpoints on the Nature and Structure of Texts.* Paris: L'Harmattan.

Martin, J. R. (1992a). *English Text: System and Structure.* Amsterdam: John Benjamins.

Martin, J. R. (1992b). Theme, method of development and existentiality: The price of reply. *Occasional Papers in Systemic Linguistics* 6: 147–83.

Martin, J. R. and Rose, D. (2003). *Working with Discourse.* London: Continuum.

Matthiessen, C. M. I. M. (1995). THEME as an enabling resource in ideational knowledge construction. In *Thematic Development in English Text*, M. Ghadessy (ed.), 20–54. London: Pinter.

Reszkiewicz, A. (1966a). *Ordering of Elements in Late Old English Prose in Terms of their Size and Structural Complexity.* Wroctaw: Ossolineum.

Reszkiewicz, A. (1966b). Split constructions in Old English. In *Studies in Language and Literature in Honour of Margaret Schlauch*, M. Brahmer, S. Helsztynski, and J. Krzyzanowski (eds), 313–16. Warsaw: Polish Scientific Publishers.

Swales, J. (1990). *Genre Analysis.* Cambridge: Cambridge University Press.

Thompson, G. (2004). *Introducing Functional Grammar* (2nd edition). London: Arnold.

Thompson, G. and Zhou, J. (2000). Evaluation and organization in text: The structuring role of evaluative disjuncts. In *Evaluation in Text: Authorial Stance and the Construction of Discourse*, S. Hunston and G. Thompson (eds), 121–41. Oxford: Oxford University Press.

Winter, E. (1994). Clause relations as information structure: Two basic text structures in English. In *Advances in Written Text Analysis*, M. Coulthard (ed.), 46–68. London: Routledge.

2 | Theme, Subject and the unfolding of text

Geoff Thompson and Susan Thompson
University of Liverpool

2.1 Starting points

Our interest in Theme originates directly from our work with Flo Davies: her enthusiasm for discourse analysis, and for the study of thematic choices in particular, inspired a rewarding concern with this area of linguistic enquiry; and the contentious issues that we debated with her in numerous, sometimes heated, discussions – not only at seminars, but in our offices or the corridor, on train journeys, over coffee or dinner, and so on – have continued to occupy us. One set of issues that remain particularly salient in the field centre around the identification of Theme in text. In this chapter we explore some of these issues, focusing especially on the effect of grammatical metaphor and on the relationship between Theme and Subject. Our aim is to clarify some of the factors that should be considered in deciding what to include in Theme, and to argue the case for specific guidelines for establishing the boundary between Theme and Rheme.

It is useful to begin by providing a brief sketch of how Theme is identified in the Systemic Functional Linguistics (SFL) model within which we work. In this approach (see, for example, Halliday and Matthiessen, 2004: 85) Theme (in English) is taken as comprising everything up to and including the first experiential ('content') constituent of a clause. Anything following the Theme in the clause is termed Rheme. Example 1, from a text which will be discussed later in the chapter, illustrates some of the basic categories – the Themes are highlighted:

(1)   [1] **A hefty challenge on Barmby by Mark Pembridge** led to the opening goal. [2] **From the resultant free-kick**, Christian Ziege's cross to the far post was met by the head of Barmby, whose header in acres of space found the Everton net to send the Reds fans wild. [3] **However, the Blues** quickly rallied.

In Sentence [1], the first experiential constituent is simultaneously Subject and Theme. In Halliday's terms, this is 'unmarked Theme': the choice that is made unless there are particular reasons for choosing something other than Subject as Theme. In [2], the Theme is a 'marked Theme' (i.e. non-Subject Theme), realised by an initial Adjunct. In both [1] and [2], the initial constituent comprises the whole of Theme; they thus represent cases of 'simple Theme'. In [3], on the other hand, we have an example of what Halliday calls 'multiple Theme': the experiential constituent *the Blues* is preceded by a textual element, the conjunct *however*. Multiple Themes may also include interpersonal elements such as comment Adjuncts expressing the speaker's evaluation of the following proposition (**Fortunately, the Blues** quickly *rallied*); and both interpersonal and textual elements may appear together (**Fortunately, however, the Blues** *quickly rallied*). These elements contribute to the Theme but do not 'exhaust the thematic potential of the clause' (Halliday 1994: 52): it is only when the first experiential constituent has been reached that the thematic function is fully realised.

A further point about the identification of Theme concerns the level at which the analysis is worked out. This can be illustrated with another sentence from the text from which Example 1 above is taken:

(2)   As Liverpool picked up the tempo, Everton's rearguard began to lose its shape.

If the analyst is working at the level of the clause, this sentence has two Themes, both unmarked: *As Liverpool* and *Everton's rearguard*. However, following Fries (1981/1983), many analysts work at the level of the T-unit (Hunt 1965), identifying a single Theme for each clause complex centred around an independent clause. With this approach, the whole of the dependent clause *As Liverpool picked up the tempo* is the Theme, providing the framework within which the following independent clause is interpreted. On the whole, the clause-by-clause approach is taken by those interested in the grammar of Theme, whereas the T-unit approach is taken by those studying the thematic development of texts (though there are notable exceptions, such as Matthiessen (1995a, b) who undertake text analysis on the basis of identifying Theme in every clause).

2.2   Issues in the delimitation of theme

The picture as outlined above is deliberately simple; but there are a number of complications. One of the main areas of disagreement between analysts is the decision on where the boundary between Theme and Rheme should be placed. In a sense this is not a question that can be given a definitive answer: Halliday (e.g. 1994: 337) has always stressed that it is misleading to think in terms of a distinct Theme-Rheme boundary and that thematic prominence does not end abruptly but fades in a diminuendo (see also Fries, this volume). Nevertheless, many kinds of analyses rely on counting the occurrences of the different types of Theme, for example in order to arrive at a thematic characterisation of particular registers; and the use of different methods of identifying Theme clearly has the unwelcome effect of making it much harder to compare different studies. While accepting that the boundary is inherently indeterminate, it is still possible to approach the identification of Theme in terms of degrees of thematic prominence, and to focus primarily on the elements of the message which have greatest prominence. Thus, the question is where the thematic diminuendo should be seen as starting. There are many factors which affect the answer that may be adopted; and in the following sections we will explore three that lead to the greatest variations between different analyses.

2.2.1 Theme and interpersonal grammatical metaphor

One salient issue in the delimitation of Theme that is relevant to the thematic analyses of texts is the presence of grammatical metaphor (Halliday and Matthiessen 2004, Chapter 10) in Theme. The complications arise especially in relation to interpersonal meanings. These meanings are congruently expressed through choices in interpersonal systems such as modality and Mood; but they may be 'experientialised', that is, metaphorically expressed as if they were part of the propositional content. Examples 3–7 illustrate the difference (the use of different forms of highlighting is explained below).[1]

(3)   **Probably he** was too optimistic about his prospects

(4)   **It** *is probable he* cared little about Literature, after all.

(5)   **I** *think he's* about 55, like me

(6)   **Has this** been getting worse?

(7)   **Can I** *ask you whether this* has been getting steadily worse over time?

In Example 3, the interpersonal modal Adjunct *probably* is a congruent realisation of modality. In 4 and 5, on the other hand, the writer's assessment of probability is expressed as a separate clause: in 4 it is construed as if being *probable* were an 'external' attribute of the proposition *he cared little about Literature*, while in (5) the proposition *he's about 55, like me* is explicitly projected through the writer's mental process of *thinking*. In 6 the ordering Finite^Subject signals that this is an interrogative, functioning as a question; whereas in 7 the speech function being performed is made experientially explicit through the projecting (reporting) clause *Can I ask you* (see Halliday and Matthiessen 2004: 626 on interpersonal projection).

In terms of Theme, *probably* in 3 is part of a multiple Theme which also includes the experiential constituent *he*; and *has this* in 6 also comprises a multiple Theme, with the Finite *has* as an interpersonal element. However, when the kinds of interpersonal grammatical metaphor illustrated in Examples 4, 5 and 7 occur in clause-initial position, there are two main options in identifying Theme. In 4, for example, Halliday (see e.g. Halliday and Matthiessen 2004: 98) identifies *it* alone as Theme (which, for convenience, may be described as 'minimal Theme', shown by bold above), with *he* as the separate subsidiary Theme of the embedded clause. On the other hand, a number of other analysts such as Davies (1988) and Martin (1995: 251) (see also Forey and Montemayor-Borsinger, this volume) view *it is probable* as an interpersonal element in a multiple Theme (functionally equivalent to *probably*) and therefore include the following experiential constituent *he* in Theme ('maximal' Theme, shown by italics above).[2] Example 5 can be treated in a similar way, either as a complex consisting of two clauses with *I* as Theme of the T-unit or as a single modalised proposition with *I think* as part of multiple Theme. A minimal Theme analysis of 7 identifies *can I* as the Theme of the clause complex; while in a maximal Theme analysis *can I ask you whether* can be seen as an interpersonal element signalling speech function (much as the Finite^Subject interrogative ordering in 6 signals the speech function), in which case the Subject of the proposition being queried, *this*, should be included.

These different analyses stem from differing degrees of emphasis on wording and meaning. Since the matrix clauses *it is probable, I think* and *can I ask you* are experientialised expressions of interpersonal meanings, they can be read both 'literally' as clauses with their own Theme-Rheme structure and metaphorically as interpersonal elements within a more extensive Theme. Neither reading is 'truer' than the other – the 'value added' of having double readings in co-existence is precisely one of the communicative benefits of grammatical metaphor (see e.g. many of the papers in Simon-Vandenbergen *et al.* 2003); and thus both approaches to analysing Theme are equally justified. However, most analysts who are working on Theme in text would accept that the use of such clauses in initial position is significant both in mapping the unfolding of texts and in characterising different registers in terms of thematic patterns. For example, in the following extract, the penultimate paragraph of a position paper by an environmental pressure group,[3] the negotiation of stance is highlighted as the argument reaches its conclusion through a cluster of interpersonal thematic elements:

(8) **Disappointingly, the World Water Council** is already planning for the 5th World Water Forum. **Yesterday** a vote was taken to hold it in Turkey in 2009. **It is regrettable that this decision** has been taken before any kind of review has taken place of the need for, the role of, and the processes within WWF4. **It is clear that there must be** significant reform of the whole WWF process if the event in 2009 is to make a more significant contribution to meeting the Millennium Development Goals on water and sanitation.

The interpersonal and experiential Themes are shown in Table 2.1.

The experiential Themes here 'scaffold' the text (Martin 1992: 436) in terms of aspects of the topic (the actions of the WWC). On the other hand, the interpersonal thematic elements, running in parallel to the experiential elements, provide an attitudinal orientation to the message. These textual frameworks draw on fundamentally different kinds of meanings and thus both need to be accounted for in a Theme analysis; and the salience of the interpersonal 'thread' (which is strengthened by the fact that it is carried by separate clauses in the third and fourth sentences) is characteristic of this kind of argumentative discourse (see e.g. Thompson 2007: Section 3.2.5).

Given the recognition that such cases are textually significant, it would clearly be useful to have an agreed way of handling the analysis: comparisons between different studies and generalisations across their findings would be made easier (see comments in e.g. Fries 1995; North 2005; Boström Aronsson 2005, on the difficulties of matching results from different studies). From this perspective, it would seem helpful if textual studies report their findings using maximal Theme involving interpersonal grammatical metaphor as outlined above, since minimal Theme can normally be deduced from maximal Theme, but the reverse is often not

Table 2.1 Interpersonal and experiential 'threads' in Theme

Interpersonal	Experiential
Disappointingly	the World Water Council
	Yesterday
It is regrettable that	this decision
It is clear that	there must be

the case. Some analysts will doubtless continue to need to use minimal Theme, for various purposes; but it would be relatively straightforward to include at least a summary of maximal Themes in their data to allow for comparison.

In most cases the identification of such maximal Themes is relatively straightforward. However, there are, inevitably, problematic cases. In some instances the experientialisation of the interpersonal assessment can reach an advanced stage, making it difficult to decide whether or not the matrix clause should be treated as metaphorical. This can be illustrated with Examples 9 and 10:

(9)   It strikes me as a distinct possibility that all the MPs that are to vote 'nay' in the upcoming vote are actually religious bigots

(10)   We face the disturbing possibility that this turbulence has so strained nurses that their interactions with patients have become superficial.

The case for analysing Example 9 in terms of maximal Theme (i.e. everything up to and including *the upcoming vote*) seems reasonably clear, not least because the *it ... that* structure is intimately associated with the interpersonal evaluation of propositions (see e.g. Hunston and Sinclair 2000). With 10, on the other hand, the nominalisation of the modality is more thoroughly integrated into the propositional content, and it would seem more plausible not to think in terms of a maximal Theme up to and including *turbulence* but to see just *We* as Theme. This kind of indeterminacy is inherent in interpersonal grammatical metaphor: the balance of experiential and interpersonal meaning is a matter of degree, and it is not possible to establish a distinct point at which the experiential meaning dominates sufficiently to justify ignoring the interpersonal (or vice versa). In many registers, the number of borderline cases is likely to be small; but in those where interpersonal concerns are more salient, the indeterminacy has to be accepted as a feature of the register.

A further, structure-based problem that has been discussed for example by North (2005) is when the target of an initial comment clause is a non-finite clause, as in Example 11:

(11)   It is possible to reduce exposure to these vulnerabilities by using a different web browser

In such cases, there is no Subject in the embedded clause to include in maximal Theme. However, if we take a minimal approach, *it* is identified as Theme in the matrix clause; while the embedded non-finite clause has no Theme (see Halliday and Matthiessen 2004: 100). This suggests that we can see maximal Theme as including the comment clause (*it is possible*) as an interpersonal element but as not having an explicit experiential element. This is a meaningful choice on the part of the speaker, since there is the option of including an experiential element either by making the Subject of the embedded clause explicit or by introducing a circumstantial Adjunct (maximal Themes highlighted):

(12) **It is possible for the client** to request keyword expansion/**It is possible, when causing a link to open in a different window**, to name that window

It may be useful to indicate the absence of an experiential element in cases like 11 above for the purposes of counting frequencies of different kinds of Theme.

2.2.2 Theme and projection

A further, more difficult, issue arises with clause complexes involving projection. In the following extract from a news report,[4] the minimal Themes at clause level are highlighted:

(13) **A sexual charge between pupils and teachers** is sometimes a feature of good teaching, **an academic** has claimed ...
Pat Sikes, of Sheffield University, concluded **that 'erotic charges'** were common in schools, particularly as a result of good teaching 'which provokes a positive and exciting response.'
Her 25-year study stressed **that exploitative relationships** were wrong, **but** added **that it** was not always a case of teacher exploiting pupil, **the Times Education Supplement** reported. ...
She said **teacher-pupil affairs at her school in Leicestershire** were neither uncommon, nor seen as sordid. **The study** found **it was often pupils** who initiated relationships **and that most teachers and pupils** knew of teachers and pupils who had married or were living together.

Table 2.2 shows the Themes grouped according to whether they are in the projecting or projected clause.

It is clear from Table 2.2 that the Themes in the two sets of clauses perform different functions. Those in the projecting clauses highlight the source of the information (there is an added layer of projection, in that the whole story is presented as reported from the *Times Education Supplement*, but that does not affect the basic pattern). On the other hand, those in the projected clauses signal the aspects of the content of the study being reported, centred around the topic of *sexual charge* (repeated as *erotic charges* and *teacher-pupil affairs*), with reference to the instantially contrasted *exploitative relationships* and to the people involved in the relationships (*pupils, teachers and pupils*).

Table 2.2 Theme in projecting and projected clauses

Projecting clauses	Projected clauses
	A sexual charge between pupils and teachers
an academic	
Pat Sikes, of Sheffield University	that 'erotic charges'
Her 25-year study	that exploitative relationships
but	that it
the Times Education Supplement	
She	teacher-pupil affairs at her school in Leicestershire
The study	it was often pupils
	and that most teachers and pupils

This complementary distribution reflects the special nature of projection as a logico-semantic relation: from one perspective, the projecting clause is dominant both structurally and semantically; but from another it is the content of the projected clause that has greater informational weight and the projecting clause serves as a kind of subsidiary 'source tag' – this comes out particularly clearly with parenthetical or final projecting clauses, such as the first sentence of the extract and, especially, the reference to the *Times Education Supplement* as the source of the story (see Thompson 2005: 781 on this dual perspective). The text thus has a double thematic pattern; and it seems clear that both strands need to be picked up in order to trace the textual development. This is typical of many texts in which reporting of information from other sources is important, such as news reports, academic articles and workplace texts (Forey, this volume).

If the analyst is working at clause level, it is not a problem to follow both strands – indeed the issues raised by projection can be seen as an argument in favour of the clause-by-clause approach even for text analysis. However, many studies of Theme in text work at T-unit level, which means that many of the projected clause Themes are not included: see Table 2.3.

This certainly reflects the fact that the text is a report of the study: apart from the first Theme, the writer makes the 'point of departure' (Halliday

Table 2.3 T-unit Theme in projection complexes

A sexual charge between pupils and teachers
Pat Sikes, of Sheffield University
Her 25-year study
but
She
The study

and Matthiessen 2004: 64) of each T-unit the study (rather than, as a possible alternative, the findings). Nevertheless, it gives a somewhat distorted picture of the way the text unfolds, in that the reader is likely to focus at least as much, if not more, on how the findings are described – it is worth noting that the title of the article is 'Erotic charge "is feature of good teaching"' (rather than, say, 'Study highlights "erotic charge" in good teaching').[5]

One way of capturing both threads of thematic development while keeping the T-unit as the basis of analysis has been suggested by Davies (1988, 1997) as part of her broader concept of 'Contextual Frames' (see Section 2.3 below) and taken up by, amongst others, North (2005), Forey (this volume) and Montemayor-Borsinger (this volume). This is to place emphasis on the idea of the projecting clause as a 'source tag' and to treat it as a kind of interpersonal grammatical metaphor, essentially similar in kind to those illustrated in Examples 4, 5 and 7 above. Thus, if it comes in initial position, the whole clause is analysed as part of Theme but the first experiential element of the following projected clause also needs to be included: see Table 2.4.

While this solution is clearly attractive in practical terms, the theoretical basis is uncertain. It is less easy to overlook the experiential status of the projecting clauses than with the kinds of interpersonal grammatical metaphor discussed in Section 2.1. As noted above, the interpersonal 'source tag' reading is in fact typically stronger when the projecting clause follows the projected clause (and therefore does not appear in Theme anyway). This objection is the basis for the proposal by Thompson (2004: 162) that the Theme of both clauses in a projection complex should be

Table 2.4 'Maximal' Theme in projection complexes

Theme		
Textual	*Interpersonal (projecting clauses)*	*Experiential (projected clauses)*
		A sexual charge between pupils and teachers
	Pat Sikes, of Sheffield University concluded	that 'erotic charges'
but	Her 25-year study stressed	that exploitative relationships
	added	that it
	She said	teacher-pupil affairs at her school in Leicestershire
	The study found	it was often pupils
		and that most teachers and pupils

included even when working with T-units. However, this means treating these as different in kind from other clause complexes; and, although it can be argued that there is a justification in terms of the differences in the logico-semantic relationships involved, such an approach introduces a perhaps unnecessary discrepancy in a phenomenon which is already inherently fuzzy.

Whereas there is a strong case for taking maximal Theme as the normal baseline when interpersonal metaphor is involved, the preferable analysis is less easy to decide with projection. However, the weight is perhaps towards maximal Theme again. As with interpersonal assessment, there will be borderline or doubtful cases, especially when the projecting clause is fairly elaborate (e.g. *A former associate suing Michael Jackson for alleged unpaid debts suddenly claimed on the witness stand that he ...*). Whichever solution is adopted, the logic of the arguments advanced in Section 2.2.1 suggests that, on practical grounds, it would be helpful for analysts working with minimal T-unit or clause-by-clause Themes to report results for maximal Theme in cases of projection, even if only as extra information; and, conversely, analysts working with maximal Theme of this kind should report the findings in a way which allows Theme in projecting and projected clauses to be retrieved separately.

2.2.3 Marked Theme and Subject

The final issue relating to the Theme-Rheme boundary that we wish to explore is the most controversial of the ones that we address: the status of Subject following a marked Theme consisting of one, or occasionally more, circumstantial Adjuncts in initial position. Halliday's position is that Theme should include only one experiential element, and therefore should extend only as far as the circumstantial Adjunct; on the other hand, Davies (1997), along with other analysts (e.g. Enkvist 1973; Downing 1991), argues that marked Themes of this kind perform different textual functions from unmarked Themes, and that, if, as typically happens, the Subject follows immediately after a marked Theme, this should also be included as obligatory unmarked Theme.

Certain kinds of texts appear to lend themselves well to this latter approach: a case can be made that the inclusion of Subject following marked Themes allows the analyst to capture more fully certain aspects of the way in which thematic choices construe the unfolding of text. This can be illustrated with Example 14, an extract from a history website for schoolchildren.[6] The marked Themes are in bold and the Subjects are in italics.

(14) **In their daily life**, *most Americans* witnessed far less change. **In 1800** *most Americans* were farmers by occupation; **in 1899** *most Americans* were still farmers, or at least were living in tiny towns in rural areas. **In 1800** *women* often spent 15 or 20 hours a week doing laundry by hand; **in 1899** *they* were doing the same. **In 1899** *most Americans* might be cooking on a wood or coal stove rather than in an open fireplace, but *the amount of work needed to haul the fuel and keep the fire going* was almost the same.

The text is clearly simple to an unusually extreme degree – and the simplicity is above all in the almost naïve way that the resources of marked Theme and Subject are deployed. This has the advantage that it represents a kind of baseline: these resources have been stripped to the minimum, so that they signal a single textual pattern and virtually no extraneous material distracts from the pattern as it unfolds. The patterning comes out even more clearly if the marked Themes and Subjects are presented separately in a table: see Table 2.5.

The first marked Theme establishes the focus of this paragraph, in contrast with the preceding paragraph which was about the USA as *a large and powerful nation* – i.e. from a political perspective. The remaining marked Themes signal the comparison between daily life in the two periods around which the paragraph is structured. The Subjects, with the exception of the last, refer to the people involved. Thus each set of elements has a very simple semantic unity, and both serve to frame the information in different ways: the marked Themes are associated with switches in the temporal framework, and the Subjects are associated with continuity in the entities about which predications are being made.

However, we have deliberately started with a simple example. More typical of sophisticated written text is Example 15, an extract from a medical report.[7] Again, Themes are in bold and Subjects are in italics (in two cases Subject is Theme).

Table 2.5 Marked Theme and Subject in a simple text

Marked Theme	Subject
In their daily life,	most Americans
In 1800	most Americans
in 1899	most Americans
In 1800	women
in 1899	they
In 1899	most Americans
	[but] the amount of work needed to haul the fuel and keep the fire going

(15) **In a multicentre observation** *the efficacy and tolerability of Allergodil nasal spray* was studied in patients suffering allergic rhinitis. **During a period of observation from February to November 1992** *a total of 4018 patients* was included in the investigation. *The results described below* refer to 280 children of up to 12 years of age who were treated in approximately 200 medical practices. **In 21.5% of these children,** *rhinitis* was diagnosed as 'perennial', **and in 67.7%** as 'seasonal'. *7.9%* exhibited a 'mixed' form.

Table 2.6 shows the marked Themes and Subjects separately.

Here the textual functions of the two sets of elements are much less easily separated. In particular, elements relating to what can be seen as the main 'topic' thread, the experiment – shown in bold in Table 2.6 – appear in both marked Themes and Subjects. The Subjects by themselves are all in the same broad semantic area, but no clear topical pattern emerges across the extract. On the other hand, if we focus only on the Themes in Halliday's narrower definition, we can trace a coherent unfolding framework, which starts with the methodological context of the study (where and when), and then moves to the *results*, with the last three Themes detailing these:

In a multicentre observation

During a period of observation from February to November 1992

The results described below

In 21.5% of these children

and in 67.7%

7.9%

Table 2.6 Marked Theme and Subject in a 'sophisticated' text

Marked Theme	Subject
In a multicentre observation	**the efficacy and tolerability of Allergodil nasal spray**
During a period of observation from February to November 1992	**a total of 4018 patients** **The results described below**
In 21.5% of these children **and in 67.7%**	rhinitis [it] **7.9%**

(Compare Fries 1981/1983, who found that the distinction of marked and unmarked Theme did not seem significant in signalling the method of development of the extracts that he analysed.) Any approach to the relationship between Theme, Subject and the way a text unfolds will need to be able to account satisfactorily for both simple cases like Example 14 and more complex cases like Example 15.

The justifications outlined earlier for treating interpersonal metaphor and projection as having special thematic status do not apply to experiential Adjuncts like *In 1800* and *In 21.5% of these children*. Whereas the former can be seen from one perspective as outside the propositional content of the message, locating the message in an interpersonal and textual context, the latter are part of the propositional content – the part which has been chosen as the first experiential element. Thus other arguments are needed if a case is to be made for including Subject automatically as unmarked Theme.

This issue has been approached from two main angles. In Davies's (1988, 1997) view, the marked Themes function as Contextual Frames, or CFs (see also Downing 1991, who establishes a similar category of 'circumstantial frameworks'), while the Subject Themes carry forward the 'topic' of the text. The category of CFs in fact includes interpersonal metaphor and projecting clauses, as discussed in Sections 2.2.1 and 2.2.2 above, as well as interpersonal and textual elements in multiple Themes: the aim is to bring together all the kinds of elements that may precede Subject. This allows functional similarities between the various elements to be highlighted, while the differences are handled through sub-categorisation at a more delicate level. Davies argues that all CFs share the function of contextualising the message in different ways, and that different patterns of CFs, in terms of type and frequency, are characteristic of different registers. If a distinction is made between CFs with textual and interpersonal elements (including grammatical metaphor of the types discussed in Sections 2.2.1. and 2.2.2 above) and those with experiential elements (i.e. marked Themes), important generalisations are missed.

The other main arguments in favour of systematically including Subject in Theme are based on an exploration of what thematic status means. Berry (1996) identifies meanings which are inherently thematic – those which locate the clause in its textual and interpersonal context; and she suggests that the 'weight' of such meanings 'will be located in the portion of the clause up to and including the lexical verb' (1996: 31). Her proposal is therefore that Theme should be taken as normally including Subject (as well as modal elements following Subject, such as auxiliaries and negative markers). Ravelli (1995) explores the implications of taking a dynamic perspective on language, seeing Theme from the point of view of the receiver processing utterances. Expanding on Halliday's gloss on Theme as the 'point of departure' of the message, she argues that the receiver can only be sure that the point of departure has been passed when the Predicator is reached: 'until a potential Subject element is confirmed, the Theme analysis is still relevant, as the message is not yet fully "off the ground"' (Ravelli, 1995: 227). Thus she also views Subject as inherently thematic, irrespective of what elements – interpersonal, textual or experiential – precede it.

Strong as these arguments are, there are equally strong counter-arguments. The key ones, from a systemic perspective, are to do with choice and the metafunctional hypothesis. If the constituent functioning as Subject is specified as an obligatory experiential element in Theme, a fundamental aspect of the concept of Theme – that its meaning depends on its being the result of a choice on the part of the speaker or writer as to which experiential element should form the point of departure for the message – is lost. Similarly, if Subject is taken as Theme because it is Subject, this means that the distinction between the metafunctions in terms of their different contributions to meaning is blurred. Whereas Theme is the 'starting point of the message', Subject is the '"resting point" of the argument'; Subject 'specifies the entity in respect of which the assertion is claimed to have validity' (Halliday and Matthiessen 2004: 117, 118). As Halliday consistently argues, there is a natural affinity between Subject and Theme, since it makes sense to start a message with reference to the entity in which modal responsibility for the success of the interchange of meaning is vested (hence the categorisation of Subject as unmarked Theme); but the two kinds of meanings cannot be simply merged.

At the same time, it seems clear that Subject has a special role to play in the construction of texture (cf. MacDonald 1992; Gosden 1993). For instance, in Example 14 above (see Table 2.5), the contribution of successive Subjects to the dynamic unfolding of the text cannot be ignored: the marked Themes indicate where the following information is to be located in the 'conceptual map' (Thompson 2004: 167) of the text, while the Subjects signal that in each case the information is valid for the same group of entities as in the preceding clause complex. However, rather than viewing that as a justification for including Subject in Theme, it would seem theoretically more secure to consider the possibility that the two threads of meaning, while both contributing to texture, operate independently, and that, in order to gain a full picture of the logogenetic growth of the text, both need to be traced separately. Martin (1992 Chapter 6) provides fuller arguments in favour of this approach and shows how it can be implemented.

Of course, as noted earlier, Example 14 is unusual in that the two threads are kept completely apart. Example 15 above is more typical in that here, as Martin (1992: 475) puts it, 'distinct, though partially overlapping, strings are woven through Theme and Subject'. This overlapping, together with the affinity between the functions of Theme and Subject, certainly makes it less straightforward to disentangle the two threads. Nevertheless, it should, in principle, be possible to track the development of both threads separately. From this perspective, the choice of conflating Subject and Theme remains a choice (even if it is the usual choice); and the reasons why this conflation happens at particular points in the text, and why it does not happen at others, can then be explored and can lead to a deeper understanding of how the texturing resources have been deployed.

It is worth noting that the issue of the unit of analysis which should be used comes up with Subject as it does with Theme: it can be tracked by clause, or by T-unit. In order for the threads to be comparable, it is clearly necessary to use the same unit as for the thematic analysis. If this is based on T-units, it is the Subjects of independent clauses which are relevant.

2.2.4 Marked Theme and Subject in text: an illustrative analysis

In order to illustrate and extend the discussion, we will examine a complete text which has a relatively high percentage of marked Themes, and which therefore raises with particular sharpness the question of how Themes and Subjects operate and interact (it also has the advantage, for our present purposes, that there are no cases of grammatical metaphor in Theme to distract us). In Text 16 below, T-unit Themes are in bold (keeping to Halliday's approach with Subject following marked Theme not included), and independent clause Subjects are in italics.

(16) Liverpool 3 : 1 Everton
      3.00pm 29/10/00
      by Dave MacBryde for *The Liverpool Echo*
      It was *Liverpool* who claimed all three points in the 163rd Merseyside derby, as the script was – for once – well and truly adhered to.
      After a typically frenetic opening in which Everton enjoyed the best of the early exchanges, it took only 12 minutes for *Nick Barmby* to find the net against his old club.
      A hefty challenge on Barmby by Mark Pembridge led to the opening goal. **From the resultant free-kick**, *Christian Ziege's cross to the far post*

was met by the head of Barmby, whose header in acres of space found the Everton net to send the Reds fans wild.

However, *the Blues* quickly rallied and were level six minutes later. **Following sustained pressure,** *an Idan Tal corner* was met by the head of David Weir – the ball falling to Kevin Campbell, to present the Blues striker with an easy chance from close range. **With Sander Westerveld stranded,** *Campbell* duly dispatched the chance to put Everton on level terms and to prove that Liverpool's art of throwing away leads is still not lost.

At 1-1, *this fierce encounter* soon began to settle down, with both sides enjoying more time on the ball in midfield.

The second-half saw Liverpool start the brighter side, with the Reds controlled possession forcing Everton on to the back foot. **However, *Everton*** battled back, winning a corner on 52 minutes, but failing to capitalise.

As Liverpool picked up the tempo, *Everton's rearguard* began to lose its shape. ***They*** weren't helped when Michael Ball limped off on 54 minutes, to be replaced by newboy Gary Naysmith at left-back.

The pivotal moment of this passionate contest arrived on 56 minutes – Nick Barmby's header teeing up Emile Heskey, whose screamer from 30 yards left Paul Gerrard with no chance. ***Heskey's fifth goal in three league games*** will no doubt be one to treasure, as he continued his rich vein of form.

Just as Everton needed to find their way back into this game, *Liverpool* turned it up a gear. ***The Reds*** now looked the sharper side, with a number of Everton passes going astray.

Everton did press briefly, with a Gascoigne effort parried by Westerveld. **Then on 76 minutes,** *Liverpool* broke again, with Smicer taking up the pace. **As the Czech bore down on goal,** *Thomas Gravesen* intervened, bringing him down inside the penalty area. ***Gravesen*** was immediately shown the red card by Durkin as the Reds were duly awarded a penalty – Patrik Berger stepping up to convert the spot-kick.

When the final whistle did come, *it* was a welcome relief for Walter Smith, as Gérard Houllier and the majority of a packed Anfield celebrated his second derby win as a Liverpool manager. **For the next six months at least,** *the Red half of Merseyside* can revel in the pleasure of a derby win, which has been 18 months coming.

Table 2.7 shows the Themes separately.

It is clear that the text is organised as a chronological account of the match, and that the primary role in signalling this method of development is performed by the marked Themes, which locate the key events in an unfolding time frame. It is worth noting, however, that there are some departures from this norm (as one would expect: extreme regularity in thematic patterns is rare). Two of the marked Themes (*From the resultant*

Table 2.7 Marked and unmarked Themes

Marked Theme	Unmarked Theme
	It was Liverpool[8]
After a typically frenetic opening in which Everton enjoyed the best of the early exchanges,	
	A hefty challenge on Barmby by Mark Pembridge
From the resultant free-kick,	
	However, the Blues
Following sustained pressure, With Sander Westerveld stranded, At 1-1,	
	The second-half However, Everton
As Liverpool picked up the tempo,	
	They The pivotal moment of this passionate contest Heskey's fifth goal in three league games
Just as Everton needed to find their way back into this game,	
	The Reds Everton
Then on 76 minutes, As the Czech bore down on goal,	
	Gravesen
When the final whistle did come, For the next six months at least,	

free-kick and *With Sander Westerveld stranded*) mainly refer to events in the match – though they still have some temporal meaning in that they locate the events in the Rhemes as following or simultaneous with the thematised event; and two of the unmarked Themes (*The second-half* and *The pivotal moment of this passionate contest*) function as signals of chronological stages.

When we look at the Subjects separately, an equally clear pattern emerges – see Table 2.8, in which the Subjects have been divided into three categories (Subjects functioning as Theme are in italics).

With the exception of the two cases in the 'Time' column, the Subjects all refer to the teams, players or events in the match, thus maintaining a semantic continuity. This is not surprising in itself, but it is significant that Tables 2.7 and 2.8 show a clear division of informational labour, with

Table 2.8 Subjects

Teams/players	Events	Time
Liverpool[9]		
Nick Barmby[9]		
	A hefty challenge on Barmby by Mark Pembridge	
	Christian Ziege's cross to the far post	
the Blues		
	an Idan Tal corner	
Campbell		
	this fierce encounter	
		The second-half
Everton		
Everton's rearguard		
They		
		The pivotal moment of this passionate contest
	Heskey's fifth goal in three league games	
Liverpool		
The Reds		
Everton		
Liverpool		
Thomas Gravesen		
Gravesen		
	it [the final whistle]	
the Red half of Merseyside		

the meanings which dominate in Theme occurring relatively infrequently in Subject, and vice versa. This could be seen as supporting the argument that the Subjects should be included consistently in Theme, even when preceded by a marked Theme. However, it could equally well be used as evidence for the hypothesis that Subjects carry topic through the text as an independent thread of development. In order to substantiate this latter claim we need to consider whether it is possible to establish a textual rationale for the writer's decision at each point to separate or conflate Subject and Theme.

In order to do this, we can first map the Themes on to what appear to be the main stages of the match as construed in the report. Leaving aside the first sentence which acts as a prefatory summary outside the chronological sequence (a hyper-Theme – see Martin 1992: 437), the Themes can be grouped according to the stages as shown in Table 2.9 (unmarked Subject Themes are in italics).

This largely bears out the claim that major textual transitions are associated with marked Themes, which occur at transitions between six of the eight stages. None of the 'teams/players' Subject Themes occurs at the boundaries. The two unmarked Themes at transitions (Stages 3 and 4) are

Table **2.9** Stages and Themes

Stage	Initial Theme in stage	Other Themes in stage
1: 1st half fluctuating fortunes	After a typically frenetic opening in which Everton enjoyed the best of the early exchanges,	
		A hefty challenge on Barmby by Mark Pembridge From the resultant free-kick, However, *the Blues* Following sustained pressure, With Sander Westerveld stranded,
2: stable phase	At 1-1,	
3: 2nd half starts	*The second-half*	
		However, *Everton* As Liverpool picked up the tempo, *They*
4: climax	*The pivotal moment of this passionate contest*	
		Heskey's fifth goal in three league games
5: reaction	Just as Everton needed to find their way back into this game,	
		The Reds *Everton*
6: the clincher	Then on 76 minutes,	
		As the Czech bore down on goal, *Gravesen*
7: the end	When the final whistle did come,	
8: the aftermath	For the next six months at least,	

the Subjects referring to time (see Table 2.8). Their presence suggests that, as Fries (1981/1983) argues, semantic considerations (here, reference to time) are more important in thematic choice than formal ones (marked vs. unmarked). However, it is worth noting that they are also 'anomalous' in that they do not belong to the main Subject groupings of players and events: thus they have a doubly special status within the text. The instantial foregrounding of these two Themes can perhaps be seen as reflecting their significance within the unfolding account: the first of them corresponds to the major 'real-world' division of the match into two halves, and the second (which includes salient evaluation) signals the climax of the match.

The Themes within stages show a less clear-cut pattern: eight are unmarked and five are marked. The unmarked Themes occur as would be predicted, in that they signal topic continuation within the temporal framework established by the 'stage' Theme: the sentences provide details of what happened in that stage of the match. For example, in Stage 6 the final goal comes *on 76 minutes* and is the result of a foul by *Gravesen*. The marked Themes, on the other hand, appear at first sight more of a stumbling-block for the approach that we are advocating: if the main reason why marked Themes occur is to signal transitions, it seems odd that they appear within a stage functioning at the same textual level as unmarked Themes. However, we would argue that in each case it is possible to identify a rationale, which hinges on the fact that writers work at several levels in choosing their Themes: they need to signal the major staging of the text but also to reflect lower-level concerns, on a T-unit by T-unit basis. One simplified way of picturing the patterns is that, once a major stage has been signalled, the writer is 'free' to deploy thematic resources to reflect more local communicative pressures until the next transition point is reached (cf. Thompson (2003) for a similar view of discourse organisation in spoken monologue). In this text, the marked Themes within a stage mainly appear to contextualise the events of that stage at a more micro-level. For example, the reports of the two first-half goals both show a similar pattern: the goal is announced in a structurally simple sentence with an unmarked Theme: *A hefty challenge ... led to the opening goal*; and *However, the Blues ... were level six minutes later*. Then the text fills in the details of how the goal was scored, in structurally more complex sentences. Part of that complexity comes from the fact that the actions around the scoring of the goal are contextualised by marked Themes which explain the crucial factors that resulted in the goal: *From the resultant free-kick* for the first, *Following sustained pressure*, and *With Sander Westerveld stranded* for the second.

Some of the other choices of marked vs. unmarked Theme are less straightforward, and require a delicacy of analysis that we can only sketch very briefly. To take one example, in the report of the last goal, set in the time frame of *Then on 76 minutes*, there is linear thematic progression (see Daneš 1974) at a local level: *Smicer* in the Rheme of the first sentence is picked up as *the Czech* in the Theme of the next sentence, with attention switching to *Gravesen* in the Rheme; then *Gravesen* is Theme in the third sentence, with the rhematic focus shifting to *the Reds* and *Berger* for the report of the goal (this switching from team to team is perhaps also designed to mimic the action on the pitch). The thematic patterning interlocks with the writer's decision to centre the clause complexes structurally around three of the details that are included: *Liverpool broke, Gravesen intervened,* and *Gravesen was shown the red card.* The processes by which writers decide to distribute information in independent or dependent clauses are not well understood; but in the third sentence here one factor appears to be the writer's tendency (which may be idiosyncratic, or a feature of the register of football reporting) to present the actual scoring of the goals obliquely, in dependent (and in two of the three cases, non-finite) clauses, in final or near-final position in the clause complex. This means that the independent clause comes in initial position and *Gravesen,* the prime candidate for Theme in terms of thematic progression, is unmarked Theme.

Thus, it is possible to establish a rationale for separate functions of the Theme and Subject threads and for the ways in which they are interwoven across the text with overlappings (conflation) and separations; and in our view treating the two threads separately allows a more illuminating and theoretically better-grounded analysis of how texture is constructed. However, we recognise that some analysts will continue to argue for the inclusion of Subject as obligatory unmarked Theme; and, in line with our suggestions in the case of interpersonal metaphor and projection, we would recommend that, whichever approach is adopted, results are as far as possible reported in ways which allow researchers using a different approach to re-analyse them for comparison with their own results.

2.3   Conclusion

What we have aimed to do in this chapter is to explore some of the key issues in the identification of Theme which have proved problematic in theoretical terms and, which in practical terms, lead to unhelpful differences in analyses by different researchers. The main dimension along which the aspects that we have focused on vary is that of degrees of experientialisation. Based on Halliday's notion of multiple Theme, we have argued that, when a clause-complex initial element can be seen as realising interpersonal meaning, even if this is expressed in relatively experientialised terms, it should not be treated as filling the slot of required experiential constituent in Theme. Conversely, once this slot has been filled, even if it is by an Adjunct (or Complement, though we have not illustrated this above) rather than by the Subject, that is best treated as the boundary of Theme. One useful consequence of this approach is that the distinct contribution of Subjects to the texture of a text is highlighted, together with the need for more extensive study of how Theme and Subject interact across texts. While, inevitably, borderline cases remain (e.g. where there is more than one circumstantial Adjunct in initial position), we feel that the approach proposed here is theoretically grounded and has the advantage of combining clarity with flexibility.

Our discussion of experientialised interpersonal meanings in Theme is an attempt to make explicit the justification for what we see as the current mainstream practice of analysts working within the SFL paradigm. On the other hand, we recognise that the position on marked experiential Theme that we have arrived at, after much hesitation between this and rival analyses, runs counter to that adopted by a number of researchers in recent years. In particular, as noted above, Flo Davies has consistently argued for the inclusion of Subject – indeed it was the discussions with her that originally prompted our interest in, and doubts over, this problem in the identification of Theme. We feel that, on balance, the main arguments for requiring an unmarked Theme in all cases are less conclusive if Subjects are seen as constituting a separate thread of development running through the discourse; but we accept that there are well-founded arguments on both sides. We look forward to continuing what will no doubt be a long-running debate on the issue.

Notes

1. All isolated examples in this chapter have been taken from the internet.
2. Thompson (2004: 152) argues that the experientialised interpersonal meaning *it is probable* functions alone as a type of enhanced Theme which he calls 'thematised comment'. However, this has the disadvantage of setting up a constituent which is different from any others used in the categorisation of Theme; and it seems more defensible to follow Davies and Martin in

seeing the clause as a metaphorical interpersonal element within multiple Theme.

3. http://www.wdm.org.uk/wwf/finalverdictonwwf.doc, last accessed 25.3.06.
4. From *Guardian Unlimited* Friday 11 November 2005. Some sentences have been omitted in order to focus on the projection complexes.
5. The title was almost certainly added by a sub-editor; but this means that it reflects one expert reader's assessment of the main focus of the text (and of its main interest for other readers).
6. http://www.alri.org/curric/Page2.html, last accessed 10.12.05.
7. From *Current Medical Research and Opinion* (1996), 13 (7), 391–5; available online at: http://www.priory.com/cmro/cmro1101.htm, last accessed 10.12.05.
8. The first Theme is a predicated Theme (Halliday and Matthiessen 2004: 95), which is technically outside the marked/unmarked distinction. It has been included as unmarked here for the sake of simplicity.
9. Identification of the independent clause Subjects in the first and second sentences is not straightforward. Structurally the Subjects in each case are *it* plus the deferred embedded clause; but it can be argued that the Subjects of the non-cleft equivalents are more relevant for the present analysis.

References

Berry, M. (1996). What is Theme? A(nother) personal view. In *Meaning and Form: Systemic Functional Interpretations*, R. Fawcett, M. Berry, C. Butler and G. W. Huang (eds), 1–64. Norwood, NJ: Ablex.

Boström Aronsson, M. (2005). Themes in Swedish advanced learners' written English. Unpublished PhD thesis, University of Gothenburg.

Daneš, F. (1974). Functional sentence perspective and the organisation of the text. In *Papers on Functional Sentence Perspective*, F. Daneš (ed.), 106–28. The Hague: Mouton.

Davies, F. (1988). Reading between the lines: Thematic choice as a device for presenting writer viewpoint in academic discourse. *The ESPecialist* 9 (2): 173–200.

Davies, F. (1997). Marked Theme as a heuristic for analyzing text-type, text and genre. In *Applied Languages: Theory and Practice in ESP*, J. Piqué and D. J. Viera (eds), 45–79. Valencia: Universitat de Valencia.

Downing, A. (1991). An alternative approach to Theme: a systemic-functional perspective. *Word* 42: 119–43.

Enkvist, N. (1973). Theme dynamics and style: an experiment. *Studia Anglica Posnaniensia* 5: 127–35.

Fries, P. H. (1981). On the status of theme in English: arguments from discourse. *Forum Linguisticum* 6: 1–38. Reprinted, 1983, in revised form in *Micro and*

Macro Connexity of Texts, J. S. Petöfi and E. Sözer (eds.), 116–52. Hamburg: Helmut Buske.

Fries, P. H. (1995). Patterns of information in initial position in English. In *Discourse and Meaning in Society: Functional Perspectives,* P. H. Fries and M. Gregory (eds), 47–66. Norwood NJ: Ablex Publishers.

Ghadessy, M. (1995). *Thematic Development in English Texts.* London and New York: Pinter.

Gosden, H. (1993). Discourse functions of Subject in scientific research articles. *Applied Linguistics* 14 (1): 56–75.

Halliday, M. A. K. (1994). *An Introduction to Functional Grammar* (2nd edition). London: Arnold.

Halliday, M. A. K. and Matthiessen, C. M. I. M (2004). *An Introduction to Functional Grammar* (3rd edition). London: Arnold.

Hunston, S. and Sinclair, J. (2000). A local grammar of evaluation. In *Evaluation in Text: Authorial Stance and the Construction of Discourse,* S. Hunston and G. Thompson (eds.), 74–101. Oxford: Oxford University Press.

Hunt, K. (1965). *Grammatical Structures Written at Three Grade Levels.* Champaign, IL: NCTE.

MacDonald, S. P. (1992). A method for analyzing sentence-level differences in disciplinary knowledge making. *Written Communication* 9: 533–69.

Martin, J. R. (1992). *English Text: System and Structure.* Philadelphia, PA and Amsterdam: John Benjamins.

Martin, J. R. (1995). More than what the message is about: English Theme. In *Thematic Development in English Texts.* M. Ghadessy (ed.), 223–58. London and New York: Pinter.

Matthiessen, C. M. I. M. (1992). Interpreting the textual metafunction. In *Advances in Systemic Linguistics: Recent Theory and Practice,* M. Davies and L. Ravelli (eds), 37–81. London: Pinter.

Matthiessen, C. M. I. M. (1995a). *Lexicogrammatical Cartography: English Systems.* Tokyo: International Language Sciences Publishers.

Matthiessen, C. M. I. M. (1995b). THEME as an enabling resource in ideational 'knowledge' construction. In *Thematic Development in English Texts,* M. Ghadessy (ed.), 20–54. London and New York: Pinter.

North, S. (2005). Disciplinary variation in the use of Theme in undergraduate essays. *Applied Linguistics* 26 (3): 431–52.

Ravelli, L. J. (1995). A dynamic perspective: implications for metafunctional interaction and an understanding of Theme. In *On Subject and Theme: A Discourse Functional Perspective,* R. Hasan and P. H. Fries (eds), 187–234. Amsterdam and Philadelphia, PA: John Benjamins.

Simon-Vandenbergen, A.-M., Taverniers M. and Ravelli, L. J. (eds) (2003). *Grammatical Metaphor: Views from Systemic Functional Linguistics,* Amsterdam: John Benjamins.

Thompson, G. (2004). *Introducing Functional Grammar* (2nd edition). London: Arnold.

Thompson, G. (2005). But me some buts: a multidimensional view of conjunction. *Text* 25: 763–91.

Thompson, G. (2007) Unfolding Theme: the development of clausal and textual perspectives on Theme. In *Continuing Discourse on Language: A Functional Perspective*, Volume 2, J. Webster, C. M. I. M. Matthiessen and R. Hasan (eds). London: Equinox.

Thompson, S. (2003). Text-structuring meta-discourse, intonation and the signalling of organisation in academic lectures. *Journal of English for Academic Purposes* 2: 5–20.

<table>
<tr><td>3</td></tr>
</table>

Theme, field and genre: thematic realisations in academic articles and their popularisations

John Corbett
University of Glasgow

3.1   Introduction

The study of Theme and thematic choice remains a constant concern of systemic-functional linguistics, as is evident, for example, in Francis (1989), Downing (1991), Fries and Francis (1992), Ghadessy (1995) and Davies (1997). These papers consider the nature of Theme, its relation to cohesive harmony and its usefulness as a marker of genre. The present chapter adds to the literature by considering the realisation of Theme across three academic genres and their popularisations. The recasting of peer-group academic texts for a broader audience has been a useful means of clarifying the concept of genre, both within and outside systemic-functional linguistics. Young (1990) gives a detailed comparison of university textbooks and lectures. Nwogu and Bloor (1991) focus on thematic progression in popular and professional medical texts, concluding tentatively that linear thematic progression is suited to explanation and exposition, and therefore is found more frequently in popular texts than professional ones. Themes are more frequently repeated in adjacent clauses in professional texts than popular ones; this frequency can be linked to the professional texts' need to spell out their methodological procedures. Myers (1990) focuses less on the detailed linguistic analysis of his texts; instead he offers a detailed ethnographic investigation of the writing practices of biologists who write both for peer-group and popular readerships, concluding that the ideologies underlying the academic 'narrative of science' and the popular 'narrative of nature' are qualitatively different. The present chapter is an attempt to extend the analysis of Nwogu and Bloor by combining an analysis of Theme with the ideological insights offered by Myers.

3.2 The nature of theme

The definition of Theme has varied over the years. A statement by Weil (1887) argues for a 'division' in the 'statement' in the classical languages, on the grounds that:

> it was necessary that a word of introduction should precede the remark which it was intended to utter; it was necessary to lean on something present and known, in order to reach out to something less present, nearer or unknown. There is then a point of departure, an initial notion which is equally present to him who speaks and to him who hears, which forms, as it were, the ground upon which the two intelligences meet; and in another part of the statement (*l'énonciation*), properly so called. (Weil 1887; trans. Super 1978: 29)

This statement contains much of what later came to characterise Prague School Functional Sentence Perspective and 'Communicative Dynamism' (e.g. Daneš, 1974, 1987), specifically the references to 'a point of departure' and 'something present and known'. Halliday (1976), of course, separates these two concepts into the grammatical system of Theme and the intonational system of Given. In a recent revision of the key account of functional grammar, Halliday and Matthiessen state that:

> The Theme is the element which serves as the point of departure of the message; it is that which locates and orients the clause within its context. The remainder of the message, the part in which the Theme is developed, is called in Prague school terminology the Rheme. (Halliday and Matthiessen 2004: 64–5)

In Halliday's functional grammar, the Theme can be identified by its initial position in the clause; it extends to the first circumstance, participant or process that is realised in any clause. In unmarked clauses, the Theme will be conflated with the Subject of the sentence; however, it is very possible for the Theme to be realised by an Adjunct expressing a circumstance, or a verbal group expressing a process, in which case the Subject falls into the Rheme. This chapter follows Halliday's mainstream definition of Theme, despite the availability of alternatives, for example that of Davies (1997), which argues that Theme should always be extended to include the Subject of the clause. Since the criteria used in defining functional constituents are primarily semantic, they are seldom uncontroversial, and a good case can often be made for reworking or conflating proposed constituents whilst exploring a particular aspect of textual organisation. However, for the purposes of the present chapter, I shall assume that the systems of Theme/ Rheme and Subject/Mood are distinct, and that Subject can be non-thematic (cf. Thompson and Thompson, this volume).

3.3   Field and genre

In the remainder of this chapter, I shall use Halliday's concept of Theme to explore the ways in which popular and academic texts in three fields – computing, biology and history – orient their respective readerships. The exploration of the 'ground upon which the two intelligences meet' is likely to be of interest to text analysts, not only as a heuristic for differentiating between genres. Myers (1990: 142) argues that when a biologist or journalist recasts academic work for popular audiences, specialist 'narratives of science' are transformed into 'narratives of nature', which do not merely simplify the scientific process – they imply different conceptions of scientific activity. Narratives of science are linguistically organised to make and sustain claims to knowledge; for example, their discourse structures tend to articulate problem-solution patterns rather than chronological events. Moreover, their vocabulary and syntax emphasise 'the conceptual structure of the discipline' by, for example, preferring impersonal constructions and nominalisations that transform events into abstractions. In this respect, Myers' view of scientific writing concurs very much with that of Halliday and Martin (1993). Myers goes on to argue, however, that popular 'narratives of nature' take concrete phenomena rather than scientific methodology as their subject, they prefer chronological narratives to non-chronological problem-solution patterns, and their 'syntax and vocabulary emphasize the externality of nature to scientific practices' (Myers 1990: 142).

This chapter explores whether Myers' distinction between narratives of science and nature is evident in thematic realisation across academic and popular biological articles. Furthermore, it questions whether this distinction is evident in other fields – one scientific (namely, computing) and the other from the humanities (namely, history).

3.4   Materials and methods

The present study identified a small selection of texts whereby an academic article written for a peer-group readership is recast for a more general audience, either by one of the original authors, or by a journalist. The full list of texts is given in the appendix, and, for convenience, the articles are given a number and a coding:

B: Biology   P: Popular

C: Computing   L: Learned/Academic

H: History

Thus BL1 and BP1 refer to two articles, the first (Aronson and Sues, 1987) being a justification for using palaeoecological evidence in an argument that predation was a factor in the near destruction of the population of undersea ophiuroids, or brittlestars, in the Mesozoic period. The second article (Aronson 1987) recasts this argument as a narrative in which the destruction of the brittlestars is presented as a 'murder mystery'. In BP2, a journalist offers an explanation of a controversial article in *Nature* on the use of mitochondrial DNA to date the existence of *super-Eve* the mother of all living humans. The other articles are paired up along similar lines, a minor exception being CL1 and CP1 – here the 'academic' article was an as-yet unpublished journal submission, whose origins in a conference presentation were still evident in its colloquial register.

The history articles were more difficult to match up. However, in a phone conversation with J. K. Walton, he impressed upon me the fact that he regarded his 1981 paper on the rise of working-class seaside resorts to be more scholarly than his 1985 return to the topic for the popular magazine *The Historian*. Similarly, Stevenson's account of the Bishops' Wars for a Sunday newspaper supplement aims for a more popular readership than his chapter on the same subject for a scholarly book, and Bailey reworks similar material from his earlier bibliographical essay on crime into a popular article for another magazine, *History Today*.

During the analysis it became clear that although the fields and in several cases the authors remained stable, the articles as a whole would prove difficult to compare. The academic articles were generally much longer and more explicit than their popular counterparts. As Nwogu and Bloor (1991) found in their exploration of medical texts, the scientific articles contained much more extended descriptions of 'methods' than the popular texts. Therefore, rather than analyse the Themes present in the texts as a whole, I identified 'parallel passages' from each matched pair. The introductory and concluding passages are always analysed, along with passages that overlap in information or function. For example, I analysed passages from BL1 and BP1 that deal with constraints on the formation of brittlestar beds, experimental procedure, and the role of predators in the brittlestars' near-extinction. Parallel passages from the body of CL1 and CP1 deal with the nature of intelligence (human and artificial), descriptions of parallel distributed processing, and the advantages and weaknesses of a PDP model of human intelligence. And parallel passages from HL1 and HP1 deal with the universality of seaside holidays, class conflict at the seaside, and changing holiday patterns (the full texts are given in Corbett (1992) from which the present chapter is in part derived). The focus on parallel passages makes a comparison between the popular and academic articles more robust: the extracts chosen communicate similar information, or introduce, or conclude each article. Therefore any systematic difference in the realisation of Theme should reflect the difference in the discourse community at which the text is directed: lay folk or specialists.

The analysis to some extent follows Francis' (1989) qualitative study of Theme in newspaper editorials and letters. In particular, our focus is on three aspects of Theme in academic and popular articles: the types of thematic participant in material and relational processes, thematic settings in time and space, and modal Themes. In the texts selected, the dominant choices as Theme are participants in material and relational processes, and circumstantial settings. Modal Themes are rarer, but are nonetheless interesting for the light they cast on direct expression of the writers' attitudes.

3.5   Results and discussion

3.5.1 Thematic participants in material and relational processes

In this section, I shall consider three aspects of Theme that are realised by participants in material and relational processes: (a) the degree to which these participants are themselves nominalised processes; (b) those Themes that direct the reader towards a research context; and (c) the explicit nature of the information articulated in the Theme.

Nominalisation has long been widely recognised as an issue in factual writing, and scientific writing in particular. Francis (1989: 202) identifies nominalisation as a means of differentiating between the genres of News and Editorial/Letters in newspapers:

> The typical and most predominant themes in News are material and verbal, while far fewer relational participants and processes are selected

as point of departure for the message. This reflects the fact that in News there is less nominalisation which as Halliday (1987) points out, means there is more ideation and more information.
(Francis, 1989: 202)

In contrast, in both the academic and popular texts in the fields considered here, there is a predominance of material and relational process, and a high incidence of nominalised Theme. To give one example: both BP2 and BL2 use a nominalised Theme to explain the increase in wildcat population in recent years (emphases added):

BP2:

Only a *relaxation* in the zeal of gamekeepers,
and the rapid *spread* of coniferous plantation
after the First World War

have allowed the wildcat to recolonise many of its former haunts in Scotland.

BL2:

This *increase*

may have been partly due to changes in availability of habitat and food ...

The popular and learned articles organise their information in different ways, largely because the clauses function in different immediate contexts. The clause from BP2 is taken from the beginning of the article, and the behaviour of *gamekeepers* and the *spread* of forests is taken as the point of departure for information about the increase of the wildcat population. The academic article uses the nominalised process, *increase*, as the point of departure for information about the habitat, *the coniferous plantations*, and also the subject of *cross-breeding*, which is key to this article. As we would expect, following Myers (1990), the nature-oriented popular article focuses on things (*gamekeepers* and *forests*) while the science-oriented academic article focuses on an abstraction (*increase*), but both Themes include nominalisations.

While it must be borne in mind that all the articles in this study employ nominalised Themes, there are occasions, particularly in the description of scientific procedure, when the realisations in the popular and academic articles diverge. For example, in the articles on *super Eve* we find the following:

BP2:

Second, they	find that each geographically distinct population stems from many lineages connected to the tree at widely separated points ...
Third, they	calibrate their 'genetic clock' with archaeological data on the likely dates of the colonisation of New Guinea ...
The Berkeley researchers	then extrapolate back to the likely date of the 'common ancestral mitochondrial genotype'.

BL2:

The second implication of the tree (Fig. 3) – that each non-African population has multiple origins –	can be illustrated most simply with the New Guineans.
Asian lineage 50	is closer genealogically to this New Guinea lineage than to other Asian mtDNA lineages ...
Six other lineages	lead exclusively to New Guinean mtDNAs, each originating at a different place in the tree ...
This small region of New Guinea (mainly the Eastern Highlands Province)	thus seems to have been colonised by at least seven maternal lineages ...
Each estimate	is based on a number of region-specific clusters in the tree ...
These numbers, ranging from 15 to 36 (Tables 2 and 3)	will probably rise as more types of human mtDNA are discovered.
A time scale	can be affixed to the tree in Fig. 3 by assuming that mtDNA sequence divergence accumulates at a constant rate in humans.

One way of estimating this rate	is to consider the extent of differentiation within clusters specific to New Guinea (Table 2; see also refs 23 and 30), Australia and the New World.
People	colonised these regions relatively recently: a minimum of 30,000 years ago for New Guinea, 40,000 years ago for Australia, and 12,000 years ago for the New World.
These times	enable us to calculate that the mean rate of mtDNA divergence within humans lies between two and four percent per million years;
a detailed account of this calculation	appears elsewhere.

In this matched pair of articles, none of the academic authors was involved in the writing of the popularisation, and perhaps this explains the tendency in the popular version to thematise the researchers when explaining the research procedure. Certainly, the focus in the popular article is on a group of Berkeley researchers who have come up with a startling theory. The academic original is different: there are non-nominalised participants as Theme, *Asian lineage 50, people, these times* and so on, but these participants exist at a higher level of generality than the small group of named researchers in the popular article. That is, they are more difficult for the reader to visualise or to grasp, and so they are less likely to act as points of departure in a popularisation. Moreover, the academic article also has a range of nominalised Theme: *the second implication, each estimate,* and *a detailed account of this calculation.* A tendency in academic articles is to move from a description of a process e.g. *these times enable us to* **calculate**... to a nominalised use of it as a participant in its own right *a detailed account* **of this calculation**. This kind of patterning – a focus on researchers and other *agents* in popular articles and on research *claims* in academic articles – is also evident in the computing texts, for example CP1 and CL1:

CP1:

Researchers	devised programs that did well at individual tasks.
Computers	played chess at a level close to world class;

they	rediscovered one of Kepler's laws and Ohm's law.
They	learnt to re-use successful planning strategies to meet new demands.
CL1:	
Mixed models	thus require multiplex forms of psychological/computational explanation.
Not just different *tasks* but different aspects of the *same* task	now look in need of different kinds of computational explanation.
Insofar as human beings are required to negotiate some truly rule-governed problem domains (e.g. chess, language mathematics)	some form of mixed model may well be nature's most effective solution.
The apparent success of thoroughly soft PDP systems in negotiating some such domains (e.g. the model of past-tense acquisition)	may be due to the presence of a concealed 'bolt-on' symbol processing unit – us!

Here the thematised participants in the popular article have referents in the physical universe – researchers and computers – while the academic article thematises an abstraction, a model, and then moves to a nominalisation *apparent success* via two cognitive Themes: *aspects, look* and a circumstantial subclause *insofar as* ... .

The situation, as we would expect, is complex, but from the evidence of the biology and computing texts, there is a greater tendency in the popularisations to focus on physical agents and thus to revert to non-nominalised Theme; in the academic articles the focus is firmly on the research claim and Themes are likely to exhibit a higher degree of nominalisation. This pattern is, however, not easy to find in the history articles. In this field, both popular and academic genres have a high number of nominalised Theme, often similar. If there is a noticeable difference between them, it is not evident from the small sample analysed here. A brief example serves to illustrate:

HP1:

Developments in the resorts themselves	were more to the point ...
The policies of the landowners	were particularly important in the early stages of resort growth ...
Large landowners	might also subsidise the promenades, utilities and drainage systems which were essential ...
and they	might step in to support pier and entertainment companies when the latter faltered or were slow to materialise.
Large scale entertainment	was rarely profitable in the long run at the seaside, except at Blackpool ...
... most such towns	owed their attractiveness, in part, to municipal socialism
The rising demand for seaside holidays	owed much to the attractiveness of the resorts themselves ...

HL1:

The evolution of this distinctive Lancashire holiday system	had important implications for the resorts.
The demand for seaside visits	was spread over several weeks of the summer, as different towns took their holidays at different times;
and this accidental stagger effect	made it possible for a working-class holiday industry to emerge at an early stage.
... the longer season	enabled some of the resorts to make themselves attractive to the working-class visitor ...
Rhyl, Douglas, New Brighton and Scarborough	were among the resorts which responded to these developments.

Here, in both the popular and academic version, the author moves between nominalised Theme e.g. *Developments ..., the rising demand, the evolution ..., the demand for seaside visit* and non-nominalised Theme e.g. *large landowners, the longer season.* Out of context, it would be difficult to assign, say, the Themes *the rising demand for seaside holidays* and *the demand for seaside visits* to either a popular or an academic genre. This apparent divergence in the field of history from the more scientific fields, computing and biology, has significant ideological implications, as we shall see.

3.5.2 Research-oriented themes

A feature of the academic genres is the tendency of the writer or writers to thematise the article itself and/or the procedures used in it. Examples from the articles analysed here include:

this paper (BL3)

My strategy (CL1)

The matching process presented in this paper (CL2)

The structure of this paper (CL3)

Section 3 (CL3)

The majority of such Themes are found in the opening or closing passages of the article: the writers are announcing what they aim to accomplish or what they claim to have achieved. Such a self-conscious concern with the research article as a construct, as an embodiment of a research instrument, is largely lacking in popularisations.

Another, perhaps minor but still significant, feature of the orientation towards research in academic genres is their naming conventions. In popularisations, researchers are usually referred to by their surnames and sometimes institutional affiliations; in academic articles, researchers are usually identified via their publications, e.g.

Popular	*Academic*
Brendan Keegan (BP1)	Warner (1971) (BL1)
Cann and her colleagues (BP2)	Vevers (1952) (BL2)
French and her co-workers (BP3)	Corbett (1978, 1979) (BL2)
H. J. Eysenk (HP3)	Cockburn (1977b) (HL3)

This point might seem slight; nevertheless, when popular articles thematise researchers, they usually refer to the person or persons, whereas when academic articles do the same, they refer to published work. This fact is consistent with the depersonalised research-orientation of Themes in academic articles.

Orientation towards research rather than researchers can cause difficulties when writers wish to refer to themselves in academic genres. In popularisations, this seems to be less of an issue: first-person singular and plural pronouns are freely used. In academic articles there is a greater variation in self-reference strategies: writers may say *this paper* or refer to their own published work, e.g. Richard Aronson refers to *Aronson and Harms (1985)* as an agent. Single authors refer to themselves as *we* (e.g. HL3), which involves reader and writer in the research process. While Myers (1990) considers such distancing as part of the objective style of academic writing, it can equally be explained in terms of research orientation.

3.5.3 Explicitness of content in themes

In the few cases where there is a near one-to-one correspondence of clauses in the academic and popular genres, there is often a higher level of explicitness in the Themes of the academic article. Some examples from all three fields can be seen below:

BP1:

| Many beds in the western English channel | have disappeared since 1970. |
| Not one brittlestar in a Jurassic population from Dorset | was regenerating an arm. |

BL1:

| In fact, fluctuations in the occurrence of dense beds of *Ophiothrix fragilis* in the English Channel over a period of several decades | have been correlated with changes in predation pressure exerted by two species of the starfish *Ludia* (Holme 1984). |

Of 55 well-preserved specimens of *Ophiomusium weymouthiense* from the Late Mid-Jurassic of Weymouth, Dorset, housed in the collections of the British Museum (Natural history),	only one showed arm regeneration (Aronson, personal observation).

CP2:

The first step in recognition	is to find a promising correspondence between a few features of the image and a few features of the object.

CL2:

The initial viewpoint estimate for the model (shown in figure 6a in dark blue)	is made by using simple linear approximations.

HP3:

Changes	have taken place in the types of non indictable offences, reflecting changes in social and economic conditions.

HL3:

Of course, changes in the administration of justice	were a vital influence upon this pattern, of which more in the next section.

The above examples, from all three fields, suggest that academic articles are generally more explicit in their Themes than their popular equivalents. This explicitness takes a number of forms. First of all, modifiers and qualifiers give additional information e.g. *Changes **in the administration of justice**. Second, where modifiers and qualifiers are present in both genres, a more technical and/or precise term is used in the academic text e.g. *many beds* versus *dense beds*; *several skull measurements* versus *skull measurements of these three groups*. Third, relexicalisation means that the popularisation uses less technical, more accessible vocabulary e.g. *Ophiothrix fragilis* versus *brittlestar; the initial viewpoint estimate* versus *the first step in recognition*. By relexicalisation, I mean here the selection, in different contexts, of alternative lexical items to express the same or very similar entities or concepts. No temporal significance is intended, although all the academic articles predate the popularisations. Finally, we even find in the popular article an exaggeration of the claim made in the academic equivalent. For example, in BP1 we learn of the *disappearance* of brittlestar beds and that the author found *not one brittlestar* regenerating an arm in a Jurassic community. In the corresponding academic article, we read of *fluctuations* rather than disappearance, and discover that the writer found *only one* brittlestar regenerating an arm in what seems to be the same Jurassic community.

Before leaving the topic of relexicalisation, it is worth noting in passing the impact that technical terms have on tenor as well as field. Eggins (1994) categorises field into 'technical' and 'everyday' based partly on vocabulary selection. However, it is evident that this choice has an equal impact upon tenor, that is, upon the writer's relationship with his or her intended readership. Precision is related to formality. Both technical and formal texts use latinisms, for example, to identify carefully-delineated concepts, but also for decoration (a feature that extends back to the use of *aureate* or *golden* latinate vocabulary in high-style mediaeval poetry). And so we find that some colloquial terms that popularisations use to increase accessibility are avoided in academic texts not only because they are imprecise but because they are considered inappropriate for the formal tenor. The following examples illustrate this point:

BP1:

The top carnivores in Sweetings pond	are octopuses.
They	eat the small crustaceans and clams that live in the lake but leave brittlestars alone.
Octopuses	are relatives of the shelled cephalopods, *Nautilus* for example, that were predators before the Mesozoic marine revolution.

BL1:

Another aspect of the lake's anachronistic character	is its high density of *Octopus briareus,* the Caribbean reef octopus.
The population density of this cephalopod	is also orders of magnitude greater in Sweetings Pond than off the coast.

The obvious marker of informality in the above example is the use of *top* in the popularisation. This colloquialism implies a kind of league table of predators as the point of departure for messages about octopus' ancestry and behaviour. The academic article conveys similar content by thematising an abstraction (*aspect*) to establish a peculiar characteristic of the lake as a point of departure. Again, thematic selection serves a number of functions: establishing a rapport with a readership through the use of the appropriate tenor, and directing readers towards salient, stage-setting information – things in the popular example, characteristics in the academic text – and giving them the amount of information they would be expected to need.

3.5.4 Circumstantial themes

In the texts analysed here, the most frequent circumstance realised at Theme is locational. A further consideration of the kind of location realised supports the argument that academic articles favour an orientation towards research. Simply put, the locational Themes of academic articles – again particularly in the scientific fields of biology and computing – are more likely to direct the reader towards the article itself. A full list of the locational Themes in the academic and popular articles from the fields of biology and computing is given below:

Popularisations	*Academic texts*
In 1885	During the last few years
A century later	In this chapter
Here	Where information is available
From Chadwick's century-old	Under certain rare circumstances
account and studies by a student	By the end of the 19th century
in the 1960s	Over the past 60 years or so
today	In this paper
This time	In PCA [Principal Component
As the Scottish wildcat was	Analyses]
ruthlessly eradicated from Britain	and particularly in CVA [Canonical
Once the wildcat began to recover	Variates Analyses]
from man's persecution	In the present paper
Recently	In this paper
To an evolutionary theorist	
To many cognitive scientists	
Before we recognise an object	

It is evident from the absence of any locational Theme in the popularisations directing the reader towards the article or sections thereof that research-orientation is achieved by thematised circumstances as well as participants in academic texts. Popular articles generally direct the reader towards periods and points of time, physical locations in space, and salient agents. In other words, the circumstances selected in popularisations provide the points of departure for a narrative, for episodic sequences of action to unfold. Academic texts also do this – but to a lesser extent – and they also direct the reader towards the text itself.

Again, the field of history proves an exception, at least in this small sample. None of the extracts of the academic history texts contains a single locational Theme directing the reader towards the research. Not surprisingly, the history texts contain a high proportion of Themes of temporal location, and the articles on the development of seaside resorts contain a considerable number of Themes of spatial location. However, the concern with explicit procedures – with self-reflexively constructing an article in accordance with a set of conventions – seems to be absent in academic history texts. Again, I shall consider the reasons why this should be so in the conclusion.

3.5.5 Modal themes

Modal Themes are few enough in our extracts to show in their entirety. The majority are attitudinal adjuncts; some are style adjuncts (shown with an asterisk):

Popularisations		*Academic texts*	
BP1:	Strangely	BL1:	In fact
			In fact
			In particular*
BP3:	Unfortunately	BL3:	Indeed
			Without any doubt
CP1:	Perhaps	CL1:	In short*
	Perhaps		Perhaps
			in fact
CP2:	In fact	CL2:	In fact
	In fact		
	Fortunately		
	In fact		
	In fact		

			Of course
			Unfortunately
		CL3:	in fact
			In any event
HP1:	As will be clear	HL2:	Not surprisingly
			Ironically
			Clearly
			probably
			obviously
			Of course
HP3:	Indeed	HL3:	Of course
			Of course
			Broadly speaking*
			Without doubt
			More specifically*
			Inevitably

There are two tendencies that are suggested by this list: (a) that there is a greater range of modal adjuncts in academic than in popular texts; and (b) that thematic adjuncts found in history texts are markedly different from those found in computing and biology. In the academic scientific texts, the most common modal Theme is *in fact*, which Halliday and Matthiessen now label as 'factual' (2004: 130), although an earlier and perhaps more useful label was 'verifactive' (Halliday, 1985: 50). Other attitudinal Themes in the academic biology and computing texts express assertion *Indeed* and probability *perhaps*. The academic history texts have a different bias: the most common thematic attitudinal modals express presumptions *of course* and assertions *obviously, clearly, without doubt*, followed by predictions *inevitably, not surprisingly*. Like their scientific counterparts, the academic history texts have their fair share of probability Themes *probably*, and there is one instance of a modal adjunct that still does not fit neatly into Halliday and Matthiessen's categories *ironically*. The academic texts also have a monopoly of the style adjuncts, whose purpose is to make explicit the degree of specificity *in particular, broadly speaking* and *more specifically* or to indicate a summary *in short*.

The popularisations have their share of factual, probability and presumptive Themes, in a similar distribution across the fields of computing, biology and history (i.e. propositional in history texts, speech-functional in science texts), but they also range more widely (e.g. to include the desirability adjuncts, *fortunately* and *unfortunately* and a strong expression of unpredictability, *strangely*. This evidence suggests that popularisations express a broader and more intense set of attitudes than their academic equivalents. Academic science is largely confined to expressing probabilities and verifying facts; academic history texts are confined to expressing probabilities and asserting presumptions. Popular history extends the range to expressing desirability and irony – and selecting lexis that will express these attitudes intensely.

The greater incidence of style adjuncts at Theme in academic texts supports the thread of our argument that academic texts demonstrate an explicit concern for their own structure. Quirk and Greenbaum (1973: 42) suggest that style adjuncts 'convey the speaker's comment on the form of what he is saying'. By using style adjuncts, academic texts are again directing the reader towards the form of the message, because the construction of the article is a self-conscious embodiment of a robust research procedure which will be judged by the academic discourse community (cf. Bazerman, 1988). Popularisations, which convey information more dramatically to a less critical readership, can afford to be less self-conscious.

3.6 Summary and conclusion

This chapter offers a broad survey of thematic types in matched extracts from academic and popular articles across three fields – biology, computing and history. The survey suggests that there are various similarities between academic and popular articles in these fields: both generally favour participants in material and relational processes as Theme; the 'points of departure' privilege actions, events and states of being. Circumstantial Themes favour settings in time and space. Both academic and popular articles have a low frequency of modal adjuncts whose realisation is nevertheless note-worthy – neither genre has the monopoly of expressions of attitude, although popular texts tend to have a wider range and more dramatic lexis.

We have also seen differences: academic biology and computing texts tend more frequently than their popular counterparts towards abstractions, often in the form of nominalised Themes, particularly when they are describing complex processes and experimental procedures. In such passages, popularisations drift towards concrete participants as Theme, less frequently nominalised. In addition, academic texts will have a greater degree of explicitness in the Theme, often realised by complex strings of modification and qualification in the nominal group. The greater degree of technical precision expected in academic texts can, however, become a feature of tenor – an expression of appropriate formality. (An exception to this rule is CL1, which is an unpublished draft of an academic article whose lexis still betrays its origins as a conference paper – expressions such as 'hot topic' are relics of the spoken idiom).

The regularities that we find distinguishing academic and popular genres in the fields of biology and computing are less apparent in the field of history. Here both academic and popular articles use nominalisations frequently, and it is difficult to tell between them. Popularisations can show a high degree of explicitness in long, heavily-modified Themes, while the corresponding academic text can sometimes show quite a low degree of explicitness. The level of formality in the popular and academic genres seems roughly equivalent.

Some degree of 'research orientation' is evident in the Themes of the academic articles in all three fields; such 'points of departure' are largely absent from the popularisations. Research orientation is also evident in the convention of identifying researchers through their publications. In academic genres, the text itself is an agent in the construction of knowledge.

It is interesting, finally, to compare the above findings with more ethnographic explorations of academic and professional genres as performed, for example, by Myers (1990), Hyland (2000) and the contributors to Candlin and Hyland (1999). Following Swales (1990), much genre analysis outside systemic functionalism has explored the concept of the 'discourse community', a tightly or loosely-knit group of readers and writers sharing some common discursive practices. These practices are driven by a shared ethos and set of communicative purposes, that members are socialised into and which they continually negotiate and maintain. Myers' (1990) description of the 'narratives of nature and science' can be related to two distinct discourse communities – a close-knit peer-group of biologists whose conception of the academic research article is as an instrument of knowledge creation, and a more diverse and a loosely-knit 'popular' readership, whose conception of the article is as an entertaining and instructive vehicle for revelation about the natural world. This view of two divergent discourse communities, with different understandings of the purpose of the texts, is clearly compatible with the findings of the present study. Research-orientation in particular directs the specialist reader towards the abstract agents found in the 'narratives of science' and away from the physical agents more often found in the 'narratives of nature'. If Theme is about 'points of departure', then academic articles in the two scientific fields are 'about' research whereas popularisations are 'about' the physical universe. Researchers in 'narratives of science' tend to be impersonal, but they still state probabilities, verify facts, and make presumptions. Only in popularisations do scientists state what they desire – whether by noting that something is *(un)fortunate* or *(un)lucky*.

However, the Themes of the academic and popular history articles can less easily be used to distinguish two types of narrative. One conclusion might be that historians do not distinguish between popular and academic readerships, although Megill and McCloskey would disagree:

> A work of history that satisfies the wider public is unlikely to satisfy a professional audience; and only a few works that satisfy a professional audience manage to have a wider appeal. In other words, divergent historiographic audiences now exist.
> (Megill and McCloskey 1987: 223)

Even if perceived audiences vary in the history articles, there does not seem to be the same degree of variation that is found in the biology and computing articles, perhaps because, as Megill and McCloskey state, professional historiography is a comparatively new development. This tiny trawl through academic and popular history texts might well have netted three pairs of conservative texts. By contrast, Bazerman (1988) and Halliday (1988) argue that professional science writing has been developing since the time of Newton. Another possible reason for the lack of divergence in the history texts is that professional historiography, like most disciplines in the humanities, can be characterised as a 'rural' discourse community in Becher's (1989) terms. Becher argues that, unlike the sciences, in which comparatively large groups of individuals work on a small, and therefore highly-populated set of problems, the humanities proceed by a dispersed group of people working on largely different (and therefore low-populated) problems. In other words, more people are likely to be working in well-resourced teams on the problems of computer vision than on the rise of working-class seaside resorts. This difference in the composition of the discourse communities of the sciences and humanities must have an impact on the genres that each produces – humanities researchers can presumably take fewer concepts than their scientific counterparts for granted, they must continually make a case for their own particular research territory amidst colleagues with widely differing interests, and in the absence of agreed experimental techniques, they must proceed by assertion *of course* rather than verification *in fact*. In other words, the discourse community of professional historians has much in common with that of that of the general public – and this is possibly why the professional and popular discourses are so similar in their thematic realisations.

References

Bazerman, C. (1988). *Shaping Written Knowledge: The Genre and Activity of the Experimental Article in Science.* Madison, WI: University of Wisconsin Press.

Becher, T. (1989). *Academic Tribes and Territories.* Milton Keynes: Open University Press.

Candlin, C. and Hyland, K. (eds) (1999). *Writing Texts: Processes and Practices.* London: Longman.

Corbett, J. (1992). Functional Grammar and genre analysis: a description of the language of learned and popular articles. Unpublished PhD thesis, University of Glasgow.

Daneš, F. (1974). *Papers on Functional Sentence Perspective.* Janua Linguarum Series Minor, 147. Prague: Academia.

Daneš, F. (1987). On Prague School Functionalism in linguistics. In *Functionalism in Linguistics*, R. Dirven and V. Fried (eds), 3–37. Amsterdam: John Benjamins.

Davies, F. (1997). Marked Theme as a heuristic for analysing text-type, text and genre. In *Advances in Systemic Linguistics: Recent Theory and Practice.* T. Piqué and D. J. Viera (eds), 105–35. London: Pinter.

Downing, A. (1991). An alternative approach to Theme: a Systemic-Functional perspective. In *Word* 42, pp. 119–43.

Eggins, S. (1994). *An Introduction to Systemic Functional Linguistics.* London: Pinter.

Francis, G. (1989). Thematic selection and distribution in written discourse. In *Word* 40: 1–2, 201–21.

Fries, P. H. and Francis, G. (1992). Exploring Theme: problems for research. In *Occasional Papers in Systemic Linguistics*, 6. 45–59.

Ghadessy, M. (ed.) (1995). *Thematic Development in English Texts.* London: Pinter.

Halliday, M. A. K. (1976). Theme and Information in the English clause. In *Halliday: System and Function in Language.* G. Kress (ed.), 174–88. Oxford: Oxford University Press.

Halliday, M. A. K. (1985). *An Introduction to Functional Grammar*, 1st edn. London: Edward Arnold.

Halliday, M. A. K. (1987). Language and the order of nature. In *The Linguistics of Writing.* N. Fabb, D. Attridge, A. Durant and C. MacCabe (eds), 135–54. Manchester: Manchester University Press.

Halliday, M. A. K. (1988). On the language of physical science. In *Registers of Written English.* M. Ghadessy (ed.), 162–78. London and New York: Pinter.

Halliday, M. A. K. and Martin, J. R. (1993). *Writing Science: Literacy and Discursive Power.* London: The Falmer Press.

Halliday, M. A. K. and Matthiessen, C. M. I. M. (2004). *An Introduction to Functional Grammar*, 3rd edn. London: Edward Arnold.

Hyland, K. (2000). *Disciplinary Discourses: Social Interactions in Academic Writing.* London: Longman.

Megill, A. and McCloskey, D. N. (1987). The rhetoric of history. In *The Rhetoric of the Human Sciences: Language and Argument in Scholarship and Public Affairs.* J. S. Nelson, A. Megill and D. N. McCloskey (eds), 221–38. Madison, WI: University of Wisconsin Press.

Myers, G. (1990). *Writing Biology.* Madison, WI: University of Wisconsin Press.

Nwogu, K. and Bloor, T. (1991). Thematic progression in professional and popular medical texts. In *Functional and Systemic Linguistics: Approaches and Uses.* E. Ventola (ed.), 369–84. Berlin: Mouton de Gruyter.

Quirk, R. and Greenbaum, S. (1973). *A University Grammar of English.* London: Longman.

Swales, J. (1990). *Genre Analysis: English in Academic and Research Settings.* Cambridge: Cambridge University Press.

Weil, H. (1887; 1978). *The Order of Words in the Ancient Languages, Compared with that of the Modern Languages,* trans. C. W. Super. Amsterdam: John Benjamins.

Young, L. (1990). *Language as Behaviour, Language as Code: A Study of Academic English.* Amsterdam/Philadelphia: John Benjamins.

Appendix

Articles used in this paper, with codings.

Biology

BP1: Aronson, R. (1987). A murder mystery from the Mesozoic. In *New Scientist,* 8 October, 56–9.

BL1: Aronson, R. and Sues, H-D. (1987). The Palaeoecological significance of an anachronistic Ophiuroid community. In *Predation: Direct and Indirect Impacts on Aquatic Communities,* W. C. Kerfoot and A. Sih (eds). Hanover, NH: University Press of New England, 355–66.

BP2: Poulton, J. (1987). All about Eve. In *New Scientist,* 14 May, 51–3.

BL2: Cann, R. L., Stoneking, M. and Wilson, A. C. (1987). Mitochondrial DNA and human evolution. In *Nature* 325 (1 January), 31–6.

BP3: Kitchener, A. (1988). No domestic bliss. In *The Guardian,* 7 June.

BL3: French, D. D., Corbett, L. K. and Easterbee, N. (1988). Morphological discriminants of Scottish Wildcats (*Felis silvestris*), domestic cats (*F. catus*) and their hybrids. In *J. Zool. Lond.* 214, 235–59.

Computing

CP1: Clark, A. (1987). Cognitive science meets the biological mind. In *New Scientist* 8 October, 36–8.

CL1: Clark, A (no date). PDP or not PDP: Is that the question? Unpublished MS: University of Sussex.

CP2: Lowe, D. (1987). Vision leads robots from the factory. In *New Scientist,* 10 September, 50–2.

CL2: Lowe, D. (1987). The Viewpoint Consistency Constraint. In *International Journal of Computer Vision.* 1, 57–72.

CP3: Wilson, G. (1988). Computing in parallel. In *New Scientist,* 11 February, 54–7.

CL3: Forrest, B. M, Roweth, D., Stroud, N., Wallace, D. J. and Wilson, G. V. (1987). Implementing neural network models on parallel computers. In *The Computer Journal* 30 (5), 413–19.

History

HP1: Walton, J. K. (1985). The seaside resort and its rise in Victorian and Edwardian England. In *The Historian,* 16–22.

HL1: Walton, J. K. (1981). The demand for working-class seaside holidays in Victorian England. In *Economic History Review* 2nd series, 34, 249–65.

HP2: Stevenson, D. (1988). The Bishops' Wars. In *The Sunday Mail Story of Scotland* 2 (16): 434–7.

HL2: Stevenson, D. (1981). *Scottish Covenanters and Irish Confederates* Belfast: Ulster Historical Foundation [Chapter 1].

HP3: Bailey, V. (1988). Crime in the twentieth century. In *History Today*, 38 (May), 42–8.

HL3: Bailey, V. (1980). Crime, criminal justice and authority in England. In *Bulletin of Society for the Study of Labour History* 40 (Spring), 36–46.

4 | Thematic content in peer reviews of scientific papers

Hugh Gosden
Formerly Tokyo Institute of Technology

4.1 Background

Peer review is a central gatekeeping process in academic publication and in recent years the ethics of this rather 'occluded' procedure (Swales 1996) have been the subject of much debate, particularly in the professional science literature (e.g. Fletcher and Fletcher 1997; Godlee *et al.* 1998; Godlee and Jefferson 1999; Goldbeck-Wood 1998, 1999; Smith 1999; some Websites – http://bmj.bmjjournals.com/cgi/collection/peer_review; http://www.ama-assn.org/public/peer/peerhome.htm – also offer useful background and further links). In the field of English for Academic Purposes (EAP), discourse analysts have become increasingly interested in 'research process genres', such as peer reviews and academic correspondence, since they are seen as sites of disciplinary engagement (Hyland 2000) which reveal aspects of social interaction in academic life. However, predominantly due to their occluded and often confidential status, such genres have been relatively little studied compared with the publicly available products of mainstream research writing activities.

As a teacher-researcher in the field of EAP, my primary interest lies in the analysis of episodes of spoken and written interaction in research communication between members of the international scientific community, and in the application of insights gained from such analysis to EAP contexts. An important area for research is to understand better how novices become acculturated into this international community and how cross-cultural and linguistic variation impacts on this complex process. On a practical level, since my teaching role involves me with research students who are non-native speakers of English (NNSE) and who are preparing their first papers for publication in English-language journals, relevant insights from analysis of research genres help to guide the content and structure of EAP courses at this advanced level. In previous related work, one example of this is the analysis of how successfully published research writers use appropriate text-structuring devices to organise the flow of information in their texts, that is, how writers make thematic choices and control thematic development across stretches of a research article in response to the changing rhetorical demands of that genre (Gosden 1992, 1993). How novices' own research writing processes and products can be improved by providing them with tools to handle more expertly this crucial means of text organisation was subsequently the focus of practical application (Gosden 1998).

However, in the case of a research process genre such as academic peer reviews, the primary focus of discourse analysis is not to provide insights to help 'train' novices to write peer reviews – the main objective is not for them to 'model' their own writing on specific characteristics of these texts, but for analysis to reveal the subtle complexities of this occluded genre so that, as relatively inexperienced novices, they may be able to frame their replies to referees' criticisms more effectively.

This article is part of a broader study based on a corpus of 40 peer reviews of manuscripts following submission by NNSE researchers to an international scientific journal for publication (Gosden 2001, 2003). The following section contains background information on the study, starting with the form of scientific research articles known as Letters and particular aspects of the review process of Letters, followed by details of the corpus on which this study is based. As suggested above, this report focuses on one important functional component of language, namely, thematic content, and Section 4.3 gives a brief overview of Theme with a description of the functional categorization of Theme adopted in this study. Section 4.4 illustrates the approach taken with a coded example of one complete review, followed by overall corpus results and comments.

4.2   The study

Short papers in various scientific fields, typically limited to 2000 words, are known variously as Letters, Research Notes, Rapid Communications or Brief Reports. The main concern of such journals which often appear weekly is the rapid publication of new findings. In such cases, the review process is usually streamlined in order for scientists to be able to establish priority for their research claims in fast-moving fields. The present data come from the review of submissions to an international Letters journal, with its main editorial offices in the UK and USA, which publishes approximately 30 papers weekly in English, in a hard science field. Given the emphasis on rapid publication, the Letters journal has regional advisory editorial boards in 20 countries worldwide to handle local submissions – here, I am dealing with papers submitted to a member of the advisory editorial board in Japan. However, English is used for all official journal correspondence, which includes referees' reports, authors' responses with re-submissions, and editorial records and correspondence. As is common practice in many scientific fields, referees know the identities of the authors and their affiliations from the submitted manuscripts and covering letter – the review process can therefore be described as 'anonymous' (the referees know the authors' names), rather than 'blinded' (neither party knows) or 'open' (both parties know).

Any analysis of gatekeeping discourse, such as peer reviews, inevitably involves issues of confidentiality and how data may be exploited. After explaining my specific objectives, I asked a local advisory editor whether I might have access to a corpus of referees' reports. I was given 21 envelopes, comprising the editor's most recently completed 'batch' of submissions, completed in that they had either been through the full review process and had been accepted for publication, or the papers had been withdrawn by the authors after review. Envelopes were chronologically ordered by date of original receipt in the editor's office, and I kept to this simple arrangement for the purposes of numbering referees' reports and authors' replies in my corpus. Thus, it can be concluded that there was no actual gathering, selection, or randomization of data involved in the corpus of papers.

The corpus consists of reports by 40 referees – 15 non-native speakers of English and 25 native speakers (as far as could be judged) – divided into two groups depending on the initial judgement of referees regarding their suitability for rapid publication:

Group I consists of 22 reports (average length 199 words) on 15 papers which were all initially marked 'accept with revisions' (some reviewers had added with 'minor' or 'major' revisions). Seven papers had two reports each, eight papers only one. In all 15 cases, the revised versions of the manuscripts were accepted for publication. For Group I papers, the average time from receipt of paper to acceptance for publication was 14.6 weeks.

Group II consists of 18 reports (average length 185 words) on six papers which were initially deemed 'unacceptable'. One paper had one report, one had three, two had two, and two papers had five reports, indicating multiple revisions and re-submissions. However, only one paper was satisfactorily revised and accepted. The other five were withdrawn and were untraceable by author or title computer search, which implies that the technical content and/or format of those papers was considerably re-worked due to the reasons for rejection. Gosden (2001) discusses these six papers in greater detail.

4.3   Thematic choice

4.3.1 Background

Why look at thematic choice in texts, and in scientific research writing in particular? The foregrounding of certain types of information, i.e., thematic choice, is an important resource in helping a writer stage the appropriate, genre-specific flow of social interaction in a text, where there may be a need to balance interactional, 'human face' discourse with more impersonal, topic-based technical discourse. In the mainstream genres of professional scientific research, it may be thought that there is little presence of interactional 'human face' discourse, and hence little need to foreground this kind of information for readers. The same might be thought to be the case in related scientific process genres, such as referees' technical reports. However, due to a variety of factors such as issues of confidentiality and lack of access to data, there is in fact little reported research on less visible genres such as peer reviews. Given their importance in the traditional culture of scientific publishing, it is naturally of interest to explore how peer reviews 'work' on a variety of levels.

4.3.2 The analysis of Theme

What count as Theme elements? Halliday (1985: 36) states that the typical unmarked thematic form in a declarative clause in English is one which conflates three separate and distinct functions: SUBJECT, the grammatical subject, 'that of which something is predicated'; the THEME, the psychological subject, 'that which is the concern of the message'; and the ACTOR, the logical subject, 'the doer of the action.' Since Theme is realised as the element which serves as the 'point of departure' (Halliday 1985: 38) of the message, the conflated grammatical/psychological/logical subject functions as unmarked Theme, unless a writer has a good reason for choosing something else. The majority of Themes in the typically declarative statements of scientific written discourse conform to the predominant unmarked pattern. This conflated subject/unmarked Theme pattern characterises much scientific writing and thus it can be suggested that generic distinctiveness itself appears to be strongly encoded in thematic choices.

However, researchers, many predominantly working within a Hallidayan systemic-functional tradition, inevitably disagree about aspects of multi-layered, metafunctional analysis, and the elasticity of thematic interpretation is an example of this. If Theme is glossed as the 'point of departure', which elements realise Theme and up to which components does it actually hold? Should analysis be of all clause Themes or only sentence-initial Themes? In this chapter, as in previous work by Davies (1988, 1991), I have adopted a simplified, discourse-functional approach to the analysis of Theme, i.e. I take unmarked Theme as grammatical subject and focus on this, ignoring for the present purposes any elements which may precede it. Moreover, only Themes in sentence-initial clauses are coded here, since the intention is to give a clearer picture of thematic patterns without secondary organisation. As demonstrated in Gosden (1998), this approach is guided by the practical need to gain a transparent view of textual development in written scientific discourse. In this way, any textlinguistic analysis and labels employed aim to capture commonsense insights that can be directly applied in the classroom, where EAP students often have an immediate need for their use in understanding their own research writing (and importantly post-review re-writing) processes.

4.3.3 Functional categories of Theme

The rationale behind the current model of unmarked Theme/subject domains based on Davies (1988, 1991) was outlined in Gosden (1993), and further adapted by McKenna (1997). Briefly, this model consists of four main domains:

- Participant
- Discourse
- Hypothesised and Objectivised
- Real World

These four categories represent a continuum from the Participant to the Real World domain. Towards one end, it is typified by the presence of the writer (e.g. *we, our argument*) as a visible participant in the research and research reporting process, as well as the intended target audience (e.g. *the reader*); towards the other end of the continuum, there is a focus on research-based, real-world physical entities and processes (e.g. *the sample pressures, the procedures applied*). Thus, these two poles of the continuum can be seen to reflect a potential balance between the more 'human face' interactional Themes of the Participant domain and the more impersonal topic-based thematic choices of the Real World domain. Within each domain, there are several sub-categories, each related by the primary focus of the domain. For example, *we* and *the reader* can be viewed more distinctly as part of a Discourse Participant sub-category, and *our argument* as a Participant Viewpoint. Likewise, *the sample pressures* is a Real World Entity and *the procedures applied* a Real World Process. Between the two poles of the continuum, there are two further domains which represent more subtle realisations of interactional thematisation. The Discourse domain represents the research products of participants (e.g., *this manuscript* which can be subcategorised as a Macro Discourse Entity; *the reference in (1) above* functions as an Interactive Discourse Entity). The Hypothesised and Objectivised domain represents more subtle means by which writers' hedged comments on hypotheses and viewpoints can be realised (e.g., *one reservation regarding the paper, it is curious that...*).

The categories and sub-categories outlined in Gosden (1993) are used as the baseline for analysis in this chapter and are adapted according to the present corpus of peer reviews. Examples of unmarked Themes in each sub-category noted in the corpus are given below (Themes are in bold).

PARTICIPANT DOMAIN

- Discourse Participant

    The reader needs Tables of numbers that go into eq. 6.

- Participant Viewpoint

    One's major concern is with the analysis.

- Interactive Participant

    Ottinger has just published another paper (+TD) that should be added.

DISCOURSE DOMAIN

- Discourse Event/Process

    This conclusion is well-supported by their observations.

- Macro Discourse Entity

    This manuscript reports interesting work.

- Micro Discourse Entity

    The statement referring to the reference should read ...

- Interactive Discourse Entity

    The reference in (1) above provides an easy way to measure (+TD).

HYPOTHESISED AND OBJECTIVISED DOMAIN

- Objectivised Viewpoint

    One reservation regarding the paper is that...

- Empty H & O Theme

    It is curious that... (+TD).

REAL WORLD DOMAIN

- Real World Entity

  The sample pressures should be given.
- Real World Event/Process

  The procedures applied should be applied in greater detail.

In order to illustrate the approach taken here to analysis of the thematic content of referees' comments under these functional categories, the next section presents a fully coded example, followed by results drawn from the corpus as a whole.

4.4   Analyses

4.4.1 Example of coding of Themes

This section presents the coded analysis of sentence-initial unmarked Themes contained in one referee's report marked 'accept after revisions'. Working through an example of analysis in the EAP classroom is an invaluable way for students to appreciate how to derive functional categories and, in turn, to apply simplified discourse-analytic tools to their own writing in order to develop a greater awareness of thematic patterns in texts.

For reasons of space, the report below is not reproduced in full; (+TD) indicates technical detail in the report that has been omitted here. Sentence-initial unmarked Themes/subjects are underlined, and the thematic choices are described by functional category (and sub-category) in Table 4.1.

(1)   [1] <u>This manuscript</u> reports interesting work. [2] However, <u>it</u> needs significant improvement before being published. [3] Furthermore, <u>the work</u> is questionable for a Letter format. [4] <u>The phenomena being studied</u> are not particularly new, although it is useful. [5] <u>The manuscript</u> reports (+TD). [6] However, <u>this reader</u> regards these numbers with some suspicion because the authors do not give sufficient detail and they do not consider the possible cumulative errors. [7] <u>The authors</u> should consider the following specific points.

[8] <u>The values from ref. 21</u> are probably too large. [9] See (+ new ref.) for a new measurement of (+TD).

[10] The authors quote (+TD) value as 0.25. [11] That in fact was for a different study. [12] The reference in (1) above provides an easy way to measure (+TD) and it should be done.

[13] The data are referenced to (+TD). [14] How good is this reaction ±10%, ±20% etc?

[15] No information is given about the band width of the laser or (+TD).

[16] How were the experiments actually done?

[17] The reader needs Tables of numbers that go into eq. 6. [18] No one could ever do comparable experiments and check back for verification of data.

[19] Eq. 6 needs attention. [20] The reader needs the (+TD) factors too.

[21] Finally, the reader deserves (+TD) in Table 1. [22] Also, the authors should summarize (+TD). [23] Are these branching factors reliable to a factor of 2? [24] Why not give us the full story?

Table 4.1 Analysis of Theme/subjects

S	Theme/subject	Functional category
1	The manuscript	Discourse (Macro Discourse Entity)
2	it *(manuscript)*	Discourse (Macro Discourse Entity)
3	the work *(re. format)*	Discourse (Macro Discourse Entity)
4	The phenomena being studied	Real World (Real World Entity)
5	The manuscript	Discourse (Macro Discourse Entity)
6	this reader	Participant (Discourse Participant)
7	The authors	Participant (Discourse Participant)
8	The values	Real World (Real World Entity)
9	*See	*imperative form
10	The authors	Participant (Discourse Participant)
11	That *(value)*	Real World (Real World Entity)
12	The reference	Discourse (Interactive Discourse Entity)
13	The data	Real World (Real World Entity)
14	*How good ...?	*question form
15	No information (i.e. *TD*)	Real World (Real World Entity)
16	*How ...?	*question form
17	The reader	Participant (Discourse Participant)
18	No one	Participant (Interactive Participant)
19	Eq. 6	Discourse (Micro Discourse Entity)
20	The reader	Participant (Discourse Participant)
21	the reader	Participant (Discourse Participant)
22	the authors	Participant (Discourse Participant)
23	*Are these branching factors ... ?	*question form
24	*Why not	*question form

In Example 1, 19 of the 24 (79 per cent) sentences are declarative statements, with additionally four interrogatives and one imperative form. For present purposes, cases of non-declaratives are excluded from analysis. However, the review above illustrates the typical thematic content of interrogatives with Real World subjects (*Are these branching factors reliable to a factor of 2?*), although the closing 'question' (*Why not give us the full story?*) obviously functions at a different level as more of a general closing comment. Nevertheless, it can be suggested that non-declarative forms such as questions in reviews are relatively unambiguous in terms of interpreting implied revisions. Additionally, five of the 19 sentence-initial elements include textual Themes, such as *However, Furthermore, Also*. Obviously such 'context frames' (Davies, 1991; Gosden, 1992) have important text-structuring functions, but they are not dealt with here.

By functional domain, we can organise the 19 unmarked Themes in the coded example above as follows:

- Participant domain   =   8
- Discourse domain   =   6
- Real World domain   =   5

It can be seen that 14 (74 per cent) of the 19 statements relate to non-Real World domains. The dominance of Participant domain Themes, especially under the sub-category of Discourse Participant, e.g. *The authors, The reader* followed in frequency by Discourse domain Themes, e.g. *the manuscript*, is clear. These thematic choices consequently give great rhetorical weight to this individual referee's main concerns regarding the authors' lack of sufficient attention to making their paper fully accessible and convincing to readers. There are clearly technical questions that need to be addressed in any revised version, but one can readily speculate that the poor interactional orientation of the submitted paper was also one major reason why it was marked 'accept after revisions'.

4.4.2 Results

All 40 reviewers' reports were analysed for Theme in the same way as the example above. The results of the analysis are shown in Table 4.2. As can be seen, the vast majority (88 per cent) of sentences in the corpus were declarative statements, with little distinction in the proportions between Group I and Group II in the corpus (i.e., whether the submitted papers were initially marked 'accept with revisions' or 'unacceptable', respectively).

Table 4.2 Sentence-initial elements in the 40 reports

	Overall	*Group I*	*Group II*
Declaratives	458 (88%)	285 (89%)	173 (87%)
Non-declaratives	60 (12%)	35 (11%)	25 (13%)
Total	518 (100%)	320 (100%)	198 (100%)

With a focus on the corpus of 458 sentence-initial unmarked Themes, Table 4.3 gives their overall distribution (both Groups I and II) according to the four main domains outlined earlier.

It is particularly worth noting that the entities and processes/procedures of Real World Themes, i.e. the technical subject matter, account for just one-third of the total of Themes. In the Participant domain (25.6 per cent), the majority of cases (103 of 117) were examples of Discourse Participant with frequent mentions of *authors* and *readers*, as exemplified in Section 4.4.1 above. In the Discourse domain (32.1 per cent), 106 of the 147 examples referred to Macro (*This paper*) and Micro (*This point*) Discourse Entities. Real World references (33.4 per cent) were predominantly to technical Entities (*The molecule*). No examples of Hypothesised and Objectivised Themes occurred in the coded example in Section 4.4.1, but Table 4.3 indicates that overall the figure was 8.9 per cent (*One reservation regarding the paper is that ...; It is curious that ...*).

In order to verify whether the overall judgement of papers by referees (i.e. whether manuscripts were accepted or rejected for publication) affected the ratio of technical Real World vs. non-Real World interactional comments, I broke down the data by group. The results are shown in Table 4.4.

As can be seen, there are some small differences in Table 4.4 that may be attributed to referees' judgement regarding the rejection of Group II papers. For example, there is more emphasis on technical Themes (36.4 per cent as opposed to 31.6 per cent), i.e. the (problematic) research topic itself

Table 4.3 Distribution of Themes by domain

	N	%
Participant	117	25.6
Discourse	147	32.1
Hypothesised/Objectivised	41	8.9
Real World	153	33.4
Total	458	100

Table 4.4 Distribution of Themes by domain and group

	Group I	*Group II*
Participant	26.7%	23.7%
Discourse	30.5%	34.7%
Hypothesized & Objectivized	11.2%	5.2%
Real World	31.6%	36.4%
Total	100%	100%

is the focus. In addition, the reviews of rejected papers contain slightly more Discourse Themes – highlighting the problems with the papers themselves – and fewer Participant Themes – a possible means for referees to distance themselves from authors whose work they are rejecting. In the minor category of Hypothesised and Objectivised Themes, when giving reasons for rejecting papers, scrutiny of the reports suggests that the critical comments required demand less of a hedged approach in order for referees to distance themselves from authors/papers, and hence there are fewer Hypothesized and Objectivized thematic choices.

Finally, we can summarize the data in Table 4.4 by separating the Real World category from the other three, as in Table 4.5.

It can be seen from Table 4.5 that the more strongly interactional domain Themes of the three non-Real World categories accounted for 66.6 per cent of the overall total. This broad generalisation allows us to make a powerful statement about the overall interpersonal orientation of the thematic content of referees' comments.

4.5   Conclusions

The results from this small-scale study indicate that two-thirds of all sentence-initial unmarked Themes in the corpus focused on non-Real World interaction. The fronting of thematic choices relating to the roles

Table 4.5 Overall % of Real World vs. non-Real World Themes and by group

	Overall (%)	*Group I (%)*	*Group II (%)*
Real World	33.4	31.6	36.4
Non-Real World	66.6	68.4	63.6
Total	100	100	100

as *authors* and *readers* and the shared medium of *manuscripts* and *papers* emphasises referees' continued focus on the degree to which they believed *authors*, and more objectively their *papers*, had been successful or not in making a convincing presentation of their research findings to intended target readers.

In their efforts to publish their first papers, many novice research writers may initially believe that the successful revision of papers is mostly about improving technical details of 'the science', thereby satisfying referees about their knowledge of the topic. In this way, novices may tend to misread or underestimate referees' concerns regarding the need to remedy in revised manuscripts any 'interactional' deficiencies, which may be pointed out by referees in a number of both explicit and subtler ways. For example, one way of thematically fronting referees' evaluation of manuscripts could be by means of what are labelled here as Hypothesised and Objectivised Themes (e.g., *one reservation regarding the paper*). However, the data show that evaluation was relatively rarely realised in this way, which means that interpretation of evaluative comments may be more challenging for novice NNSE researchers who, as less experienced readers, may be expecting mostly transparent signals of evaluation in referees' thematic content. The present approach to the analysis of referees' thematic choices reveals quite clearly that the motivation behind their comments is typically more to do with the way in which the content has been presented, and the way in which the interaction between the writer and reader has been handled; and it also highlights the variety of forms the evaluations may take.

From a pedagogical perspective, the analytical approach is a way into exploring the issues outlined above with novice writers. Based on my own experience, NNSE research writers can beneficially be taught how to use the linguistic tools of analysis adopted here. The obvious proviso is that the levels of description used are circumscribed according to students' current – and future – needs. After all, the time is surprisingly short between one day being doctoral candidates attending EAP classes in 'Research Writing and Conference Presentations in English', and then, as post-docs or assistant professors, finding themselves with the responsibility for their own young research students, charged with teaching them writing skills in L2 English. Without the facility to access and verbalise intuitions gained through the experience of cross-cultural research communication, these young novices will themselves have to divine a learning process from their own reading and from the supervisor's red ink covering their own initial efforts at writing up their research, a frustrating process all too familiar to countless NNSE researchers around the world. The kind of socio-rhetorical knowledge resulting from this study, i.e. revealing aspects of how a particular set of texts 'works', can be seen as just one more professional skill for young NNSE researchers to learn, and the application of insights from such analysis in EAP support courses is a means of helping them reduce already considerable barriers to effective participation in the international scientific community.

References

Davies, F. (1988). Reading between the lines: Thematic choice as a device for presenting writer viewpoint in academic discourse. *The ESPecialist* 9 (2): 173–200.

Davies, F. (1991). Writing across text-types and genres: The potential of marked Theme as a device for structuring text. *ELU Working Paper No 2*, University of Liverpool, English Language Unit.

Fletcher, R. and Fletcher, S. (1997). Evidence for the effectiveness of peer review. *Science and Engineering Ethics* 3 (1): 35–50.

Godlee, F., Gale, C. and Martyn, C. (1998). Effect on the quality of peer review of blinding reviewers and asking them to sign their reports. *JAMA* 280 (3): 237–40.

Godlee, F. and Jefferson, T. (1999). *Peer Review in the Health Sciences.* London: BMJ Books.

Goldbeck-Wood, S. (1998). What makes a good reviewer of manuscripts? *British Medical Journal* 316. 10 January. p. 86.

Goldbeck-Wood, S. (1999). Evidence on peer-reviews: scientific quality control or smoke screen? *British Medical Journal* 318. 2 January: 44–5.

Gosden, H. (1992). Discourse functions of marked Theme in scientific research articles. *English for Specific Purposes* 11 (3): 207–24.

Gosden, H. (1993). Discourse functions of Subject in scientific research articles. *Applied Linguistics* 14 (1): 56–75.

Gosden, H. (1998). An aspect of holistic modelling in academic writing: Propositional clusters as a heuristic for thematic control. *Journal of Second Language Writing.* 7 (1): 19–41.

Gosden, H. (2001). 'Thank you for your critical comments and helpful suggestions': Compliance and conflict in authors' replies to referees' comments in peer reviews of scientific research papers. *IBÉRICA* 3: 3–7. Madrid: AELFE.

Gosden, H. (2003). 'Why not give us the full story?': Functions of referees' comments in peer reviews of scientific research papers. *Journal of English for Academic Purposes,* 2 (2): 87–101.

Halliday, M. A. K. (1985). *An Introduction to Functional Grammar.* London: Edward Arnold.

Hyland, K. (2000). *Disciplinary Discourses: Social Interactions in Academic Writing.* London: Longman.

McKenna, B. (1997). How engineers write: An empirical study of engineering report writing. *Applied Linguistics* 18 (2): 189–210.

Smith, R. (1999). Opening up BMJ peer review. *British Medical Journal* 318 (2 January): 4–5.

Swales, J. (1996). Occluded genres in the academy. In *Academic Writing*, E. Ventola and A. Mauranen (eds), 45–58. Amsterdam: John Benjamins.

Text-type and texture: the potential of Theme for the study of research writing development

Ann Montemayor-Borsinger
Cuyo National University

5.1 Introduction

Over the years the study of text flow and organisation has gained importance in educational, professional, and research contexts, with a view of furthering genre-based support for specialised English instruction. The structural features of Theme and Information combine together with the cohesive features of reference, ellipsis, substitution, conjunction and lexical cohesion to give *texture* to a piece of discourse (Halliday 1994: 334). This chapter analyses changes in thematic structure that affect the texture of research articles as researchers gain experience.

An important reason for studying the ways in which the thematic texture of research articles changes with time is to help novice researchers enter more successfully the publishing *arena*. In the author's experience with academic writing workshops, young researchers are often eager to know how their published work compares with that of leaders in their field, not only regarding results per se, but also regarding ways of presenting results. Researchers publishing their first papers are acutely aware of the importance of mastering optimal writing strategies in a highly competitive publishing world. Rather than just seeking advice at the editing level, there comes a point when they want to discuss deeper systemic levels of options that affect the texture of their texts. A greater focus on Theme can be a very effective way of helping, especially when time is short and the pressures to publish are great. Devising optimum thematic elements is an important step towards giving a more expert tone to research articles, where writer choices are especially strategic as they affect the way in which findings are perceived by the research community at large.

The present analysis adopts a systemic-functional view based on the Davies (1988, 1997) formulation of Theme in declaratives that includes Subject as an obligatory component. Within this approach Subject may be preceded by an optional 'Contextual Frame', i.e. non-obligatory elements that serve as a contextual framework for the rest of the sentence. In the present analysis changes in Subject and Contextual Frame are studied in research articles as scientists, already familiar with research article conventions, develop over time as writers. Ten scientists were asked to provide three articles each, written during the course of their careers and published in international physics journals. To trace changes of texture in Theme, this study modifies the original Davies (1988, 1997) criteria by introducing the notions of *Conventional* and *Instantial* wordings. Conventional wordings, both in Subject and Contextual Frame position, are identified as commonly used terms in the fields concerned, readily available to research writers as soon as they start publishing. Examples of Conventional wordings are illustrated both in the Contextual Frame *Under a magnetic field H* and in the Subject *the compound* in the following example: *Under a magnetic field H the compound undergoes a transition to a ferromagnetic state.* In contrast, Instantial wordings are identified as expressions especially created by authors to fit given stretches of text, once they have made their own the matter with which they are working. The following example shows Instantial wordings in Subject position: *The failure in achieving a satisfactory representation of the selected data leads to various kinds of modifications.* The next two sections examine the procedure leading to these notions that provide a basis for the discussion of results of the corpus analysis developed in the final part of the chapter.

5.2 Setting up the notions of 'conventional' and 'instantial' subjects

5.2.1 Davies (1988) on Subject

Davies originally distinguishes four possible choices of Subject (or unmarked Theme) that go along a cline of writer visibility for presenting viewpoint in academic discourse: Participant, Discourse, Hypothesised and Objectivised and Real-World Subjects. She suggests that differences in Subject choices are an indication of how committed and visible writers appear in relation to their research, with writers being most visible in Participant and most invisible in Real-World Subjects.

The notions of Participant and Discourse Subjects are relatively straightforward to recognize on the basis of lexical clues. Participant Subjects focus on writers, and are mostly worded as *we.* Discourse Subjects focus on the terms writers use for naming the parts laid out in their research paper, and belong to a well defined lexical set mainly comprised by the words *Figure* (x), *Table* (x), *Section* (x) and *(this) paper/work.*

More problematic to distinguish are the last two notions of Hypothesised and Objectivised and Real-World Subjects, both of which focus on phenomena the scientist is writing about. The Hypothesised and Objectivised Subject option is when writers establish as objective entities in Subject role the theories, hypotheses, models and classes they have set up, although they know such entities have a hypothetical status. Examples given in a study of scientific research articles that built upon Davies (1988) are the following: *the apparent contradiction ... the most striking influence of the P-phase ...* (Gosden 1993: 66). The 'Real-World Subject' option is when writers choose to 'hide' entirely behind the actual physical entities and the actual procedures executed on these entities. An example of a Real-World Subject is the following: *the AlFeNi alloy system ...* (Gosden 1993: 67).

However, when looking at my corpus, I sometimes found it extremely difficult to distinguish between Hypothesised and Objectivised and Real-World Subjects because Real-World, physical entities and procedures were very often theories, hypotheses or models that were subsequently being theorised and hypothesised upon, and then remodelled. Was it then reasonable to consider *the AlFeNi alloy system ...* as belonging to the Real-World domain and *the apparent contradiction ... the most striking influence of the P-phase ...* to the Hypothesised and Objectivised one?

I went back to talk to the author of the paper and other physicists. On the basis of these further interviews, it appeared that *the AlFeNi alloy system ...* could be just as much of an abstraction as *the apparent contradiction ... the most striking influence of the P-phase ...* as it might be part of constructing a model. Actually, most of the Subjects that appeared to be Real-World ones in my corpus were in fact models constructed by the authors. For instance *the radial velocity profile calculated with the fine mesh ...* could be seen as belonging to the Real-World of the research concerned, although in interviews it appeared as being a model constructed by the researcher who probably wanted to 'objectivise' it, and should then probably be coded as a Hypothesised and Objectivised entity. To take another example from my corpus, a Subject such as *the upwinding imbedded in the Lesaint-Raviart method* should then also be coded as belonging to the Hypothesised and Objectivised category precisely because 'the upwinding' – which could be seen as a Real-World event – is in fact 'imbedded' in a method.

5.2.2 Peck MacDonald (1992) on Subject

Another very interesting view of differences in the texture of academic texts due to Subject choice is the one presented by Peck MacDonald (1992). She presents a method for analysing these differences by presenting a cline of abstractedness, and distinguishes between more abstract Epistemic Subjects, which have to do with methods, conceptual tools and previous studies researchers bring to bear on an object of study as in '*The New Historicism is characterized by x*', and less abstract Phenomenal Subjects, which have to do with the object of study *per se* as in '*Shakespeare did x*' (1992: 543–4). Epistemic Subject are knowledge-making elements in the field of research concerned and share some of the features of the Davies (1988, 1997) Hypothesised and Objectivised Subjects, whereas Phenomenal Subjects are the actual objects which are being studied and share some of the features of the Davies Real-World Subjects.

If we now go back to an example from the present corpus and look at it in the light of Peck MacDonald, how would *the upwinding imbedded in the Lesaint-Raviart method ...* be considered? When I interviewed researchers involved in these fields, on the one hand they said that it represented a Phenomenal Subject, in the sense that it was an object of study, but that, in turn, it could be considered as an Epistemic Subject as it also implied knowledge-making within their field of study.

One of the reasons for the difficulties encountered when using the Davies or the Peck MacDonald studies is that Real World or Hypothesised and Objectivised Subjects and Phenomenal or Epistemic ones share common characteristics. If we look at the writer visibility cline, in all cases writers are invisible, albeit in varying degrees. If we look at the cline of abstractedness, because of the characteristics of the present corpus, all the elements written about are abstractions of the real, physical world that is being studied, albeit again in varying degrees. In an endeavour to tease out differences in the types of Subjects found in Research Articles I shall now turn to Halliday's discussion of grammatical metaphor in scientific writing.

5.2.3 Halliday (1993, 1998) on grammatical metaphor

Halliday (1993, 1998) observes that there are two different types of grammatical metaphor, a referring-type and an expanding-type. He highlights the different roles both types have in scientific discourse, because of the different things they enable writers to do:

> When a figure (congruently construed as a clause) is reworded, by grammatical metaphor, in a nominalised form, a considerable amount of energy is released in terms of the two semantic potentials mentioned above: the potential for referring and the potential for expanding – that is, for transforming the flux of experience into configurations of semiotic classes, and for building up such configurations into sequences of reasoned argument.
> (Halliday 1998: 197)

So the first type of grammatical metaphor – henceforth Type 1 metaphor – is the potential for referring, and has to do with the way scientists name their objects of study. This Type 1 metaphor has also been referred to by Martin (1993) as *distillation*:

> Perhaps the best metaphor for technical language is that of **distillation**. Technical language both *compacts* and *changes the nature* of every day words – just as a vat of whisky is both less voluminous and different in kind from the ingredients that went to make it up.
> (Martin 1993: 172).

In the present corpus, Type 1 referring metaphor (that refers via heavily 'distilled' technical classes) has often to do with the actual things being studied, and sometimes shares some common ground with the Peck MacDonald (1992) Phenomenal Subjects. Examples from the present corpus are technical terms such as *Fluorescence Photobleaching Recovery Spectroscopy* (or *FPRS* as it is referred to in the corresponding literature) that coins an experimental method currently used in optics, *Non-Newtonian Fluid Mechanics* (or *NNFM*), *High-ir Superconductors, the three-dimensional Josephson junction array model* (or *3D JJA model*) etc. ...

The second type of grammatical metaphor distinguished by Halliday – henceforth Type 2 metaphor – is the potential for expanding used for building up the heavily 'distilled' technical classes into flows of argument. Examples we gave from the present corpus are *the upwinding imbedded in the Lesaint-Raviart method* and *the radial velocity profile calculated with the fine mesh* where scientists have nominalised their reasoning processes. What is interesting about Halliday's distinction between Type 1 referring/taxonomising metaphor and Type 2 expanding/reasoning metaphor is that Type 1 is already part of the enduring technical jargon of a given field of research, whilst Type 2 has had to be constructed for the needs of a particular instance of text, it is *instantial*.

What is even more interesting, and explains the difficulties encountered when using either the Davies or the Peck MacDonald views on Subject, is the continuum Halliday observes between the two types of grammatical metaphor. With time, the instantial form of Type 2 expanding/reasoning metaphor may end up as a Type 1 referring/taxonomising metaphor, because it has become part of the language system:

> If we view the discourse of science in the longer term, we can observe the instantial *becoming* the systemic ... instantial effects flow through into the system – because there is no disjunction between system and instance: what we call the 'system' of language is simply the potential that evolves over time. Thus any wording that is introduced discursively as a resource for reasoning *may* gradually become *distilled*; ... it becomes a new 'thing'.
> (Halliday 1998: 221).

There often exist such continua, which of course explains in part the difficulties encountered not only with Subjects, but also as I discuss below with Contextual Frames. In the present case of Subjects, Davies sees a continuum of writer visibility choices, going from Subjects where writers choose to be totally visible to ones where they progressively become invisible. Peck MacDonald perceives it as a continuum of abstractness, going from less abstract to more abstract nouns. Halliday's continuum has to do with time. He distinguishes three different types of time. The first is the time of unfolding of the text – logogenetic time. The second is the time of evolution of the language – phylogenetic time, and the third the time of growth and maturation of the user of the language – ontogenetic time (cf. Halliday 1998: 222–3), the latter being the main concern of the present research.

Hence for changes in texture related to time the distinction of interest is not so much the Real-World vs. Hypothesised and Objectivised, or the Phenomenal vs. Epistemic. In fact, the Subjects in my corpus are always related with abstractness and with the phenomena being discussed. My claim is that writers change the texture of their texts over time with increased knowledge related both to subject-matter and to ways of writing about it. Writers can base their Subject choices on the readily accessible wordings conventionally used in their field. On the other hand, writers may want to create tailored wordings that precisely fit into a particular stretch of discourse to convey complex and sometimes controversial reasoning processes. They are in a position to do so once they have deeply reflected upon and assimilated the substance with which they are working, and have made the material their own, as it were. Hence my Conventional vs. Instantial notions to differentiate these last two types of Subject.

5.2.4 Subjects revisited

Table 5.1 presents the different types of Subjects with examples of their realisations. Participant and Discourse Subjects are those originally presented and discussed in Davies (1988). Conventional Subjects are technical terms such as *Fluorescence Photobleaching Recovery Spectroscopy* (or *FPRS* as it is referred to in the corresponding literature) that refer via heavily 'distilled' technical wordings to methods, models, and phenomena. Further examples are given in Table 5.1. Instantial Subjects, on the other hand, are nominalisations of reasoning processes. To take the first example of Instantial Subjects in Table 5.1, *the minimising of F with respect to* ξ_c *and* $\xi_{ab...}$ the author has chosen to put in Subject role a mathematical operation, in order to give it greater objective status. The complete sentence goes *the minimising of F with respect to* ξ_c *and* ξ_{ab} *allows one to obtain the* $\xi_c(T)$ *and* $\xi_{ab}(T)\$$ *functions, which in turn are used to detect the superconducting transitions.* Instead of writing 'I have minimized F with respect to ξ_c and ξ_{ab} so that I can obtain the new functions I need to detect superconducting transitions' s/he presents *the minimising of F with respect to* ξ_c *and* ξ_{ab} as an entity in its own right. It looks as if it is not the

Table 5.1 Subjects revisited

Participant	Discourse	Conventional	Instantial
We ... Our work ... Our results ...	Figure (x) ... Table (x) ... Section (x) ... (The/this) paper/work ...	Fluorescence Photobleaching Recovery Spectroscopy (FPRS) ... Non-Newtonian Fluid Mechanics (NNFM) ... The mesh ... the compound ... High-ir Superconductors ... The three-dimensional Josephson junction array model (3D JJA model) ...	The minimizing of F with respect to x_c and $x_{ab...}$ The upwinding imbedded in the Lesaint-Raviart method ... The radial velocity profile calculated with the fine mesh ... Whether a chiral gauge theory with an arbitrary fermion content can be consistently quantised or not ... The failure in achieving a satisfactory representation of the selected data... Attempts to free the results from the selection of distorting potentials ... The other extreme approach valid in principle only for good metals ...

researcher that minimises F so that s/he can obtain $\xi_c(T)$ and $\xi_{ab}(T)$, but rather that it is the minimisation of F – presented as an entity independent of the researcher – which 'allows' the researcher to do things, when it is actually the other way round.

5.3 Setting up the notions of 'conventional' and 'instantial' contextual frames

5.3.1 Davies (1997) on Contextual Frames

As a reminder, Davies (1997) extends the boundaries between Theme and Rheme by arguing that Subject should not merely be seen as the unmarked choice of Theme, but as an obligatory element in Theme. Obligatory Subject may be preceded by an optional thematic element that she calls 'Contextual Frame'. For instance, rather than seeing certain types of Textual and Interpersonal Themes, such as conjunctives and modal Adjuncts, as having to come initially 'if they are to be present in the clause at all' (Halliday 1985: 56) and the sequence of textual^interpersonal^experiential being 'the unmarked one' (ibid.), Davies postulates that 'from a semantic perspective, they may be regarded as a marked choice if they are present' (1997: 78). Hence her criterion is not one of obligatory or optional position in Theme, but one of 'the presence or absence of the semantic notions expressed in conjunctive and modal Adjuncts' (1997: 78). She sees those conjunctive and modal Adjuncts as inherently Circumstantial and proposes that 'the marked choice is represented primarily through the presence or absence of a Circumstantial element in Theme and, at a secondary level, through reference to a classification of Circumstantial elements based on functional semantic criteria rather than traditional grammatical class' (1997: 78). Her justification for doing so is that Halliday's distinction between conjunctive and modal Adjuncts (serving the Textual and Interpersonal function), on the one hand, and Circumstantial Adjuncts (serving the Experiential function), on the other, cannot be maintained with consistency because there is an important degree of overlapping 'with this apparently transparent division of functions' (ibid.).

Hence, Davies views the constituents of Theme with reference to the categories of obligatory Subject/Topic, representing the basic Experiential element, and of optional Contextual Frame, preceding the Subject/Topic, which may or may not include additional Experiential elements. Davies distinguishes four main types of Contextual Frame, i.e. Logical Relations,

Location, Goal and Process and Evaluation Contextual Frames. Her discussion is a delicate and semantically based reappraisal of marked Theme, which seeks to identify distinctive features of text-types, texts and genres. More specifically, in her 1997 paper Davies explores

> the potential of the analysis of marked Theme as a means of differentiating amongst Interactive and Topical units of *Texts* as a constituent of *Genres* and as a means of signalling the progression of a text.
> (Davies 1997: 53, italics as in the original)

My present purpose, as stated above, is different: changes in the texture of Theme are analysed in order to discern signs of increasing writer expertise in texts that belong to the same genre of the Research Article in hard sciences. It was necessary to encounter a method that would capture these signs of writer development in Contextual Frame, and the Conventional/ Instantial distinction also proved useful for such an analysis.

5.3.2 Contextual Frames revisited

Contextual Frames may be conjunctions, noun groups, non-finite clauses or whole hypotactical clauses that precede the Subject of the main clause. Some Contextual Frames show signs of being much more elaborate than others. Here again an important means of distinguishing Conventional from Instantial wordings is that in one case writers opt for commonly used terms, and in the other compose more complex, multifunctional elements.

Conventional Contextual Frames may be worded as conjunctive Adjuncts, modal Adjuncts or coordinating conjunctions, all of which tend to be, or even sometimes have to be, thematic (Halliday 1994: 48), in which case they are coded here as 'Typical' Contextual Frames. Conventional Contextual Frames may also be worded as Circumstantials without postmodification, in which case they are coded as 'Circumstantial' Contextual Frames.

On the other hand Instantial Contextual Frames are heavily crafted, postmodified wordings of a 'Clausal' type. Contextual Frames entailing an added Interpersonal strand are 'Expressive' and grouped together with Clausal ones under the 'Instantial' heading. Conventional and Instantial Contextual Frames with examples of their different realisations are shown in Table 5.2.

Table 5.2 Contextual Frames revisited

Conventional Contextual Frames		Instantial Contextual Frames	
Typical Contextual Frames realised by Conjunctions, Conjunctive and Modal Adjuncts	Circumstantial Contextual Frames realised by Circumstantials without postmodification	Clausal Contextual Frames prototypically realised by Clauses and postmodified Circumstantials	Expressive Contextual Frames prototypically realised by Projecting Clauses (optionally embedded)
However, Therefore, Moreover, Actually, In general, In particular, etc...	For condition (ii) ... In Equation 4 ... At the quantum level... From Equations (25) and (46) ...	Since the phase factor describes general properties of the electron flux such as its average value and first moments,... Therefore selecting O' to coincide at time t = 0 with the centre of charge defined by zs'-zp' = O,... For the diffusion experiments through an unoriented LC sample within a quartz capillary,...	This is a rather peculiar system, in the sense that ... Taking into account the result for the following commutators, (18) we conclude that ... Obviously, if ~Eq...~ is expanded over a complete basis, ...

Contextual Frames have been ordered from left to right, going from more typical and conventional to more crafted and expressive wordings. Contextual Frames are either realised or prototypically realised by different elements. When I use the word 'Realisation', it means that Typical Contextual Frames *are* conjunctive and modal Adjuncts. When I use the words 'Prototypical realisation', it means that Expressive Contextual Frames are *generally* realised, or characterised, by projecting clauses, but that these are not necessarily the only possible wordings. In this respect it is particularly interesting to note that as we move away from Conventional Contextual Frames towards more fashioned Clausal and Expressive ones, there are no more 'Realisations' *tout court* but rather 'Prototypical realisations' of these more complex wordings.

5.4 Results: modifications in the texture of theme in first and later papers

This section outlines changes in Theme texture between first and subsequent papers published by ten physicists. Preliminary results for individual cases were discussed in previous works (see for instance Montemayor-Borsinger 2001a, and 2003). The whole set of results is considered here as one sample, in order to offer more comprehensive and systematic insights into changes in Theme as researchers become more experienced in writing their research papers. The corpus of 30 research articles written by ten different authors was tested for representativity and randomness (Montemayor-Borsinger 2001b). It includes 4,531 Themes that imply within the Davies (1997) approach the same number of Subjects. As we saw above, Davies postulates two potential functions for Theme. These are 'identification of [obligatory] *Topic*, realised by Subject, and provision of [optional] *Contextual Frame*, realised by elements preceding Subject' (Davies 1997: 55, italics as in the original, text in brackets added). In the present corpus there are 2,435 Contextual Frames.

5.4.1 Changes in Subject

At first, Conventional Subjects are by far the most common, representing about 55 per cent of total Subjects, while Instantial and Participant Subjects each represent about 20 per cent. As time goes by, Instantial Subjects increase while Conventional and Participant Subjects decrease. The texture of papers published about 12 years after a first paper shows quite different choices of wordings in Subjects: Conventional Subjects diminish by 10 per cent and even out at around 45 per cent, Instantial Subjects nearly double at just below 40 per cent, and Participant Subjects diminish by half at just above 10 per cent. These trends are especially significant for Conventional and Instantial Subjects. In both cases the confidence level of the fitting is nearly 100 per cent. In the present corpus Discourse Subjects were the least frequent (under 5 per cent) with no significant changes in their use, which is why they will not be discussed further.

Initially, Conventional and Participant Subjects do not appear to be as difficult to use as Instantial Subjects. Researchers make their choices more from one or another of these two types of Subject especially in their earlier papers where the percentage of Instantial Subjects is still low. Regarding Participant, choosing a comparatively high proportion of *we* might not necessarily indicate researchers have decided to take open responsibility for their work and decided to be visible. Rather, especially in first papers, they might have chosen to appear because it could be easier to organise their writing by stating *we compare ...* or *we observe ...* in the manner some narratives are constructed.

Regarding Conventional Subjects, it is also of course a readily available option. In research papers these Conventional Subjects, overall the most frequent, are of a more obligatory nature than Participant ones. The more optional character of Participant Subjects surfaced in the analysis of individual cases (Montemayor-Borsinger 2001b). Some of the writers of the corpus had managed to make choices in such a way that Participant Subjects were virtually non-existent.

In contrast, and because of the very nature of the Research Article in physics, it would be impossible for authors to strive to eliminate Conventional Subjects. A hypothetical option could be to compose all the obligatory meanings needed in Subject position as Instantial wordings. However, this would prove far too cumbersome for the general flow of discourse, because of the extensive pre- and post-modification generally present in Instantial Subjects. Such an article, if writable, would be unreadable.

To sum up, we have:

- Conventional Subjects – obligatory – readily available choice at the onset of publishing research articles in physics because they are part of the common vocabulary of the field of research concerned. They decrease over time, but still remain the most important wordings in Subject.

- Instantial Subjects – obligatory – more difficult Subjects to manage effectively. As time goes by and as researchers become more experienced, their relative weight nearly doubles.

- Participant Subjects – optional – a readily available choice at the onset of publishing research articles in physics. Over time, the tendency is for Participant Subjects to diminish by half.

If we now look at these general trends with Halliday's metafunctions in mind, it could be suggested that there is a tendency for Experiential meanings in Subject position to increase, with no fewer than 40 per cent of Conventional Subjects *and*, increasingly, as writers gain experience, Instantial Subjects. The tendency for Interpersonal meanings in Subject position is not necessarily that it decreases, but that Interpersonal meanings in Subject be shifted from the overtly Interpersonal Participant Subjects to the more subtle and covertly Interpersonal Instantial Subjects.

5.4.2 Changes in Contextual Frames

Contextual Frames are optional elements and because of this, changes in their texture as writers gain experience are more difficult to track than changes in the Subject. Nevertheless, it has been possible to identify interesting changes. Results show that there is a tendency for Typical Contextual Frames to increase as time goes by from under 30 per cent in a first paper to 35 per cent for the last papers. One explanation could be that although Contextual Frames are in general 'optional', some Contextual Frame elements, such as conjunctions, are mostly obligatory. This is shown by the fact that physics papers as a whole tend to have around half of their Subjects preceded by Contextual Frames, with at least one third of these being 'Typical'. These elements are primarily conjunctions and conjunctive Adjuncts and as researchers gain experience in writing their papers, they increase their use of these more common thematic elements of a 'Textual' and 'Logical' nature, which are actually necessary for text flow and organisation. Results also show that experienced researchers significantly increase their use of Location Contextual Frames, the most numerous and distinctive type of meaning within Circumstantials, from 10 to 16 per cent. These Location Contextual Frames also have an important role to play in enhancing text flow and organisation.

The next question is whether, in a similar way to Instantial Subjects, there is an increase in the use of Clausal or Expressive Contextual Frames of an Instantial character. Interestingly, the analysis provides no evidence of such an increase. On the contrary, results show in particular a decrease in non-finite clauses in pre-Subject position, which are the most frequent type of Clausal wordings. An example of such pre-Subject wordings (the main subject is in bold underlined) is *taking the covariant divergence on both sides of the first equation of motion and using the second one **we** get Equation 1.* The general trend indicates a decrease from 12 per cent to 7 per cent, suggesting that experienced writers tend to reduce their use of these more complex Contextual Frames. This is further confirmed when looking at the results of the analysis for Expressive Contextual Frames that decrease from 15 per cent to 10 per cent as writers gain experience. Results thus suggest that as writers gain experience, they will tend to decrease their use of complex and multistranded framing elements of an Instantial character. These trends will now be examined in relation with the trends that appeared for Subjects.

5.5 Changes in theme texture as writers gain experience: the interplay of subject and contextual frame

When looking at results for Subjects and Contextual Frames together, interesting interaction patterns emerge, the main one being the differing behaviours of Instantial wordings according to whether they are in Subject or in Contextual Frame position. Instantial wordings increase in Subject and decrease in Contextual Frame. These results indicate that as researchers gain experience, they become more proficient at moulding the more complex Instantial Subjects needed to express the kind of information they want to pass on to their research community. As Subjects start incorporating rising amounts of complexity, a natural outcome is not to burden the reader with similarly intricate Instantial Contextual Frames. Experienced researchers are seen to concentrate complex meanings, whose best position is in Theme, in Subject rather than in Contextual Frame position. The corpus analysis indicates that later papers will have of the order of 20 per cent more Instantial Subjects, and 10 per cent fewer Instantial Contextual Frames. When bearing in mind the more hidden strands of Interpersonal meanings which are typical of Instantial wordings, the increase in Instantial Subjects and the decrease in Instantial Contextual Frames with increased experience point towards the fact that some subtle and covert signs of fronted interpersonality will tend to flow towards the 'nub of the argument' realised by Subject.

Quite the reverse happens in the more commonly used wordings represented on the one hand by Conventional Subjects, and on the other by Conventional Contextual Frames. Findings show a decrease in Conventional Subjects of about 10 per cent as writers gain experience, whereas Conventional Contextual Frames show an increase of the same order. Results thus suggest that there will be a tendency for more expert writers to make full use of the simpler and necessary Contextual Frames that are crucial for optimum text flow, rather than use this pre-Subject slot for strategic meanings that are best either in Subject as the 'nub of the argument' or in Rheme as 'News'.

5.6 Conclusion

The present longitudinal study of a corpus drawn from the research writing genre provides further insights about ways in which texts written at different times of growth and maturation of authors use different texturing resources in Theme. The corpus analysis indicates that more experienced writers tend to signal forthcoming information, sequence of events or changes of topic by simple conjunctions, conjunctive Adjuncts, and Circumstantials of Location. The analysis further suggests that as writers gain experience, more complex Instantial wordings are transferred towards the 'nub of the argument' realised by Subject.

Berry suggests that the priority meanings that are being enabled by the textual metafunction in pre-Subject position would be interpersonal and logical (or 'transitional') meanings (Berry 1996: 46). The present corpus analysis points indeed towards a prioritisation of logical/transitional meanings at the very beginning of the clause, and indicates that interpersonal meanings start to be interwoven with other strands of meaning from Subject onwards as writers gain experience. In general, interpersonal meanings seem to be much more 'moveable' to different parts of the sentence. As Halliday has repeatedly pointed out, there is a tendency for interpersonal meanings to be scattered prosodically throughout the unit, whether the unit considered is a group, a phrase, a clause or a clause complex (see for instance Halliday 1994: 190). Interpersonal meanings can adapt to different structures and move to different parts of the sentence to such an extent that they have been seen as being parasitic on other structural elements (Thompson 1996: 65). Moreover, their study covers a broad range of meanings such as evaluation (Thompson and Ye 1991, Hunston and Thompson 2000) and appraisal (Martin 2000; Martin and Rose 2003; Martin and White 2005).

With pedagogical applications in mind, raising awareness of changes in texture in research writing can be done by selecting articles, considered as being classics within a given field, for examination regarding the type of Subjects used and how they are framed. One interesting outcome is that when devising such tasks, applied linguistics becomes an important support for the teaching of language and provides an illustration of how to bridge the gap between theoretical linguistic input and practical methodology in language teaching. Another interesting outcome for the ESP/EAP practitioner is that a dialogue can naturally be established with specialists from other research communities, whose help is crucial in selecting and analysing relevant texts from their fields.

References

Berry M. (1995). Thematic options and success in writing (revised). In *Thematic Development in English Texts*, M. Ghadessy (ed.). London and New York: Pinter, 55–84.

Berry M. (1996). What is Theme? A(nother) personal view. In *Meaning and Form: Systemic Functional Interpretations*, M. Berry, C. Butler, R. Fawcett and G. Huang (eds), 1–64. Norwood, NJ: Ablex.

Davies F. (1988). Reading between the lines: thematic choice as a device for presenting written viewpoint in academic discourse. *ESPecialist* 9 (1/2): 173–200.

Davies F. (1997). Marked Theme as a heuristic for analysing text-type, text and genre. In *Applied Linguistics: Theory and Practice in ESP*, J. Pique and D. J. Viera (eds.), 45–79. Universitat de Valencia: Servei de Publications Universitat de Valencia.

Gosden H. (1993). Discourse functions of Subject in scientific research articles. *Applied Linguistics*, 14 (1): 56–75.

Halliday M. A. K. (1985/ 1994). *An Introduction to Functional Grammar*. London: Edward Arnold Publisher.

Halliday M. A. K. (1993). Language and the order of nature. In *Writing Science: Literacy and Discursive Power*. M. A. K. Halliday and J. R. Martin (eds), 106–23. London: The Falmer Press.

Halliday M. A. K. (1998). Things and relations. In *Reading Science: Critical and Functional Perspectives on Discourses of Science*, J. R. Martin and R. Veel (eds), 185–235. London and New York: Routledge.

Hunston S. and Thompson G. (eds), (2000). *Evaluation in Text: Authorial Stance and the Construction of Discourse*. Oxford: Oxford University Press.

Martin J. R. (1993). Literacy in science: learning to handle text as technology. In *Writing Science: Literacy and Discursive Power*, M. A. K. Halliday and J. R. Martin (eds), 166–202. London: The Falmer Press.

Martin J. R. (2000). Beyond exchange: appraisal systems in English. In *Evaluation in Text: Authorial Stance and the Construction of Discourse*, S. Hunston and G. Thompson (eds), 142–75. Oxford: Oxford University Press.

Martin J. R. and Rose D. (2003). *Working with Discourse: Meaning Beyond the Clause*. London and New York: Continuum.

Martin J. R. and White P. P. R. (2005). *The Language of Evaluation: The Appraisal Framework*. London: Palgrave.

Montemayor-Borsinger A. (2001a). Linguistic choices in two research articles in physics: study of an author's development, *ESPecialist* 22 (1): 51–74.

Montemayor-Borsinger A. (2001b). Academic writing in the sciences: a focus on the development of writing skills. Unpublished PhD, University of Glasgow.

Montemayor-Borsinger A. (2003). A comparison of thematic options in novice and expert research writing, *ELA* 37 (21): 37–52.

Peck MacDonald S. (1992). A method for analyzing sentence-level differences in disciplinary knowledge making. *Written Communication* 9: 533–69.

Thompson G. (1996). *Introducing Functional Grammar.* London: Arnold.

Thompson G. and Ye Y. (1991). Evaluation in the reporting verbs used in academic papers. *Applied Linguistics* 12: 365–382.

6

'To elicit an honest answer – which may occasionally be the same as the truth': texture, coherence and the antagonistic political interview

David Hyatt
University of Sheffield

6.1 INTRODUCTION

Texture has been described as the properties that make a text a text. As Halliday and Hasan (1976: 2) note a text 'derives its texture from the fact that it functions as a unity with respect to its environment'. The emphasis is, then, on what makes a text a text within its particular context. This definition has more recently been complemented by an acknowledgement that, as well as the cohesive relations implied in a notion of texture, structure too plays a crucial role: 'texts are characterised by the unity of their structure and the unity of their texture' (Halliday and Hasan 1985/ 89: 117). Texts therefore need to be understood in terms of their function and communicative purpose as well as the cohesive resources that are employed to make them distinctive and functional.

This chapter seeks to consider the ways in which cohesive resources and communicative purpose contribute to texts that can be described as adversarial political interviews, that is the linguistic features that make a text clearly recognisable as such an interview. In this chapter, I analyse the resources employed by both interviewers and interviewees to, in their views, effectively achieve their communicative purposes. The research is grounded in an investigation of the current context of one genre of news media discourse, the genre of broadcast political interviewing, and more specifically one sub-set, or sub-genre, of this, the adversarial political broadcast interview. This analysis, however, will be tempered by the understanding that any discourse, and within this any genre, is a dynamic entity, and rather than seeking any final definition of the reality of the genre under investigation, my aim will be to emphasise the value of being able to 'unpack' such genres as a tool to understanding how language is employed to make meanings.

The chapter will first move to a consideration of the variety of approaches used in the analysis of political interviewing and the ways in which those writing from a systemic functional perspective have understood the notion and relationships between texture and coherence. Using the four part framework set up as a result of these considerations, I will then consider data elicited from a corpus of 40 adversarial interviews, broadcast between 1995 and 2001; and the insights gleaned from an analysis of this corpus regarding discourse structure and language choices are supplemented by 21 questionnaires, one letter response and 11 telephone interviews with key informants, namely interviewers working for terrestrial television channels. The analysis considers the linguistic resources creating texture in this context, including situational coherence and generic coherence. Whilst it is recognised that the linguistic resources creating cohesion, namely conjunctive relations, reference, ellipsis and lexical relations, are also fundamental aspects of the creation of texture, a detailed analysis of these features is unfortunately beyond the scope of this chapter.

Through the textual analysis, the chapter aims to illustrate how interviewers make the choices they do in order to realise the meanings they intend, and considers some of the implications of such construals for a wider audience. The chapter uses a corpus of 40 adversarial interviews. In addition, the emerging discourse structure and language choices are supplemented by 21 questionnaires, one letter response and 11 telephone interviews with key informants, namely interviewers working for terrestrial television channels. The corpus data gathered was analysed in terms of its discourse move structure and the informant data was analysed categorically.

6.2 Insights from the literature on political interviewing

This first significant research undertaken in this field was by Blum-Kulka (1983) who contended that interviewers assess responses as either supportive or non-supportive. Blum-Kulka's categories are linked with my categories of successful and unsuccessful responses discussed later. Following Blum-Kulka's lead, using a conversational analysis approach, Heritage (1985) noted that unlike everyday conversation, evaluation and receipt comments (e.g. *oh really?*) are absent in news interviewing, arguably avoiding the interpersonal alignment which is a common feature of everyday discourse, and therefore signalling that there is an audience beyond the immediate. This raises three general issues:

- Roles are pre-established with the institutional identities of the participants in the interviews.

- Heritage claims that the receipt comments propose some commitment to the truth or adequacy of the talk they receipt.

- The talk is produced for 'overhearers' (which can be interpreted as the reason for the inappropriacy of receipt comments, through which questioners would identify themselves as the primary addressees of the talk).

The next key work was that of Greatbatch (1986, 1988). Greatbatch (1988) contends that the interview turn-taking system, for British news interviews, operates through a simple form of turn-type allocation, and that the constraints on turn-taking in interviews produces systematic differences between news interview interaction and mundane conversation. The interview's character is linked to the context of the broadcasting journalistic conventions in UK broadcasting. In interviews, turns are produced in the form of questions and this structure limits the discourse. Greatbatch adds that interviewers produce statements prior to the production of question components, in order to provide contextual detail, establish relevance of and as referents for the subsequent questions. However, as I will show below, the analysis of my data would suggest that a change has taken place in both style and convention.

From a pragmatics, as opposed to a conversation analysis perspective, Jucker (1986) asserts that politicians are more likely to be asked face-threatening questions than other interviewees. He lists 13 ways in which journalists do this. The most frequently used are confirming an opinion, accepting discrepancy between your opinion and reality and taking responsibility for action. The explanation is that challenging questions produce more interesting interviews, so the journalist adopts the position of an opponent (Jucker 1986). Jucker argues that politicians are vague, hesitant and non-committal. However, the findings of the present study support Harris (1991) who points out that the politicians' main aim is political propaganda and, therefore, they do not wish to project an image of hesitancy and vagueness but of authority, knowledgeability, trustworthiness and of purpose. However, this does not mean that they are not evasive. Harris (1991) sets out to classify responses to questions from a corpus of 17 political interviews from 1984–6. She usefully raises the issue of possible dispute over the illocutionary force of a question, where questions could act as accusations. She also uses the notions of conditional relevance (the response being expectable and its non-occurrence creating a 'noticeable absence') and of situational appropriacy (e.g. in interviews, respondents are expected to offer elaborated responses, not simply short positive/negative comments).

Her frame for response consists of three categories: direct Answers, indirect Answers and challenges (to presuppositions or illocutionary force in the question). These categories of response equate directly with degrees of evasiveness. Her conclusion highlights three issues: 1. She provides empirical evidence that politicians are evasive and there is a scale of evasiveness. 2. Politicians are constrained by the semantic and syntactic properties of questions – though this lack of freedom is relative. 3. Politicians respond in different ways but these need to be interpreted in socio-historical contexts.

Harris (1991) provides a useful categorisation of response types. However she studies only the responses and does not consider prosodic patterning for the whole text (Martin and Rose 2003). Thus, I would argue that her study represents a 'common-sense' naturalised view of the relationship between interviewer and politician, perhaps suggesting that a free press is able to keep politicians in line. Her conclusions are drawn on the basis of the corpus and perhaps would have been strengthened by qualitative interviewing of interviewers to establish if this is what they actually believe. This is a critique I have attempted to address within my own methodological approach.

Whilst Jucker (1986) and Harris (1991) present a view of a hesitant and non-committal politician, or an evasive politician, this view is challenged by Simon-Vandenbergen (1996), who offers the first analysis from a systemic-functional perspective. She claims this needs to be complemented by the acknowledgement that, as well as this negative strategy, politicians also use the positive strategy of presenting a personal image of certainty and clarity. This is an attempt to assert their intellectual power as a justification for being given socio-political power. This is achieved by a cognitive commitment to the 'truth' which is achieved through modality. Her research was based on 65 interviews on BBC Radio 4, the UK's most prestigious news and current affairs radio station, broadcast between 1985 and 1990. Her analysis emphasised two areas: expressions of cognitive certainty (the speaker's knowledge) and expressions of emotional and social commitment (the speaker's credibility as a political figure).

Simon-Vandenbergen (1996) asserts that speakers claim authority by referring to 'objective sources' which links to the notion of *intertextuality*

(Fairclough 1995). Speakers also claim authority by stating or presupposing the truth without evidence. From these two categories, certainty is seen as based on:

- rationality and common-sense

- factual evidence – intertextuality through statistics, etc.

- hearsay

- majority opinion

- past experience

- 'knowledge' – signalled by the use of the factive verbs *know, realize,* etc.

These expressions of emotional and social commitment aim to increase credibility. Such commitments attempt to assert that politicians have not only intellectual superiority, but are personally involved (emotional) and aware of the democratic principles involved (social). Emotional commitment is expressed by the use of mental processes (*think, believe,* etc.) combined with strong commitment through modal adjuncts – *personally, certainly, undoubtedly, really,* etc., and by metalinguistic comments such as *I'm sad/glad to say.* Social commitment is expressed through politicians' claims to speak on behalf of others and by claiming the support or agreement of the public.

This is a significant work and links closely with many of the insights revealed from my corpus data and from my respondents' comments. However, there are some aspects with which I take issue and attempt to address in my own research. There is no admission or recognition that the corpus of radio interviews (taken it would seem entirely from the Radio 4 *Today* programme) represents just one sub-genre within the genre of political interviewing, and as such misrepresents this sub-genre's typicality for all political interviewing. Furthermore, Simon-Vandenbergen's description of Tenor (1996: 391) is questionable. The preservation of neutrality and the formality and respectfulness of tone are aspects on which the data from my questionnaire and interview respondents casts doubt.

6.3   Insights from the literature on texture

Concerns with the texture of texts are focused on the way that the message is organised and so from a systemic functional perspective fall within the textual metafunction. Texture, for Thompson (2004: 178) is 'the quality of being recognisably a text'. In the analysis of the corpus for texture, I will focus on two aspects of coherence, namely situational coherence discussed with reference to a consideration of the context of situation, and generic coherence, emerging from findings in the corpus. Coherence refers to the ways in which the producer and receiver seek an overall unity for the text in terms of their understanding of the context and purpose of the piece. Cohesion is a textual phenomenon which considers the linguistic resource used to produce the unifying features of a text.

Though it will be beyond the scope of this chapter, it would be valuable to consider in a subsequent analysis the textual resources employed for cohesion. These include conjunctive relations or the way in which differing textual units are combined to form a united semantic unit. In particular, here it would be revealing to consider the role of conjunctive adjuncts (Halliday 1985; Thompson and Zhou 2000) and wider cohesive features and textual patterns (Hoey 1983), and how they operate to create coherence.

6.4 Situational coherence

I will begin this analysis by attempting an analysis of the context of situation (Hasan, in Halliday and Hasan 1985/89). Where examples from the corpus are used these will be identified as television interviews (e.g. *Interview 1*); where examples are used from the questionnaire of informants, these will be identified as *Q* and the informant number, e.g. *Q1*; those responding to the questionnaire will be identified as *QR* (*Questionnaire Respondent*) and the case number, e.g. *QR1* and individual items within the questionnaire will also be identified where relevant e.g. *Questionnaire Item 1* will be noted as *QItem1* and where evidence is used from the telephone interviews with informants these will be identified as *IR* (*Interview Respondent*) and the case number, e.g. *IR1*.

The sets of options available in Field, Tenor and Mode will be employed to offer insights into the context of situation as it relates to the sub-genre of adversarial broadcast interviews.

6.4.1 Field

Goals (long term and short term)

The interviewer and interviewee have different goals in the interview. According to the informants, one of the key purposes of the interview is to elicit new information on the topic under discussion, e.g. *to bring out new truths, to fill in gaps to elicit the interviewee's attitude to certain things (Q.12); truth, clarity and revelation (Q.20)*; to elicit information on a particular subject – a full candid explanation of a policy incident or event, or of the interviewee's view on a subject (Q.22). However, whilst the term 'truth' was alluded to by a number of the informants, the problematic and socially constructed nature of this concept in this context was noted by one informant who identified the purpose of the interview *as to elicit an honest answer – which may occasionally be the same as the truth (Q.16)*. A long term goal that the informants did not mention was the attempt to get a 'scoop' an exclusive news story that will provide interest or entertainment for the mass audience and also hopefully raise controversial issues that could increase the viewing figures, though this was alluded to indirectly, e.g. *... news correspondents are looking for ... something which takes the story forward, or a colourful sound-bite to illustrate the kernel of a story (Q.4)* and *an informative and engaging exchange (Q.14)*. One of the main defining purposes of this type of interview is the attempt by the interviewer to force the interviewee to admit something disadvantageous to him/herself or their political cause, to contradict a colleague or the official line or to admit deficiencies in their party or their policies. *IR8* noted this in describing *the sort of interviews that are, could be regarded as, essentially hostile, in the sense that a minister or somebody else, is answering a point which they don't wish to answer, you know, they are being held to account for something, and you are trying to get an admission or a justification from them. IR11* described this more concisely as *they might just drop a nice one*. QR5 stated that the goals of the interviewer include *to get the interviewee to say something they shouldn't which is newsworthy* and another informant described this as *to gain the confidence of the interviewee in order to entice him to say more than mere party political propaganda (Q.10)*, whilst noting a degree of professional self-preservation in adding that the interviewer *tries not so to alienate the interviewee that he is never given another interview*. A number of the informants identified this process as part of what *the public-interest requires answered (Q.3)*. A further goal of the interviewer could be an attempt to maintain his/her personal or his/her organisation's reputation for effective journalism, though none of the informants identified this as a key driver.

By contrast, the interviewee is often in a difficult situation, on the defensive in the face of some sort of attack by the interviewer, perhaps seeking to avoid a politically indiscreet admission, a contradiction of the official line or an admission of political deficiencies. One informant described this process as *evading answering politically inconvenient questions and fulsomely answering politically convenient ones – regardless of whether the latter have been asked. (Q.16).* Notions of a defensive nature to the responses, coupled with an attack on political opponents, were noted by another informant who described the purpose of the interviewee as being *self/government/party preservation, propaganda points at the expense of the other side, engaging sympathy for their cause (Q.4).* Increasingly, as a number of informants put it, this is to *put over a pre-packaged message (Q.10)* through the use of the sound-bite, a view mentioned by almost all the informants. In line with this, other interviewee goals may include: the limitation of damage to his/her cause; the preservation of unity or the facade of unity, in the party; persuasion of the viewers, rather than the interviewer, to his/her point of view; and more personally the avoidance of public embarrassment or a bad performance which could be detrimental to the interviewee's career.

Acts

During the exchange, each participant performs different kinds of acts. The interviewer tries to elicit direct, or revealing answers from the interviewer, and to follow up on, and exploit, what are viewed to be 'unsatisfactory' answers. These acts are noted by many informants as being central to the interview. For example, respondents noted *interviewers must be sure they can ask the same question in a number of different ways/with different words etc. if a politician is stonewalling (Q.2); firm but courteous insistence on answering the questions, if necessary involving repeating them (Q.3).* In the event of 'successful' answers, the interviewer changes tack by advancing a new adversarial proposition in order to keep the pressure on the interviewee.

The interviewee performs a number of responding acts:

- Re-directing the agenda to their preferred line e.g. *answering questions they haven't been asked (Q.3); refusing to answer the question and producing the pre-digested propaganda instead (Q. 10).*

- Hedging, equivocating or filling available time in order to avoid potentially damaging questions through the skilled use of available language resources e.g. *interviewees often rehearse an answer on the most sensitive issue and stick to the same repetitive answer or sound-bite (Q.2); evasion (Q.5); obfuscation (Q.20); long answers – evasive answers – diversionary answers (Q. 14).*

- Utilising information, or their own evaluation of those facts, to answer or diffuse a potentially damaging exchange.

- Suggesting that the interviewer's assertions are incorrect, unfair or biased e.g. *appealing to the audience against the questioner* (*Q.3*) and *complaining to an editor after an interview has been recorded to try to block it being broadcast* (*Q.11*).

The range of language acts can then be very broad.

6.4.2 Tenor

A consideration of the context of situation as it relates to the participants in the discourse is clearly fundamental to this analysis. The main participants in the analysis are clearly the interviewer and the interviewee(s). However, as Heritage and Greatbatch (1991) point out, the interview is also addressed implicitly to the mass broadcast audience. This results in what Fill (1986) terms 'divided illocution', where the participants address each other explicitly while implicitly addressing a 'virtual' audience of viewers/listeners.

Occasionally, this addressing of the mass audience is made explicit through expressions such as in *Interview 12*, where the interviewer comments that *people listening to this I think are going to be genuinely puzzled*, though this represents a 'marked' feature in this type of interaction, and is comparatively rare in the corpus.

Agent roles

As discussed earlier, Heritage (1985) noted that within the news interview, roles are pre-established with the institutional identities of the participants in the interviews. This also resonates with Gee's consideration (1999: 12) of 'situated identities', that is identities or social positions taken up, enacted or recognised in different settings.

In the questionnaire, the respondents assigned themselves a range of job descriptions including newsreader, political correspondent, political editor, parliamentary correspondent, regional parliamentary correspondent, political reporter, presenter, anchor, reporter, home affairs correspondent, home and social affairs editor, foreign affairs correspondent, senior correspondent/newscaster. In addition to this in response to *Q Item 4*, roles identified included the representative of *the ordinary man on the street* (*Q.1, 2, 3* and *7*), goader, persuader, interrogator, confessor (*Q. 5, 10* and *17*), pupil, questioner, devil's advocate, tribune, inquisitor, outspoken critic as well as curious, well-informed viewer (*Q.21*). As can be seen later in the analysis of the potential discourse structure of the corpus of adversarial political interviewing, additional roles which can ascribed to the interviewer will include initiator of the exchange, propositioner and reiterator.

The interviewee(s) on the other hand plays a number of corresponding and related roles. *Q Item 4b* elicited a wide range of potential roles including *informant, propagandist, defendant, aggressor, victim, explainer, avoider, publicist for their position or cause, bully, enhancer of their image, sound-bite deliverer* (Q. 14), and a *figure of authority ... having to explain and be held accountable* (Q. 20). The analysis of potential discourse structure would suggest that in addition to this, the roles undertaken would include respondent, avoider of unwelcome propositions, counter-propositioner and counter-claimant, i.e. that the interviewer may be wrong or biased.

Dyadic relationship

The dyadic or hierarchical nature of the relationship between the participants can be seen as a consideration of who is in 'control' of the exchange, or who holds the most powerful position in terms of their representations of issues being addressed. The data from the questionnaire suggests that there is no uniformity among the respondents as to the nature and actuality of this hierarchical relationship. Seven respondents attested that there was a hierarchical relationship, seven respondents asserted that there was no hierarchical relationship and eight respondents offered no answer to this item or suggested that the relationship was one of equality. Such a lack of uniformity in response gives an insight into the complex nature of this issue, as noted by *QR7* with the assertion that *there is a complex pecking order.* Of the respondents who selected one or other participant as being in the stronger position, those who nominated the interviewer suggested that this was because the interviewer has control over the questions and direction of the interview and that the interviewee may not know *exactly what questions are going to be asked or what the hidden agenda, if any, is behind the interview* (Q. 19). However, for those who name the interviewee as having the stronger position, this was attributed to the understood potential that *the interviewer always knows the interviewee can walk out if pushed too far* (Q. 4), though this is an extremely marked situation (cf. the instance of the government minister John Nott walking out of an interview in 1982 as described in Greatbatch, 1988). Other reasons for ascribing the more powerful position to the interviewee include *because he/she can always refuse to answer a question* (Q. 21), and *because he can always decline to give the interview, can refuse to answer questions on specific areas and can put the interviewer at a disadvantage if the interview is conducted on the Minister's home territory, like No. 10 (Q. 10)*. Tellingly *QR 21* viewed this issue in metaphorically economic terms by noting *it's the interviewee who has a commodity the interviewer wants.*

Social distance and interpersonal relationships

As in all communication, there is a cline of relative potential social distance between the interlocutors, as noted by *QR4 most political correspondents are familiar with the figures they interview, although obviously the degree of familiarity varies.* Many interviewers may be public figures, even international figures, and in cases where the interviewee is also a public figure the participants may know each other well, and so in such cases the social distance would be minimal. *QR18* noted this, advising researchers to *allow for the human factor – perhaps to an unhealthy degree, many regulars on the political beat are friendly with politicians; moreover, interview style is about personality: in one sense, an interview is still a 'conversation'.* For some interviewees, the broadcast interview may be a rare or unique occurrence and in such cases the social distance between the participants would be more maximal, and this distance could be further lengthened dependent on the interviewer's public profile. *Q Item 3*, which asked interviewers to consider the impact of social distance on the interview, revealed that, of the 22 responses, 11 felt that social distance did have an impact, e.g. *experienced interviewers know what to expect and what's expected of them. If I am aware of the interviewee by reputation or personal contact, this is a factor in deciding my strategy. (QR20)*. Three felt that social distance possibly impacted and eight believed social distance did not impact on the interview. Those who felt familiarity was potentially negative noted the danger that *there are inevitable tendencies to go soft on the interviewees (QR13)* though such a view was tempered with assertion such as *knowing an interviewee does* not *affect your journalism. If it did we couldn't survive (QR17)*. This position was generally supported by respondents who felt that familiarity did not impact on the interview with comments such as *they have to be accountable – whether you know them or not is irrelevant (QR6)*.

6.4.3 Mode

Language role

As noted earlier, mode is concerned with the way the message in constructed or how the language is functioning in the interaction. The corpus indicates that the language role is largely a constitutive one with the language used creating the exchange. However, there are regular examples throughout the corpus of a named greeting at the outset of the interview and an expression of thanks at the end of the interview. In the introduction, there are 22 interviews which generate examples (representing 55 per cent of the corpus) of the direct naming of the interviewee(s), for example *now Paddy what do we do now? (Interview 3). Emm ... Minister – is it them or is it us? (Interview 8).*

Of the remainder of the corpus there are 13 examples (32.5 per cent) where the editing of the interview makes it unclear whether a naming of the interviewee took place and only five examples (12.5 per cent) where no naming definitely took place. In the conclusion to the interviews, there were 29 cases (72.5 per cent) where there was an expression of thanks. In 18 of these interviews, the interviewees were named directly, e.g. *Michael Russell, thank you very much (Interview 27).*

These framing devices (Goffman 1975) both serve as boundaries for the text and also play ancillary roles in representing the interview as a conversation, part of the 'masquerade' (Hyatt 1994a, b) of these interviews as 'conversations'. This conversational style contributes to the disguise of the antagonistic nature of the interview and raises the possibility of catching the interviewee 'off guard'. The degree to which this conversational masquerade is extended depends on the individual interviewing style of the journalist which cannot be viewed as a standardised convention within this genre.

Channel

The interviews in the corpus are broadcast on television and, therefore, by definition, the channel of the interviews was phonic and visual. Whilst, as Hartley (1982) noted, the inter-generic nature of media outputs, settings and camera techniques has a significant bearing on the meanings conveyed and understood, a deep exploration of the fertile terrain of semiotics and multimodality (Kress and van Leeuwen 2001) is regrettably beyond the scope of this work.

Medium

The medium within the corpus is that of spoken language. This brings in the issue of the grammatical intricacy or the lexical density of the wordings: a more grammatically intricate language is characteristic of speech, and more lexically dense language indicates an orientation to written language. The corpus displays many of the features of spoken language including a grammatically intricate and less lexically dense structure (e.g. the use of uncontracted question tags). Clearly, other semiotic influences play a role here, and an in depth multi-modal analysis would be extremely interesting although not possible in the present study.

6.5 Generic coherence

6.5.1 Discourse structure – generic structure potential

The next analytical section seeks to offer a model for the discourse structure of the adversarial interview, based on the data accumulated in the corpus. Note here that any such model can only be viewed as provisional given the fact that the model is based on a limited data set. Furthermore, it would be dangerous to ascribe fixed, immovable categories to a genre, and indeed, as Harris (1991) has claimed, the adversarial interview is a dynamic, changing genre. What this model seeks to do is to describe the data rather than classify it into fixed, universal, unchanging denominations. Genre, as a dynamic entity, is seen here in terms of its potentiality rather than in terms of fixedness. The relationship between language (system) and text (instance) can be seen as a cline of instantiation (Halliday 2001), and the potentiality is affected by the understanding that each instance minutely perturbs the possibilities within the system. Changes in the system can be brought about by single instances of text, where those instances are powerful and viewed as ground-breaking; but every instance has the potential of contributing towards both maintaining the system and changing it to some degree.

Therefore the discourse structure presented here needs to be viewed in terms of its generic structure potential (Hasan, in Halliday and Hasan 1985/89) rather than a definitive and absolute model for all adversarial interviews. However, the potential outlined in the model is a valuable tool for enabling the construction of the discourse to be viewed and reflected upon. An analysis of the corpus suggests the potential for a geometric progression of potential proposition and response movement (see Figure 6.1).

The interview begins with an *Antagonistic Proposition* from the interviewer which is met by either a successful or an unsatisfactory *Response* from the interviewee. This in turn either provokes a *New Proposition*, a *Reiteration* of the original proposition or a *New Antagonistic Proposition*, which in turn provokes a *Response* and the progression continues. The number of turns is determined by the length of the interview. The model

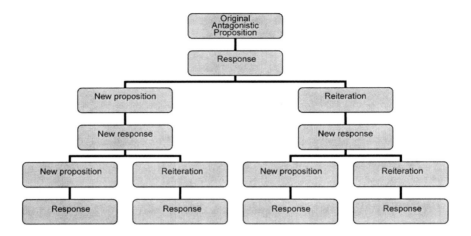

Figure 6.1: Model of potential discourse structure of adversarial interviews

and progression are determined by the choices made by the participants rather than by any pre-ordained pattern. All moves are potentially possible dependent on the course of the interview. The first two moves of *Original Antagonistic Proposition* and the *Response* to the *Original Antagonistic Proposition* are obligatory moves. The other potential moves are optional depending on the success or failure of the *Response* to the *Original Antagonistic Proposition*. The notions of success or failure in this context are fundamental, and are viewed as analytical categories determined by the participants rather than being an evaluation of the analyst.

The following section examines in detail each of the various moves that would comprise such a model of potential discourse structure. There may be some overlap between categories; and the assigning of examples to categories is an interpretive act, and as such, may be contentious and contestable. Therefore, these interpretive acts need to be seen as personal and provisional and, indeed, with the understanding that any act of interpretation is itself an act of the social construction of meaning.

6.5.2 Move 1: Original antagonistic proposition

The *Original Antagonistic Proposition,* by definition, begins the interview. In the case of an edited interview or a pre-recorded interview (transmitted as live), the proposition may be reported in the introduction and the interview itself begins with the response to Move 1, as in *Interview 31 ... I began by asking him why he thought such an esteemed economist as Gavin Davis had got it so wrong with his review of BBC funding.*

This move demonstrates the first step in which the interviewer sets him/herself up as an adversary of the interviewee. The techniques employed regularly involve presupposition in an attempt to position the interviewee. A clear example of this is the frequent use of negative interrogatives (*Isn't it fair to say that ...* and *Isn't it the case that ...*) together with the use of factive verbs (those which pre-suppose the truth of their grammatical complements), change of state verbs, and question tags.

The corpus data suggests four main ways in which the *Original Antagonistic Proposition* is realised: these are the Direct Question; the Statement; the Projected Argument of the Interviewee; and the projected Argument of a Third Party. There are 25 instances of Direct Questions, nine instances of Statement, three instances of Projected Argument of the Interviewee, two instances of Projected Argument of a Third Party and one instance where the original proposition was not recorded or reported *(Interview 20).*

Direct question

Within the corpus of 40 TV interviews, this represented the most common approach to the *Original Antagonistic Proposition,* with 25 instances. Examples of this type of Move 1 include w*hat difference Dom Phillips do you think testing would make?* (*Interview 5*) and w*hy should people like you who go around making jam and selling it to raise Party funds be allowed a vote?* (*Interview 25*). The majority of these Direct Questions include presuppositions, such as in the first example above, the proposition that the testing of the purity of illegal drugs would have an effect on the danger, or safety, of the use of such drugs and in the second the presupposition that 'rank and file' members of the Conservative Party should not have the right to vote in leadership elections. Presuppositions serve 'to anchor the new in the old, the unknown in the known, the contentious in the commonsensical' (Fairclough 1995: 107) and are key aspects of the intertextuality of the text. The use of these propositions aims to channel the interviewee into a response that will help to achieve the interviewer's goals. Seventy-six per cent of the direct questions in the original antagonistic proposition displayed overt presuppositions, whereas only 24 per cent displayed no overt presuppositions. The questions without overt presuppositions are those where the interviewer believes that a direct and honest answer will reveal information that will not be in the interests of the interviewee, and will therefore be in line with the interviewer's goals. It is on this premise that I still categorise these non-presuppositional questions as 'antagonistic.'

Statement

The second most common type of *Move 1* is the category where the interviewer makes an explicit statement. The statements all contain presuppositions which aim to suggest a particular answer in line with the interviewer's goal of challenging the expected position of the interviewee, and, as such, are often highly negatively evaluative of the interviewee's position. An example of this type of *Move 1* is: *Charles Kennedy, your strategy seems to be very clear to position yourselves quite remorselessly to the left of Labour* (*Interview 28*).

A common feature of this type of *Move 1* is the inclusion of a tag question, either at the end of the statement or embedded within the statement, to reinforce the presuppositional illocution of the statement in directing the interviewee to a preferred response e.g. *Michael Forsyth – it's not exactly building the new Jerusalem this speech is it?* (*Interview 11*).

On occasion, these tag questions are given added illocutionary force by being uncontracted, a feature unusual in other genres of spoken discourse, such as *but we have seen, have we not, in the bombing at Army HQ...* (*Interview 16*).

Projected argument of a third party

In this category of Move 1, the interviewer presents a statement or question in which he/she represents the propositional content as coming from a third party. An example of this is:

> *... you know, and you heard him, 'cause you heard him say it last week, 'I took advice on what I could or could not do. I've acted scrupulously in accordance with that advice', and the advice was, he couldn't overrule, wasn't it?* (*Interview 22*)

This technique allows the interviewer to distance him/herself from the argument while still requiring a direct answer. It is a technique which enables the interviewer to maintain a 'masquerade' (Hyatt 1994a) of neutrality.

Projected argument of interviewee

In this category of Move 1, the interviewer presents a statement or question in which he/she represents the propositional content as having the potential to come from the interviewee, e.g. *but if I'd have spoken to you a year ago, you'd have said education, education, education! And education has only got a £1bn out of this and, God knows, it needs a lot more ...* (*Interview 32*).

Again this technique allows the interviewer to project a 'masquerade' of neutrality, whilst also representing the interviewee's position as the interviewer wishes to project it in line with his/her goals, either by selectively quoting or paraphrasing the interviewee, or by suggesting a particular line of thought or argumentation as potentially coming from the interviewee.

6.5.3 Move 2: Response

This move refers to the responses made by the interviewee to the original proposition and to any subsequent reiterations or new propositions made by the Interviewer (see Figure 6.1 above). Move 2 is made up of two phases:

- The initial response to the preceding proposition, where the interviewee attempts to fend off the antagonistic proposition.

- The pre-determined agenda which the interviewee wishes to address. This has probably been researched or at least considered in advance by the interviewee (and/or his/her press officer/public relations team) and aims to represent and establish the interviewee, or his/her party or policies, in the most favourable light.

I will consider the modes of initial response first, then comment on the pre-determined point and, within this section, consider the definition of how a 'successful' or 'unsatisfactory' response is judged, in the view of the interviewer.

The initial response

There are a range of response types that can be used to categorise the rejoinders to the propositions, and each response type is outlined below and the percentage of occurrences in the data is shown.

Denial of proposition (22 per cent)

In this category of response, the propositional content of the interviewer's first or subsequent move is denied as being incorrect. *T.B. – No I'm sorry if you actually look at the average tax that people are paying in this country you will find that tax as a proportion of our national income has been rising not falling (Interview 4).*

Correctional contradiction of interviewer's proposition (10 per cent)

In this category, the content presupposition of evaluation of the interviewer's proposition is contradicted or corrected, e.g. *T.B. This is a big exaggeration there. I mean if you look at actually the policies that were ... (Interview 4).*

As will be seen in other categories, this may be signalled by the mirroring of a previous proposition, as in *Interview 13*:

> *P.S. – Competition's not a word in your vocabulary?*
> *B.C. – Competition is definitely a word in my vocabulary – we have won this franchise ...*

There may potentially be overlap between these first two categories. My distinction centres around the first being a direct refusal of the proposition and the second being a correction of the proposition being offered.

Direct answer (14 per cent)

In this category, the interviewee responds directly to the proposition indicating confidence in the potential 'success' of this mode of response, e.g. *Interview 35*:

> *J.P. – You still don't know whether an offence has been committed?*
> *B.H. – Well, I'm telling you that my advice at the moment is that no offence has been committed.*

Recontextualisation (22 per cent)

I see recontextualisation as an active and deliberate process by the interviewee of declining to share the meaning-making process of the interviewer, by purposefully choosing to interpret the proposition as being in another context. As meanings differ depending on context, this discursive strategy allows the interviewee to interpret the proposition as construing a differing illocutionary force, and therefore responding to it along lines that fit with the interviewee's own agenda.

The following example shows two recontextualising responses from *Interview 4*:

> *P.S. – ... Taxation once again you are going to tell me I'm sure that you're not going to tell us what rates of tax, fair taxation ...*
> *T.B. – It's not that I'm not going to tell you. I'm going to stop you there because people keep saying this to me that I'm not going to tell them what the rate of tax ...*
> *P.S. – You will tell us before the election – you have said so?*
> *T.B. – If there are any tax rates that we have in mind we will be open and honest with people about them.*

Recontextualisations may be textually signalled by discourse markers, such as *what I am saying is ...* as in this example from *Interview 12*:

MM – what I am saying is the Sinn Fein message to everyone ...

or by a mirroring of a previous proposition through lexical repetition:

JP – a capacity to prove you wrong when you are saying he's unmemorable perhaps?
SD – a capacity to surprise, which is why he is a remarkable man behind a slightly unremarkable exterior.

Agreement (12 per cent)

This category covers the examples where the interviewee accepts the proposition put to them, though this is often, but not always, qualified to some degree, e.g. in *Interview 4*:

P.S. – Well they haven't taken it as public ownership have they?
T.B. – No that's true, but that's not the only thing that business in industry needs and what I would say to people from industry today was that if you look at the agenda for the future in ...

Ignoring the proposition (9 per cent)

This option involves the interviewee simply disregarding the antagonistic proposition and moving to the pre-determined statement, for example:

J.P. – Would you be satisfied as a barrister with somebody who introduced as evidence of the Labour Party's softness on crime and terrorism in particular, your claim that two years ago the Labour Party voted against the renewal of the Prevention of Terrorism Act without mentioning that this year they did no more than abstain.
M.H. – well first of all do you think that abstention on the matter of this kind which touches at the very heart of the safety and security of our people, is the right approach for a party that claims to be ready for government. This is a party that ...
J.P. – that wasn't the question ... (Interview 17)

Hedging (9 per cent)

This option involves the interviewee avoiding a direct question or proposition and redirecting the discussion to his/her own agenda, for example:

J.S. – Martin McGuinness, I've got your question! I've got your question there. Did it work, for eight weeks? Yes or No, Ken Maginnis?
K.M. – Well, don't expect me to answer yes or no, quite simply. (Interview 29)

Requesting interviewer's response (2 per cent)

This rare form of response is used with the presupposition that the interviewer also will be unable to respond thereby negating the proposition. e.g. *it's far too early to say. I'd be grateful if you could give me your answer for that.* (*Interview 2*).

Inability or refusal to respond (0 per cent)

This would be the ultimate example of what would be considered an 'unsuccessful' response, and there are no examples of this from the corpus though perhaps the well-known, though extremely rare, incidents in British politics where John Nott, Michael Heseltine and Peter Mandelson have walked out of interviews would be examples of this highly marked option.

The predetermined point

The interviewee frequently uses the response move to shift to the predetermined point that they wish to make, often in the form of a sound-bite, defined as repeated phrase, clause or sentence that sums up and evaluates the topic according to the sound-bite maker's agenda. The questionnaire with broadcast interviewers revealed their perception that this element is an important aspect of the interviewees' agendas. Interestingly, the questionnaire data also revealed this was an important aspect of the interviewer's agenda as well. Responses to a question on the degree to which there was a pre-determined pattern to the interviews were that: *pre-recorded interviews designed to elicit a sound bite as the component of a political package* (QR4): that sometimes the aim is to elicit this pre-determined response *it depends ... whether I am looking for a sound-bite* (QR9); and another comment on interviewer aims *are you out to ensnare/expose over 20 minutes – or get a 'sound-bite' over three minutes* (*QR16*). QR19 evaluated this as a negative but common feature claiming that *too many interviews are about eliciting the sound-bite.*

From the interviewee perspective, again there was evidence from the questionnaire data that interviewees saw the pre-determined point as a central element of the interviewees' agenda. In questions relating to the changes over time of political interviews, *QR4* commented on *the development of the sound-bite culture* whilst *QR12* asserted that *people see the sound-bite, normally, not the original interview, so interviewees are shameless about stonewalling.* Almost all respondents noted that the techniques of interviewees related to the intent to produce a sound-bite with the following comment being typical: *Repeat the sound-bite again and again. Never answering questions directly.* Such comments locate the pre-determined message as a central element of the generic structure of the broadcast political interview.

The judgement of whether a Move 2 response has been 'successful' or not depends on a number of factors. A response may be deemed 'successful' if:

1.   it answers the proposition fully, covering all points made or charges levelled in that proposition and gives sufficient detail so as to leave no room for disagreement;

2.   the respondent may also make a successful counter-proposition which refutes the original proposition.

A *Move 2* response may be deemed 'unsuccessful' if:

1.   it does not deal fully with the original proposition;

2.   it does not address the proposition;

3.   the information in the response is deemed disputable.

The terms 'successful' and 'unsuccessful' response are not meant to give a qualitative and evaluative verdict on the content of the response, but are intended to capture how these responses are met by the interviewer: a categorisation of a response as 'successful' depends on the interviewer behaving in a way which shows that s/he sees it as successful.

6.5.4 Move 3: Reiteration

If a response is deemed by the interviewer as having been 'unsuccessful', the interviewer tends to reiterate the original antagonistic proposition, usually in greater detail through a number of options. This interviewer role is borne out by data from the questionnaire: e.g. *interviewer must represent the listener/viewer, and not be fobbed off by answers which fail to address the question. (QR3); the interviewer should try as best as possible to get full answers or explanations (QR22)*. Questions related to the role of the interviewer also elicited responses that indicated that direct addressing of the interviewer's issues may not be the prime concern of the interviewee – this interviewee was identified as someone who *usually attempts to make his/her point or that laid down by the spin-doctors regardless of the questions asked (QR3)* and *ideally evading answering politically inconvenient questions and fulsomely answering politically convenient ones – regardless of whether the latter have been asked. (QR16)*. Therefore, from the interviewer's agenda, the reiteration of questions is seemingly justified and justifiable, and is achieved through a number of mechanisms.

- **Concentrating the proposition** – where the interviewee has introduced more than one argument to dilute the original proposition, the interviewer attempts to concentrate on the issue or issues which he/she feels will bring him/her the most success, for example: (Interviewer) *let's take the pensions issue, because that is one issue which is quite fundamental to the party and what the party actually believes in now you have got a fight on your hands tomorrow, or will a deal be struck? (Interview 14).*

- **Emphasising the point** – where the interviewer believes the interviewee has not given sufficient attention to an issue that the interviewer considers to be of major significance. The interviewer thus attempts to concentrate the argument on this particular point or question and so force the interviewee to address this issue, for example:

  J.H. (Interviewer) – I take all that <u>but you didn't answer my question,</u> if and you tell me it could break down, you began this interview by talking about the danger of it all collapsing, if that happens, will you say to the IRA, 'do not start the killing again'?

  M.M. (Interviewee) – as I said in the earlier answer, my responsibility is to ensure that that doesn't happen.

  J.H. (Interviewer) – Yes indeed, <u>but you are not answering the question are you,</u> if it happens and you introduced the possibility that the whole thing might collapse<u>, you brought that up right at the beginning of this interview,</u> if it collapses will you say to the IRA,<u> it is a straightforward question,</u> will you say to the IRA 'don't go back to the gun.' (Interview 12)

- **Repetition/rephrasing** – the interviewer may repeat or rephrase the proposition with the purpose of continuing the attack. This tends to be achieved through the use of three techniques: direct repetition of the proposition in the same words; repetition with rephrasing (e.g. in *Interview 40* the interviewer asks *What policies, which policies did you get wrong in the election?* and, after the response, repeats *But which specific policies were you wrong on?*); or direct acknowledgement of reiteration (e.g. *I take all that but you didn't answer my question ... (Interview 12)*).

6.5.5 Move 4: New or changed proposition

Where the response is deemed by the interviewer to have been 'successful', the interviewer tends to change focus and either introduces a new wholly unrelated proposition, or a new proposition based on the predetermined element of the response in *Move 2*. The categories of these new or changed propositions are the same as those for the *Move 1 (Original Antagonistic Proposition)*. The differentiation between these two types of *Move 4* proposition is signalled by certain types of discourse marker. A change of focus is often signalled by a discourse marker, such as *now*, e.g. <u>*now*</u> *some MPs have said they're not going to go along with the recommendations ... (Interview 2; OK,* e.g. <u>*OK*</u> *back to the testing ... (Interview 5);* or *Right,* e.g. <u>*Right*</u> *what are we doing to chase the Excise Duty on the Thai tuna? (Interview 8).* All can be viewed as tacit evaluations of the success of the previous response.

A new proposition which is based on the predetermined element of the response in *Move 2* is often signalled by a conjunctive adjunct such as *and* or *but*, or by a reference item such as *this/these* or *that/those*. As McCarthy (1994) notes, the role of *this/these* may be to indicate that the following proposition is foregrounded or highlighted e.g. <u>*this*</u> *is empirical evidence that the current safeguards in this country are inadequate! (Interview 35).* In addition, the use of *that/those* may be used to background, marginalise or negatively evaluate the subsequent proposition, e.g. <u>*that's*</u> *kind of ancient history now though isn't it? (Interview 1).* Interestingly, the antagonistic nature of the interviews is borne out by the fact that the contrastive *but* appears more frequently that the conjunctive *and,* and that the marginalising *that* appears far more frequently than the foregrounding *this:* e.g <u>*But*</u> *why are you frightened of letting them have a direct say? (Interview 25).*

On rare occasions the interviewer may actually explicitly acknowledge that the response has been viewed as 'successful', and even in this small sample there are a number of examples of this tendency, which I had anticipated would be a highly marked occurrence.

> B.C.– *That's our real track record.*
> P.S. – *OK ... Right ...* <u>*Fair enough*</u> *... (Interview 13)*
> S.B. – *There are serious issues here...about the single currency but about economic reform in Europe as well.*
> J.S. – <u>*That I accept*</u> *... (Interview 28)*

As noted above, the new or reiterated proposition is then met with a further response, the 'success' or lack of success of which determines the form of the interviewer's next proposition. This progression continues throughout the interview.

6.6 Conclusion

In this chapter I have attempted to mirror the aims of Davies (1994, 1997) in considering the ways in which textual analyses can function as heuristic devices to illustrate the structuring of text and its contribution to the construction of meanings. In conjunction with a clear analysis and systematic understanding of the socio-historic context of the production and reception of the text, they can help to shed light on the intentions of meaning makers and also highlight the potential for resistant readings/hearings of texts. The textual analysis can only be helped by:

(a) a systematic understanding of the socio-historic context of the production and reception of the text (Wodak 2001, Hyatt 2005a).

(b) qualitative interviewing with specialist informants where possible – those engaged in the creation of the text, if one is concerned with contextualising the discourse. This does not deny the researcher's role in analysis, nor in view of social constructionist and phenomenological perspectives, should it be taken at face value. However, these informants have something to add, and some aspects of the discourse may be obscured without these insights. This could be seen as pre-empting Geoff Thompson's (2000) question in the title to his paper, *Is it enough to trust the text?*

(c) the value of an interdisciplinary study of texts. By accepting a Hallidayan perspective, we reject the view of language as an entity to be studied in experimental isolation. Other disciplines can be brought to bear – social theory and sociology, semiotics, philosophy, political theory, media studies, multi-modality studies, cognitive processing studies amongst many others.

The textual and extra-textual features elucidated so far have given insights into the meaning-making and texture within adversarial political interviewing. The antagonistic political interview provides a useful example genre with its ideational and interpersonal emphases on issues of power and social action and interaction, the analysis of which can be used, for example in educational contexts (Hyatt 2005b), to demonstrate the ways in which positions are represented, constructed and justified through choices made in the language used.

References

Blum-Kulka, S. (1983). The dynamics of political interviews. *Text* 3/2: 131–53.

Davies, F. (1994). From writer roles to elements of text: interactive, organisational and topical. In *Reflections on Language Learning*. L. Barbara and M. Scott, (eds), 170–83. Clevedon, England: Multilingual Matters.

Davies, F. (1997). Marked Theme as a heuristic for analysing text-type, text and genre. In *Applied Languages: Theory and Practice in ESP*. J. Pique and D. Viera, (eds), 45–71. Valencia: Universitat de Valencia.

Fairclough, N. (1995). *Media Discourse*. London: Edward Arnold.

Fill, A. F. (1986). *'Divided Illocution' in conversational and other situations – and some of its implications*. IRAL Vol. XXIV/1.

Gee, J. P. (1999). *An Introduction to Discourse Analysis: Theory and Method*. London: Routledge.

Goffman, E. (1975). *Frame Analysis*. Harmondsworth: Penguin.

Greatbatch, D. (1986). Aspects of topical organisation in news interviews: the use of agenda-shifting procedures by interviewees. *Media, Culture and Society* 8: 441–55.

Greatbatch, D. (1988). A turn-taking system for British news interviews. *Language and Society* 17: 401–30.

Halliday, M. A. K. (1985). *An Introduction to Functional Grammar*. London: Edward Arnold.

Halliday, M. A. K. (2001). Day Trip Boy Car Theft Fury: on the complementarity of system and text. Lecture at University of Liverpool, 14th June 2001.

Halliday, M. A. K. and Hasan, R. (1976). *Cohesion in English*. London: Longman.

Halliday, M. A. K. and Hasan, R. (1985/9). *Language, Context and Text: Aspects of Language in a Social Semiotic Perspective*. Oxford: Oxford University Press.

Harris, S. (1991). Evasive action: how politicians respond to questions in political interviews. In *Broadcast Talk*, P. Scannell (ed.). 76-99. London: Sage.

Hartley, J. (1982). *Understanding News*. London: Routledge.

Heritage, J. (1985). Analyzing news interviews: aspects of the production of talk for an overhearing audience. In *Handbook of Discourse: Discourse and Dialogue*, van Dijk, T. A. (ed.) Vol. 3, 95–117. London: Academic Press.

Heritage, J. and Greatbatch, D. (1991). On the institutional character of institutional talk: the case of news interviews. In *Talk and Social Structure*, D. Boden and D. Zimmerman (eds.), 93–137. Oxford: Polity Press.

Hoey, M. (1983). *On the Surface of Discourse*. London: George Allen and Unwin.

Hyatt, D. (1994a). The discourse of advertising. *Forum for Education*. 1/1 Bristol: University of Bristol Press.

Hyatt, D. (1994b). An Analysis of Texts and Tasks in the ESP Area of English for Politics. Unpublished M.Ed. TEFL dissertation, University of Bristol.

Hyatt, D. (2005a). Time for a change: a critical discoursal analysis of synchronic context with diachronic relevance. *Discourse and Society* 16/4: 515–34.

Hyatt, D. (2005b). A critical literacy frame for UK secondary education contexts. *English in Education* 39/1: 43–59.

Jucker, A. (1986). *News Interviews: A Pragmalinguistic Analysis* (Pragmatics and Beyond VII:4). Amsterdam: John Benjamins.

Kress, G, and van Leeuwen, T. (2001). *Multimodal Discourse: The Modes and Media of Contemporary Communication*. London: Arnold Publishers.

Martin, J. R. and Rose, D. (2003). *Working with Discourse*. London: Continuum.

McCarthy, M. (1994). It, this and that. In *Advances in Written Text Analysis*. M Coulthard (ed.), 266–75. London: Routledge.

Simon-Vandenbergen, A.-M. (1996). Image-building through modality: the case of political interviews. *Discourse and Society* 7/3: 389–415.

Thompson, G. (2004). *Introducing Functional Grammar* (2nd edition). London: Arnold.

Thompson, G. (2000). Corpora, patterns and grammar: is it enough to trust the text? Paper presented at 11th Euro International Systemic Functional Linguistics Workshop. University of Glasgow, 19–22 July 2000.

Thompson, G. and Zhou (2000). Evaluation and organisation in text: the structuring role of evaluative disjuncts. In *Evaluation in Text: Authorial Stance and the Construction of Discourse*. S. Hunston and G. Thompson (eds), 121–41. Oxford: Oxford University Press.

Wodak, R (2001). The discourse historical approach. In *Methods of Critical Discourse Analysis*, M. Meyer and R. Wodak (eds), 63–95. London: Sage.

7 | Projecting clauses: interpersonal realisation of control and power in workplace texts

Gail Forey

Hong Kong Polytechnic University

7.1   Introduction

Workplace texts within bureaucratic organisations are often primarily concerned with seemingly objective tasks. However, as pointed out by Tadros (1985: 63), in workplace texts a writer may try to 'persuade, cajole, convince and win the reader to his side'. For example, workplace texts in the form of e-mails or memos often give directives in a social environment and, to succeed, they depend highly on interpersonal relations. Indeed, workplace communication, the heart of interpersonal relations, is 'a complex interactive achievement of building consensus about what is appropriate action and what is not, what is true, and what is real' (Iedema 2003: 44). There are many different devices employed within organisations to 'build consensus', e.g. branding, logos, company ethos, mission statements, company benefits, social activities and linguistic choices within written and spoken texts help to realise the consensus. In this chapter, I focus on one specific linguistic choice, projecting clauses in thematic position. These are one means whereby a writer can encode status and viewpoint. As pointed out by Martin and White (2005), projection is dialogic in nature, part of the Appraisal system of engagement, and it functions to encode the point of view of the writer or speaker. Through the choice of projecting clauses such as *I believe, the company believes* and *it is believed* a writer may adopt a particular stance, and then in the hypotactic projected clause construe the 'correct procedure', in a way which simultaneously reflects the power relations in play and is designed to construct consensus.

   In this chapter, projecting clauses in thematic position are identified as one type of marked Theme. A projection complex is where the writer represents through a mental, verbal or fact clause what someone else has 'said or thought at a different time from the present' (Thompson 2004: 210). A marked Theme is said to be a Theme where the writer consciously or unconsciously affects the organisation of the text by choosing something other than the Subject for the starting point of their message, and as such uses it to 'signal a new setting, or a shift in major participants; that is they function to scaffold *discontinuity*' (Martin and Rose 2003: 179).

Many agree that the choice of marked Theme is important, and that it plays a crucial role in the interpretation of the message (Downing 1991; Martin 1992; Goatly 1995; Berry 1996; Stainton 1996; Davies 1997; Caffarel 2000; Martin and Rose 2003; Thompson 2004). Stainton (1996), referring specifically to workplace texts, suggests that marked Theme is not only important because it is a 'motivated' choice, but it is also important for the success of a text. The types of realisations, and the function of projecting clauses found in thematic position in an authentic corpus of memos, letters and reports, are discussed in what follows.

Research into projection based on authentic discourse data seems to be relatively limited. McGregor (1994) generally calls for the need for more research into reported speech. Drawing on Vološinov, McGregor talks of the 'enormous general linguistic and theoretical significance of reported speech' (1994: 64). For McGregor, reporting 'another person's words or meanings' is a 'pivotal' phenomenon in language (1994: 64). However, research into projection at a clause complex level in texts from the business world is rather limited, although it has considerable potential to shed light on the way in which viewpoint is constructed within an organisational setting. Martin and White (2005) present a detailed discussion of projection as part of the Appraisal System of engagement. They add that projection is one way to 'construe a heteroglossic backdrop for the text' (Martin and White 2005: 105). In their discussion of heteroglossia and the realisations that construe alternative voices and the value position of the writer, and/ or create the possibility for solidarity, Martin and White (2005) use a number of examples from media and academia to illustrate their point. The present study extends existing research by focusing on marked Theme and in particular projection in a corpus of 62 workplace texts.

In the present study it is assumed that a projecting clause in a clause complex where it functions as Theme, itself followed by a hypotactic projected clause, influences or frames the manner in which the projected clause is to be interpreted (see Davies 1997 where she introduces the term 'Contextual Frame' to describe marked Theme in written texts). In recent years a number of scholars agree that projection encodes interpersonal meaning (Davies 1988, 1997; McGregor 1994; Thompson 1994, 2004; Iedema 1995, 1997, 2000; Martin and Rose 2003, Martin and White 2005). This is perhaps clearest with impersonal types of projection such as *it is important that.* Davies, for example, states that the anticipatory *it* clause and the projecting clause 'are treated as interpersonal "projections" of the writer's message or viewpoint' (1997: 56). Thompson (2004) introduces the term 'thematised comment' for such cases, and this term is adopted in this study.

Halliday's account of projection will be extended to incorporate suggestions made by Davies (1988, 1994, 1997) who argues that the whole of the projecting clause and the Subject of the projected clause should be considered the Theme of the clause complex (in addition, see Davies 1997; Caffarel 2000; Martin and Rose 2003; Hood, this volume.

The following section establishes the position taken and the description of projection in the present study. This is followed by a brief overview of the data and methodology. In addition, in this section it is suggested that projection could be categorised in a more sophisticated manner and to this end three categories of projection are posited. In Section 7.4, the patterns and functions of projecting clauses in the corpus are discussed. The chapter then moves on to discuss the importance and relevance of projecting clauses in thematic position in construing viewpoint and identity within some example texts. Finally, the chapter concludes with a discussion of the implications and relevance of the study.

7.2 Projection in the present study

A number of studies have argued for an extension or a revision of Halliday's categorisation of projection (Davies 1994, 1997; McGregor 1994; Thompson 2004). Davies (1997) suggests that there are a number of different contextual frames which will help the analyst understand a writer's moves within a text. She outlines four main contextual frames: (a) location, e.g. *Before 1990*; (b) logical relations/progression, e.g. *by contrast*; (c) goal and process, e.g. *in a clear statement*; and (d) evaluation, e.g. *the inadequacy of this* (for a more detailed description of contextual frames, see Davies 1997: 57). She argues that by placing both the contextual frame and the Subject of the main clause within the boundaries of the Theme, the analyst is able to identify the continuity of the 'central participant' (realised by the Subject) as well as understand how the writer is framing the text and signalling changes in it. Projecting clauses are just a part of one of the evaluation contextual frame outlined by Davies. She does not fully discuss projection as a separate phenomenon, preferring to see it as part of a wider category of interactive units that fall within the boundaries of Theme.

Thompson believes that impersonal projection 'allows speakers to start their message with their own comment on the value or validity of what they are about to say' (2004: 152). As Martin and White point out, the nature of projection, as a resource within the Appraisal system of engagement, is 'dialogically directed towards aligning the addressee into a community of shared value and beliefs' (Martin and White 2005: 95). Engagement, as described by Martin and White (2005), encompasses a wide range of choices which create a dialogic expansion of the text; projection is only one of the choices within this system. Example 1 illustrates how this is reflected in the Theme analyses in the present study.

(1)   (Report 10, clause complex 29)

He envisages that	additional staff	would be required in view of the scale of the feasibility study and the subsequent implementation of the proposal.
α	β	
interpersonal Theme	Subject/Theme	Rheme

It is suggested that the projecting clause *he envisages that* in Example 1 construes interpersonal meaning, and that the main ideational element of the clause complex be considered realised in the projected clause *additional staff would be required in view of the scale* ...(see Thompson and Thompson this volume for a detailed justification of this approach).

There are three types of projection mental, verbal or factual. Halliday identifies four sub-classes of fact: cases, chances, proofs and needs (1994: 266). This form of projection is more objective; there is no human participant doing the projecting and the Subject is commonly *it*, for example, *it is believed, it is hoped*, etc. Halliday adds that *it* is not a 'participant in the projecting process but is simply a Subject place-holder' (1994: 266). The projection of a fact is a way of packaging information in a form that may appear to be more objective and factual (Davies 1988, 1994, 1997; Iedema 2003; Martin and Rose 2003; Thompson 2004; Martin and White 2005). Davies (1988) states that while the potential of 'empty subject offers a powerful tool ... it also relieves the writer of any responsibility for the viewpoint' (1988: 197). The use of *it* in projecting clauses reduces the writer's visibility and allows a viewpoint to be realised in what would appear to be a more objective manner. Davies (1988), Harvey (1995) and Hewings and Hewings (2002) argue that this is a common device used in academic discourse. In the findings presented below, fact projection gives the writer an option to present something as already packaged and decided, expressing information in what appears to be company terms and practices, and to depersonalise and objectify modal responsibility. For example, the projecting clause *it is anticipated* in the clause complex *it is anticipated that the growth in demand for video material from both students and academic staff will continue* (Report 3, clause complex 41) is basically representing an idea that has been assessed and analysed, and the projected clause is hypothesising that *the growth ... will continue.*

7.3 Data and analysis

7.3.1 Data

The data in the present study is drawn from a corpus of authentic workplace texts which is part of a more extensive analysis of Theme (Forey 2002). The corpus was gathered through my involvement with two projects, The Effective Writing for Management project (EWM) (Davies and Forey 1996; Davies *et al.* 1999), and the Communication in the Workplace project (CPW) (Nunan *et al.*, 1996; Forey and Nunan, 2002).

The corpus used in the present study is a small, specialised sub-corpus of 62 texts, comprising the text types 'memo', 'letter' and 'report'. The texts were digitised, yielding a corpus size of 31,883 words. The texts were then manually coded for their main clauses or, where a main clause was accompanied by one or more dependent clauses, their clause complexes, taking the boundaries of the orthographic sentence as a marker of structure; this analysis yielded a total of 1,486 main clauses. All names, figures, and identifying traits of the texts were anonymised, and the last step was to analyse the clauses and clause complexes for their Theme. Some of the key results are reported below.

Of the 62 texts, 33 (53.2%) originate from the EWM project (UK) and 29 (46.8%) from the CPW project (Hong Kong). The details of the 30 memos, 22 letters and ten reports are shown in Table 7.1.

Table 7.1 Details of corpus

	No. of texts	*No. of main clauses*	*No. of words*
Memos	30	504	9,788
Letters	22	248	5,652
Reports	10	734	16,403
Total	62	1,486	31,843

As outlined above, Theme at a clause complex level extends up to and includes the Subject of the main clause, and, adopting the system used by Martin and Rose (2003), a marked Theme was labelled as such, i.e. *marked Theme*, and the Subject of the main clause *Subject/Theme*. For marked Theme^Subject/Theme, the term *extended Theme* was coined to account for this type of multiple Theme in order to avoid confusion.

In the corpus used in the present study, there were 489 occurrences, i.e. nearly one third of the thematic choices were of marked Theme (comprising 32.9% of all Themes). Table 7.2 illustrates the types of extended Theme found in the corpus.

Table 7.2 shows that the two most frequent realisations of extended Theme took the form of projection and Circumstantial Adjunct. Circumstantial Adjuncts as marked Theme and hypotactic enhancing clauses appeared to be functioning as 'informing' clauses or (ideational) contextual frames (Davies 1997). On the other hand, marked Themes realised by a projecting clause in initial position in a clause complex, which, as argued above, have an interpersonal function, are the focus of the following discussion.

7.3.2 Analytical approach

Three categories of projecting Theme emerged in the analysis of the data, namely 'thematised subjective viewpoint', 'thematised comment' and 'thematised obligation/inclination', based on work by Halliday (1994) and Thompson (1994, 2004):

1.   Thematised subjective viewpoint

   This category is based on Halliday (1994: 358), but is further subdivided in a slightly different way. In cases of direct subjectivity

Table 7.2 Frequency of occurrence of extended Theme by text type

	Memo (*n*=504)	Letter (*n*=248)	Report (*n*=734)	Total (*n*=1,486)
Projecting clauses	49 (9.7%)	42 (12.9%)	112 (15.3%)	203 (13.7%)
Circumstantial adjuncts	55 (10.9%)	20 (8.1%)	92 (12.5%)	167 (11.2%)
Hypotactic enhancing clauses	43 (8.5%)	35 (14.1%)	41 (5.6%)	119 (8.0%)
Total number	147 (29.1%)	97 (39.1%)	245 (33.4%)	489 (32.9%)

I, you and *we* are used as Subject within the projecting clause, e.g. *I hope that the foregoing information provides the appropriate clarity* (Memo 11c, clause complex 23). In cases of indirect subjectivity, a nominal group realising a human participant is used in the projecting clause, and although *I* or *we* are not chosen as the Subject, the Subject choice realises indirectly a subjective construal through the choice of a human participant such as *the Director of Housing,* or of an institutional entity comprised of humans such as *the library* in *the library is also concerned that all students on distance learning courses properly understand the implications of studying for a degree by distance learning* (Report 3, clause complex 22).

2.   Thematised comment

This category is based on Thompson (2004: 152), where a proposition is encoded in what appears to be an objective viewpoint. Thematised comment is found in the form of a factual projecting clause in initial position, e.g. *it would appear that there has been no progress or further feedback to your letter of 24 May 1995 regarding the above* (Memo 11b, clause complex 1).

3.   Thematised obligation/inclination

A third category, based on Halliday (1994: 358), makes a distinction that is not based on the choice of Subject but rather on the choice of modality. The choice is between the system of modulation, with the projecting clause realising an imperative type of modality, and the system of modalisation, typically realised by probability or usuality. This third category covers cases where there is some form of obligation or inclination embedded within the projecting clause in thematic position, e.g. *we* must *therefore take the view that the activation was caused by a genuine smoke incident* (Memo 11c, clause complex 20).

7.4 Findings

7.4.1 Overview

Projection appears to be an important lexico-grammatical feature in all three text types. One or more projecting clause in thematic position is found in 61 per cent of memos, 57 per cent of letters and 90 per cent of reports. The average number of projecting clauses in thematic position per text type is 1.63 in memos, 1.9 in letters and 11.2 in reports. The highest number of projecting clauses in any one text is 18 (in Report 7). This text has 44 main clauses, of which 41 per cent are thus projecting clauses in thematic position within a clause complex. The number of projecting clauses found in each text varies tremendously; and it does not appear to be related to the size of the text, i.e. if a text has a large number of main clauses, this does not necessarily mean that the number of projecting clauses will be high.

Although projection is seen to be a part of most texts, the low frequency of projecting clauses suggests that they are used sparingly, and specifically to construe a viewpoint. Naturally, there are many choices available to a writer for the construal of interpersonal meaning and projection is only one possible choice. However, it can be argued that the influence of viewpoint, realised by projecting clauses, will to some extent affect the reader's impression and the manner in which the meaning of a text is interpreted.

Table 7.3 shows the three categories of projecting clauses found in the corpus.

In total there are 489 extended Themes in the corpus, 203 occurrences (41.5 per cent) of which involve projecting clause complexes. The type and frequency of projecting clauses appear to vary in different text types. As shown in Table 7.3, thematised subjective viewpoint is the most frequent realisation of projection in all three text types (70.9 per cent). Letters have the most frequent realisation of thematised subjective viewpoint (76.2 per cent), followed closely by memos and reports (71.4 per cent and 68.7 per cent respectively). Thematised comment appears to be realised to the same

Table 7.3 Type and number of projecting clauses by text type

	Memo (n=49)	Letter (n=42)	Report (n=112)	Total (n=203)
Thematised subjective viewpoint	35 (71.4%)	32 (76.2%)	77 (68.7%)	144 (70.9%)
Thematised comment	11 (22.4%)	9 (21.4%)	35 (31.3%)	55 (27.1%)
Thematised obligation/inclination	3 (6.1%)	1 (2.4%)	0 (0.0%)	4 (2.0%)
Total	49 (24.1%)	42 (20.7%)	112 (55.2%)	203 (100%)

limited extent in memos and letters, 22.4 per cent and 21.4 per cent respectively, whereas it is more frequently realised in reports (31.3 per cent). In all three text types, thematised obligation/inclination is the least frequent, occurring just four times in the corpus. Since so few examples of this last category were found in the corpus they will not be discussed further in the present chapter. Such projecting clauses, however, have been found to occur more frequently in other workplace genres.

7.4.2 Category 1: Thematised subjective viewpoint

The most prevalent form of projection, thematised subjective viewpoint, can be seen to be an explicit realisation of viewpoint. However, there is a difference between saying *I believe* and *we believe* and *Company X/Person X believes*. Iedema (1995) points out that the proposer's moving from the subjective *I* to the company or a part of the company, for example, *the library is also concerned that* (Report 3, clause complex 22), or *the Exco also noted that* (Report 8, clause complex 32) involves shifting the modal responsibility for the proposal.

In memos and letters, where the writer and reader generally know one another, the written word can be very influential in determining the social identity of the writer and the relations between the reader and writer. For example, when someone (an individual or a group of persons) writes in the workplace, the identity, status and power of the author are inevitably established, and often chosen to emphasise or reduce the impact of what is being projected (Fairclough, 1992; Ivanič, 1998). Conversely, as one informant interviewed on the CPW project stated, she would change her writing style to suit the person to whom she was writing, i.e. her register would be markedly different depending on whether she was writing to her English or her American superior (Nunan *et al.*, 1996). Thus consideration of the role, position, ethnic background and 'identity' of a writer and the intended reader greatly affect the language chosen, and writers frequently change register to accommodate different readers.

Projection and the use of direct - subjective *I* in workplace texts

It is worth noting that projecting clauses with *I* are present in all three text types, but are far more common in memos, while projecting clauses with *he* or a named person are far more common in reports. The writer's decision to use *I* or *we* or *Company X* is often a conscious one. As noted above, how an individual or a group wishes to construct their identity in a text will affect the subsequent relations of the author-reader developed in the text.

The choice and power invested in the selection of *I* or *we* or *Company X* may vary depending on the individual status of certain members of a company. As Clark and Ivanič put it, 'writing not only conveys a message about content but also conveys a message about the writer' (1997: 143). For example, if a projecting clause is written by a senior executive who holds an extremely powerful position within a company, then the power of using *I* in a proposal is far greater than if it were written by someone less senior. In addition, it is clear that if writers use *I* to project an idea or locution, then they are taking on the modal responsibility for their proposal (Iedema 1995, 1997), as shown in Example 2 (the projecting clauses are shown in bold):

(2) (Memo 3)

> I am uncertain whether or not you know J. E. Jones. We would have considered him for the FRD (UK) marketing role but he was unavailable because of a new attractive assignment with SSB in Switzerland. This has now miscarried, so he is available.
> Very seriously, I recommend him to you for the Sector Marketing Director role. **I think** he has all the experience and qualities you need for this except, of course, knowledge of John Brown. **I think** you will like him if you meet him.

Here the proposer feels confident and is able to put forward a personal viewpoint when recommending Jones for a position. The writer uses the two projecting clauses shown in bold to support the idea that the candidate is suitable. However, if the writer here were to use *we (at company X) think he has all the experience*, then he or she would be demonstrating support within the company and the projected information could possibly be more influential. The use of *we* in workplace and technical writing is designed to 'endorse corporate goals' (Couture 1992: 19). It might be argued that whichever identity the writer chooses to project, whether *I*, *we* or *Company X*, he or she presents an important selection in 'role identification' since, as van Leeuwen (1996: 54) puts it, 'belonging to a company or organisation begins to play an important role in identification.'

Subjective projection in reports

Even though reports are often viewed as a more formal text type, they do include projecting clauses with a first person (*I*) Subject choice, albeit infrequently. Harvey (1995) also points out that personal use of *I* seldom occurs in scientific reports. In the reports in this corpus there were 17 occurrences of *I* in projecting clauses, for example:

(3)   (Report 8, clause complex 95)

> I have recommended to the Secretary for Planning, Environment and Lands that in future a re-submission to the ExCo should be made before the award of a contract if the cost has increased significantly.

The personal pronoun *I* here, it is suggested, is chosen to directly realise the writer's involvement and viewpoint in relation to an expression of concern.

In the corpus reports, there were more than four times as many verbal projections (63) as mental projections (14). One reason for this may be that the purpose of a report is multi-functional. Iedema (1995) points out that administrative reports are a macro-genre which combines different genres; and this is supported by Harvey (1995) who found, in scientific reports, that the macro-genres included introducing, informing, describing, stating, appraising, asserting, reasserting, challenging, contending, assuming, estimating, warning, exhorting, suggesting and recommending (1995: 196–7). Thus, since the purpose of a report is multi-functional, it is possible that different types of projection, mental, verbal and fact, may be realised. However, this does not explain why there are 63 verbal projecting clauses compared with 14 mental projections in the reports analysed. Perhaps one explanation is that a report summarises activities and events which have occurred, and in doing so is required to state what others have said in relation to those activities and events. As pointed out by Iedema (2000: 47), meetings lead to minutes of meetings, which provide information for more communication, and notes from what was said in meetings are incorporated into reports which in turn lead to other linguistic and non-linguistic outcomes.

In the present corpus the majority of the verbal projections are found in only two or three of the reports. The main purpose of these reports appears to be to describe the present situation of a particular matter, and verbal processes realise what someone else has said. For example, a report by an accountant at the Housing Authority of Hong Kong has a number of verbal projections where the Director of Housing is reported to have made a number of points. This extract from Report 7 (Example 4) demonstrates a dependency by the writer on verbal projection (shown in bold) to express his viewpoint. The writer exploits verbal projection in thematic position in order to establish a particular stance on the topic discussed and to summarise/present previous decisions and statements.

(4)   (Report 7)

> Report of the Director of Audit on the results of value for money audits

> **Housing Department 9 Provision and utilization of space in the Housing Authority Headquarters (HAHQ) Building**

9.5   **The Director of Housing proposed** that some HAHQ Special Facilities (2,346 square metres net) should be relocated to a commercial complex at the Homantin South Development. **He also proposed** that the Applications Section and Commercial Properties Division (3,645 square metres net) should be relocated to the Wang Tau Hom Estate Phase, 12 Development. Both the new developments were scheduled to be completed in 1999. **The Director of Housing said** that after the relocation, the HAHQ- Special Facilities would be allocated a net area of 7,000 square metres. [...]

9.6   **An audit examination of the Director of Housing's May 1993 submissions to the Establishment and Finance Committee of the Hong Kong Housing Authority revealed** that no reference was made to the designed capacity for accommodation, 3,927 staff in the HAHQ Building. As a result, no explanation was given as to why, despite the fact that there were only 2,770 staff working in the HAHQ Building in 1993, additional space was required. **I have expressed my concern to the Director of Housing** that this information was not included in the submissions to the Establishment and Finance Committee of the Hong Kong Housing Authority.

9.7   In response to my observations, **the Director of Housing has said** that while he accepts that the HAHQ Building was planned on the basis of a projected HQ staff of 3,927 staff in 1994–95, this was only a preliminary design concept in 1985 when detailed space requirements had yet to be firmed up. For example, space requirements for the HAHQ Special Facilities were still under consideration within the Department. **Experience has shown** that more space was needed for these special facilities than had been anticipated in 1985. As a result, less space could be set aside for office use.

9.8   **The Director of Housing has also clarified** that the office space to [*sic*] staff working in the HAHQ Building, a net floor area of 3,466 square metres would have been saved. **I have therefore recommended to the Director of Housing** that he should adopt government standards in allocating office space to his staff.

9.9   In response to my observations, **the Director of Housing has explained** that the allocation of office space in the new HAHQ Building, when it was occupied in 1990 was generally on a par with the approved government standards then prevailing, whereas the standards referred to by me were new standards revised by the Government which were not promulgated for implementation until March 1992. By that time, the Housing Department has already moved into the new HAHQ Building. **The Director further pointed out** that when the revised standards were promulgated there was no requirement for all government departments to revise their existing office layouts to conform to the new standards.

This short extract, from a much larger text, has a number of projecting clauses, with most of the processes being verbal, including *inform, propose, say, express, clarify, recommend* and *explain*. Here the writer filters the report of what the Director of Housing either *said*, realised through verbal processes, or *believes* through his own disagreement with, or displeasure about, what has happened by adding his personal opinion, e.g. *I have expressed my concern to the Director of Housing that this information was not included in the submissions to the Establishment and Finance Committee of the Hong Kong Housing Authority.*

In two cases, the writer uses a Circumstantial Adjunct of Contingency, *in response to my observations*, prior to a projecting clause as a contextual frame, as background to the Director's response and to emphasise his involvement. By using thematised subjective viewpoint projection, the writer is choosing to construe his personal interpretation of the situation in initial position before reporting the 'gist' of what was said by the Director of Housing. In this text it is quite obvious that the writer is unhappy with the present situation, and has decided, whether correctly or incorrectly, to place a great deal of the responsibility for what has happened on the Director of Housing. He continually construes the Director of Housing's suggestions and words in such a way as to create a negative impression, i.e. to imply that what the Director of Housing has suggested happened, is not what did happen in reality. There are a variety of other possible linguistic choices that the writer could have made to make these meanings, but it seems he wanted to place the modal responsibility, in part if not totally, on the Director of Housing.

The words being reported may not be exactly those said by the Director of Housing. The fact that someone else is reporting his words, in a less negotiable written form compared with the less formal written or spoken text where these points were made prior to the writing of the report, allows a different interpretation to be instantiated (Thompson, 2004). The writer here uses his authority as author and certain linguistic features, such as Circumstantial Adjuncts to establish and embellish a context related to the way in which he perceives what is happening.

7.4.3 Category 2: Thematised comment

The category of thematised comment, although not as frequently used as thematised subjective viewpoint, did appear often in the data. In total there were 55 instances of thematised comment, and these occurred in all three text types. Here the writer often used a place-holder *it* to introduce the projecting Theme. In some cases the writer chooses *it is believed* rather than *I believe* to express viewpoint in a manner which superficially appears to be objective. The author could have chosen other devices to represent the same information, but in these instances chooses to start the message with an *it* projecting clause, such as *it is important* in Example 5, where the *it* clause reveals a degree of objective modality.

(5)   (Memo 19, clause complex 4)

It is important [that] AFL ensures that all costs of such assistance be accounted for honestly.

Projecting clauses in context: an example

Letter 20 (see Appendix 7.1) illustrates how projecting clauses and the writer's viewpoint and position in the message. The text, a letter to Furnish Ltd, a furniture retail store, from their legal advisers, discusses whether Furnish Ltd are liable to their landlord and other tenants for damages or losses incurred during the construction of a set of escalators. The discussion of the linguistic choices will be limited to the function and purpose of the projecting clauses in thematic position. Projecting clauses and Subject, which together act as the Theme of the independent clauses, are presented in Table 7.4, with the projecting clauses in bold.

The letter commences by creating the background and intertextuality of its contents, i.e. *Further to my letter* and *as spoken*, and states the purpose of the letter, which is to advise. In the first five clauses/clause complexes, the writer presents background information about the present situation, the contract and the parties involved. In clause complex 6, *the question is whether the other tenant's claim is 'in respect of any matters comprised by the indemnity',* the real issue of whether the other tenant has a claim is stated. It is only after the context has been established that the writer uses projection to report previous discussions, and offers their viewpoint.

In order to discuss the aspect of marked Theme further, a simplified version of the analysis of marked Theme is presented. There may also be more than one marked Theme. For example, in clause complex 7 there are two marked Themes *based on our conversation* and *you informed me that*, both of which are included in the column 'marked Theme'.

As shown in Table 7.4, it is only in clause complex 7 that the first projecting clause is realised. In line with what research into marked Theme has shown, the choice of marked Theme as a projecting clause signals a shift from statement of the law in general to the specific case, i.e. the solicitor chooses to add further background information, i.e. *based on our conversation you informed me that the other tenant.* This Circumstantial

Table 7.4 Projecting Theme in Letter 20 **(projection in bold)**[1]

CC no.	Marked Theme	Subject/Theme	Rheme
7.	Based on our conversation, **you informed me** that	the other tenant	had not yet signed the lease with the Landlord when the Landlord had allowed Furnish Ltd to do certain work as stated in paragraphs (a) to (d) of the Indemnity.
9.	**It would appear to be the Landlord's mistake** that	they	had not provided the correct plan to the other tenant.
13.	[Also,] **the indemnity given by Furnish Ltd. in clause 3, by its wording, implies** that	Furnish Ltd.	will indemnify the Landlord and/or the management company against all losses 'that may arise directly or indirectly as a result of our carrying-out such A&A works.
16.	**Furnish Ltd. cannot be expected**		to indemnify the Landlord for any impact the relocation of the escalators will have on the rental'.
19.	**Please clarify** whether	the building of the column by Furnish Ltd.	has any impact on the tenant at shops 123C?
21.	[Also,] **at the time the indemnity was being negotiated, was there any discussion** that	Furnish Ltd.	would have to bear losses in rents due to the relocation of the escalator.
22.	As spoken **the Landlord cannot expect**	Furnish Ltd.	to satisfy any claims made against them by simply taking the Landlord's word that they have suffered certain losses.
24.	[but] **that does not mean** that	the other tenant	must necessarily commence legal proceedings against the Landlord before the Landlord can claim from Furnish Ltd
29.	[However,] **I was given the impression** that	the centre	has not even officially opened yet
32.	[and] **my advice is to require the Landlord to show (from the other tenant or otherwise)** that	they	have indeed incurred such losses.
35.	**I believe**	Furnish Ltd	have a good arguable defence

(Note: In column 1, CC refers to clause complex number)

Adjunct of cause: reason is a contextual frame situating and referring to previous discussions, followed by a subjective verbal projection, i.e. *you informed me that*. A thematised subjective viewpoint is realised as the writer needs to establish the present text's intertextuality: the place of this text can be roughly paraphrased as 'we spoke, you told me X and this is how I read what you have told me in the eyes of the law'.

The writer continues with a projection of thematised comment, *It would appear to be the Landlord's mistake that they*, using both a modal finite *would* and the modal lexical verb *appear* in order to avoid making a definite statement. In the projecting clauses 9 and 13, *would appear* and *implies* are choices to demonstrate the writer's attitude: the writer seems to be hedging and not committing fully to support the issue, just in case there could be any repercussions 'covering their back' to a certain extent.

Clause complex 13 states a fact by a projection that is taken from the indemnity itself, i.e. *by its wording implies that*. The legal document here says, i.e. projects the wording, that Furnish Ltd are covered by the stipulations set down in their contract. Using legal text to project what has been said is a very powerful type of projection as the legal text is used as a tool of adjudication, and in this instance the words of the legal text state that someone else is liable. The projection in clause complex 21 is grammatically an interrogative even though there is no question mark, i.e. *was there any discussion that*, the aim of which is to establish exactly what had been discussed.

The letter then continues to list and request further details about the present situation. The two instances of projection in clause complexes 29 and 35 are both thematised direct subjective viewpoints projecting ideas, *I was given the impression* and *I believe Furnish Ltd*. Again the choice of a projecting clause appears to be a conscious one by the writer, protecting the writer by placing the onus of responsibility of the proposition at a distance, i.e. reporting, presenting information. Thus if the information is found to be questionable this is the fault of the informant not the writer. In the clause complex *however, I was given the impression that the centre has not even officially opened yet so the other tenant's sales might not in any event have been affected by Furnish Ltd works* the projecting clause could quite easily be removed without affecting the main proposition. But by including *however I was given the impression that* the writer is shifting modal responsibility to an unnamed other party. The writer adopts an authorial voice, and at the same time acknowledges, through the use of low modality *the impression that*, contingent alternatives. Martin and White classify such choices as engagement: entertain, where the writer adopts 'modals of probability', 'reality phase' and sometimes 'interpersonal metaphor' which are dialogically expansive (Martin and White 2005: 104) Note the use of the Modal Adjuncts *yet* and *even* in the clause *has not yet even officially opened*, which adds to the negative assessment of the Landlord's claim.

It is worth noting that in this text thematised projected clauses are used above all to distance the views expressed from the writer and place the responsibility for the action/information with another party.

7.5 Discussion

To date, in both workplace English pedagogy and in general English pedagogy little attention has been given to projecting clauses. Davies (1988, 1997), Nesbitt and Plum (1988), Thompson (1994, 2004), Iedema (1995) and Harvey (1995) have all discussed projection to a limited degree. However, there needs to be further research into authentic data to draw out linguistic practices and examples on which a better understanding of language in use – and a more robust approach to language pedagogy – can be based.

It is highly likely that projecting clauses play a significant role in many other discourse communities. Davies (1988), Hewings and Hewings (2002), Hood (this volume) draw on academic English for a theory of 'writer viewpoint' and 'contextual frame', a discourse where clauses such as *It is suggested by X that*, or *X argues that Y is …* are often found in the introduction, literature review and discussion sections of papers. Davies claims that contextual frames, which are realised by projecting clauses among other features, are an important feature which helps to establish the interactional nature of a text, and that contextual frames allow a writer to express viewpoint both directly and indirectly. She argues that linguistic features which realise viewpoints are very important to the meaning making of the message.

Projection is seen to be important in aiding the understanding of viewpoint. Most of the research here focuses on the types of reporting verb used (Thompson and Ye 1991; Hunston 1994) and on what Hyland (1996, 1997) calls 'hedging' and 'boosting'. The only report of such occurrences in workplace English are found in Iedema (1995), whose data are restricted to directives, and Harvey (1995), who mentions this construction but only briefly. However, as argued projection is an important feature in workplace English texts, and perhaps also in other discourses, and it deserves greater attention.

During the process of analysis, the data led to an extension of work already carried out by Davies (1988, 1997), Thompson (1994, 2004) and Iedema (1995). The three categories of projection identified, thematised subjective viewpoint, thematised comment, thematised obligation/inclination are not new and were drawn from separate theoretical descriptions. The present study used these categories in the analysis of Theme of the corpus texts and investigated the way in which they construe viewpoint in memos, letters and reports. The dialogic expansion of the text is quite clear through the use of projecting clauses, and other lexico-grammatical features which construe heteroglossia in workplace texts need to be investigated.

The findings suggest that there is indeed a pattern in the choice of projecting clauses acting as Theme: In memos and reports it is more likely that subjective direct and indirect projecting clauses will be used. Moreover, in reports there are typically far more verbal projecting clauses than mental projecting clauses. However, the corpus is relatively small and analysis of a larger sample could show that similar features may occur with a greater (or lesser) frequency in different types of text. Furthermore, this study has looked closely only at projection in thematic position, and, while there are also instances of projection occurring within the Rheme of a clause complex, these have not been investigated.

7.6 Conclusion

The findings suggest that projecting clauses are serving the particular purpose of 'framing' viewpoint, thus allowing writers to define themselves. More specifically, the findings corroborate Davies's (1988, 1994, 1997) and Thompson's (2004) views that projection as Theme acts directly or indirectly to construe interpersonal meaning. In addition, the present study supports research carried out by Brown and Herndl (1986: 22), who state that language choices in workplace writing are not randomly made, rather that they are 'logical grammatical choices – considering their syntactic, semantic, pragmatic and phonological function.' Thus, grammatical choices, such as whether to use a projecting clause, are made to some extent consciously in order to encode the message intended by the writer. It seems that in projecting clauses, which are chosen to represent a fact or to explicitly show the writer's subjective viewpoint, the 'choice is significant, communicating information about the speakers and their attitudes toward hearers, topics, contexts and so on' (Brown and Herndl, 1986: 23).

Hierarchical power is generally clearly delineated in the workplace, and clearly defined hierarchical boundaries will control a writer's selection of grammatical patterns. Whether the writer chooses thematised subjective viewpoint or thematised comment to project their ideas, and how they deploy these resources, is to some extent controlled by their position within the workplace, including their position in relation to the intended reader of the text. As pointed out by Winsor (1993), 'writers relate to texts within a hierarchical power structure that limits the control any writer has' (1993: 180). Or as Brown and Herndl point out, 'the perceived function of the writing depends upon where one stands in the production cycle' (1986: 20). Fairclough (1992) argues that one reason for such subtlety in the grammar is that the discourse of institutional practices has changed and that the overt markers of power and asymmetry have become more covert. He states that the ways of linguistically realising power are becoming 'more potent, with the result that power asymmetry becomes more subtle rather than disappearing' (1992: 203). The grammatical structures chosen by writers reflect their position within the workplace. An analysis of writers who choose to use projecting clauses and the types of projecting clause they choose in relation to their status would be very interesting, but one that is unfortunately beyond the scope of the present study.

When reading texts from the business world, subtleties such as the use of projection and, at a finer level, the type of projection chosen, may cause problems for readers. For example, a non-native English speaker may not recognise the indirect nature of such realisations and this could result in a breakdown of communication. There is clearly a need for research into the way in which control is accomplished through language within an organisation and for this to be made more explicit, and for such knowledge to be incorporated into workplace training material.

Notes

1. The presentation of data in Table 7.4 follows the model in Martin and Rose (2003) where the marked Theme column includes not only the marked Theme but also any textual or interpersonal elements which precede it (placed in square brackets in Table 7.4). This is not a fully satisfactory model and perhaps needs further attention. However, for the purpose of the present analysis textual and interpersonal Themes are classified in this manner.

References

Berry, M. (1996). What is Theme? A(nother) personal view. In *Meaning and Form: Systemic Functional Interpretations*, M. Berry, R. Fawcett and G. Huang (eds), 1–64. Norwood, NJ: Ablex Publishing Company.

Brown, R. L. and Herndl, C. G. (1986). An ethnographic study of corporate writing: Job status as reflected in written text. In *Functional Approaches to Writing: Research Perspectives*, B. Couture (ed.), 11–28. London: Pinter.

Caffarel, A. (2000). Interpreting French Theme as a bi-layered structure: Discourse implications. In *Discourse and Community*, Eija Ventola (ed.), 247–272. Tübingen: Gunter Narr Verlag Tübingen .

Clark, R. and Ivanič, R. (1997). *The Politics of Writing.* London: Routledge.

Couture, B. (1992). Categorizing professional discourse: engineering, administrative, and technical/professional writing. *Journal of Business and Technical Communication*, 6 (1): 5–37.

Davies, F. (1988). Reading between the lines: thematic choice as a device for presenting writer viewpoint in academic discourse. *The ESPecialist* 9 (2): 173–200.

Davies, F. (1994). From writer roles to elements of text: interactive, organisational and topical. In *Reflections on Language Learning*, L. Barbara and M. Scott (eds), 170–83.Clevedon, England: Multilingual Matters.

Davies, F. (1997). Marked Theme as a heuristic for analysing text-type, text and genre. In *Applied Languages: Theory and Practice in* ESP, J. Pique and D. Viera (eds), 45–71. Valencia: Servei de Publications Universitat de Valencia.

Davies, F. and Forey, G. (1996). 'Effective writing for management project.' Unpublished report. Bristol: The University of Bristol, School of Education.

Davies, F., Forey, G. and Hyatt, D. (1999). Exploring aspects of context: selected findings from the Effective Writing for Management project. In *Writing Business: Genres, Media and Discourse*, F. Bargiela-Chiappini and C. Nickerson (eds), 293–312. Harlow: Longman.

Downing, A. (1991). An alternative approach to theme: a systemic-functional perspective. *Word*, 42 (2): 119–143.

Fairclough, N. (1992). *Discourse and Social Change.* Cambridge: Polity Press.

Forey, G. (2002). 'Aspects of Theme and their role in workplace texts.' Unpublished PhD dissertation. Glasgow: Department of English Language. University of Glasgow.

Forey, G. (2004). Workplace texts: Do they mean the same for teachers and business people? *English for Specific Purposes* 23: 447–469.

Forey, G. and Nunan, D. (2002). The role of language and culture in the workplace. In *Knowledge and Discourse: Language Ecology in Theory and Practice*, C. Barron, N. Bruce, and D. Nunan (eds), 204–220. Harlow: Pearson Education Ltd.

Goatly, A. (1995). Marked theme and its interpretation in A. E. Housman's A Shropshire Lad. In *Thematic Development in English Texts*, M. Ghadessy (ed.), 164–197. London: Pinter.

Halliday, M. A. K. (1994). *An Introduction to Functional Grammar* (2nd edition). London: Edward Arnold.

Harvey, A. (1995). Interaction in public reports. *English for Specific Purposes* 14 (3): 189–200.

Hewings, M. and Hewings, A. (2002). 'It is interesting to note that …': a comparative study of anticipatory 'it' in student and published writing. *English for Specific Purposes* 21 (4): 367–383.

Hunston, S. (1994). Evaluation and organization in a sample of written academic discourse. In *Advances in Written Text Analysis*, M. Coulthard (ed.), 191–218. London: Routledge.

Hyland, K. (1996). Talking to the academy: forms of hedging in science research articles. *Written Communication* 13 (2): 251–281.

Hyland, K. (1997). Scientific claims and community values: articulating an academic culture. *Language and Communication* 17 (1): 19–31.

Iedema, R. A. M. (1995). *The Language of Administration: Write-it-right Industry Research Report Stage Three.* Sydney: NSW Dept of Education, Disadvantaged Schools Program, Metropolitan East.

Iedema, R. A. M. (1997). The language of administration: organizing human activity in formal institutions. In *Genre and Institutions: Social Processes in the Workplace and School*, F. Christie and J. R. Martin (eds), 73–100. London: Cassell.

Iedema, R. A. M. (2000). Bureaucratic planning and resemiotisation. In *Discourse and the Community*, E. Ventola (ed.), 47–69. Tübingen: Gunter Narr Verlag Tübingen.

Iedema, R. A. M. (2003). *Discourse of Post-Bureaucratic Organizations.* Amsterdam: John Benjamins Publishing Company.

Ivanič, R. (1998). *Writing and Identity: The Discoursal Construction of Identity in Academic Writing.* Amsterdam: John Benjamins.

Martin, J. R. (1992). *English Text.* Amsterdam: John Benjamins Publishing Company.

Martin, J. R. and Rose, D. (2003). *Working with Discourse.* London: Continuum.

Martin, J. R. and White, P. R. R. (2005). *The Language of Evaluation, Appraisal in English.* London and New York: Palgrave Macmillan.

McGregor, W. (1994). The grammar of reported speech and thought in Gooniyandi. *Australian Journal of Linguistics* 14: 63–92.

Nesbitt, C. and Plum, G. (1988). Probabilities in a systemic grammar: the clause complex in English. In *New Developments in Systemic Linguistics* vol. 2, R. P. Fawcett and D. Young (eds), 6–38. London: Frances Pinter.

Nunan, D., Forey, G., Fossard, R. and Foo, J. (1996). Communication in the professional workplace project, Phase 1. Research report, Part 1. Hong Kong: Hong Kong Society of Accountants & English Language Centre, University of Hong Kong.

Stainton, C. (1996). *The Technical Review as Genre*. Nottingham Working Papers no. 3. Nottingham: Department of English Studies, University of Nottingham.

Tadros, A. (1985). *Prediction in Text*. Discourse analysis monograph no. 10. Birmingham: University of Birmingham Printing Section.

Thompson, G. (1994). Propositions, projections and things. Paper presented at 21st ISFC, Ghent 1–5 August 1994.

Thompson, G. (2004). *Introducing Functional Grammar* (2nd edition). London: Arnold.

Thompson, G. and Ye, Y.Y. (1991). Evaluation in reporting verbs used in academic papers. *Applied Linguistics* 12 (4): 365–382.

van Leeuwen, T. (1996). The representation of social actors. In *Texts and Practices: Readings in Critical Discourse Analysis*, C. R. Caldas-Coulthard and M. Coulthard (eds), 32–70. London: Routledge.

Winsor, D. A. (1993). Owning corporate texts. *Journal of Business and Technical Communication*, 7 (2): 179–195.

Appendix 1
Letter 20 with projecting clauses shown in bold

Dear Elaine,

2/F & 3/F, Sun Building

Further to my letter of 30th November 1995 and as spoken, I wish to advise as follows:

Under a contract of indemnity, the holder of the indemnity (i.e. the Landlord) is generally entitled to recover the amount payable by him by virtue of any judgement recovered against or compromise reasonably made by him in any legal proceedings in respect of any matters comprised by the indemnity, including costs (Halsbury's Laws of England 4th Edition).

Therefore, generally, the Landlord is entitled to claim under the indemnity as soon as his liability to the other tenant has arisen and it may be before he has actually made payment.

However, the Landlord has to act reasonably and if he does, and the other tenant's claim is legitimate and can be related to the matters covered by the indemnity, Furnish Ltd. would be obliged to pay.

The question is of course whether the other tenant's claim is 'in respect of any matters comprised by the indemnity'.

Based on our conversation, **you informed me** that the other tenant had not yet signed the lease with the Landlord when the Landlord had allowed Furnish Ltd to do contract work as stated in paragraphs (a) to (d) of the Indemnity.

It was only subsequent to that, when the Landlord had negotiated with the other tenant a certain rent because of the (mistaken) belief that the pedestrian flow would be higher because of the position of the escalator. **It would appear to be the Landlord's mistake** that they had not provided the correct plan to the other tenant.

Based on the information you have given me, Furnish Ltd would have a good case to argue, firstly, that in terms of timing, the approval was given before any agreement was reached with the other tenant.

In any event, even if the lease had been concluded before the Landlord gave Furnish Ltd their consent, the indemnity should not extend to the knock-on effect of such relocation of an escalator because with a reduction in rents in one area, will be an increase in rents to another wherever the escalator has been moved to, so the Landlord suffers no loss. If the relocation is for the benefit of Furnish Ltd, then presumably the benefit has been factored in to the rent that FURNISH pay.

Also, the indemnity given by Furnish Ltd. in clause 3, by its wording, implies that Furnish Ltd will indemnify the Landlord and/or the management company against all losses 'that may arise directly or indirectly as a result of our carrying-out such A&A works'.

In my opinion, it is during the Period when the works are being carried out when MEA has the obligation to indemnity if losses, claims etc. are made. Once the works are completed, there is no further obligation.

Furnish Ltd cannot be expected to indemnify the Landlord for any impact the relocation of the escalators will have on the rentals. That is a separate issue not covered by this indemnity. The Landlord had given their consent to relocate the escalators.

Please clarify whether the building of the column by Furnish Ltd has any impact on the tenant at shops 123C? This may be a separate factor especially if the column was without approval.

Also, at the time the indemnity was being negotiated, was there any discussion that Furnish Ltd would have to bear losses in rents due to the relocation of the escalator.

As spoken the Landlord cannot expect Furnish Ltd. to satisfy any claims made against them by simply taking the Landlord's word that they have suffered certain losses. To an extent, they are put to strict proof but **that does not mean that** the other tenant must necessarily commence legal proceedings against the Landlord before the Landlord can claim from Furnish Ltd. But the other tenant's claim has to be related to the indemnity give and the Landlord can only compromise reasonably.

As stated in my earlier letter, there may be a variety of reasons why the rent has been revised and one factor may be due to Furnish Ltd works and Furnish Ltd may be liable for loss of rent for the period when the works were being carried out because of disruptions etc. However, **I was given the impression** that the centre has not even officially opened yet so the other tenant's sales might not in any event have been affected by Furnish Ltd works.

My advice is not to admit any loss suffered by the Landlord and require the Landlord to show (from the other tenant or otherwise) that they have indeed incurred such losses.

Their claim is very substantial in the circumstances, and potentially amounts to several millions of dollars! **I believe** Furnish Ltd have a good arguable defence and if the matter cannot be resolved amicably, the matter may have to proceed to litigation albeit Furnish Ltd may have to incur increased legal costs (for Furnish Ltd, the Landlord and possibly the other tenant) if the Landlord is able to prove their losses.

Please keep me informed of the progress of your discussion with the Landlord.

8 | What can linguistics tell us about writing skills?

Michael Hoey
University of Liverpool

8.1 Introduction

Thirty-five years ago, when I began my academic career as a Research Assistant in Communications Studies at the Hatfield Polytechnic, a tempting answer to the question posed in the title to this chapter – what can linguistics tell us about writing skills? – would have been 'Nothing at all'. Dominated as linguistics was by the theories of Chomsky and his associates, it seemed at that time as if a knowledge of linguistics might be a handicap to anyone committed to improving the writing of students, rather than a help. Actually, even then, there were linguists who were posing relevant questions for the communications teacher, notably Kenneth Pike, Robert Longacre, Randolph Quirk and my own mentor, Eugene Winter. But the 'nothing at all' answer was not unreasonable, given the climate of the time.

Thirty-five years on, the situation is markedly different. Theoretical linguists still are working away at the abstract problems that interest them, and findings from these sources remain irrelevant to the communications specialist – nor in fairness would those involved in this work claim such relevance. But in addition to this work we now have text linguists and corpus linguists, both of whom are concerned with how real language functions in real contexts, and we also have the developing and increasingly influential model of systemic functional linguistics, which places at the heart of its linguistic description the fact that speakers and writers *choose* what to say/write on a moment by moment basis, a more promising starting point from the perspective of the communications teacher who is concerned to ensure that students choose correctly for their purposes from the linguistic resources available to them.

8.2 Influences on the writer as s/he writes

I want to touch on a few of these developments, starting briefly with systemic functional linguistics (SFL for short). The most important insight this model offers for the teacher of writing skills is that every text is produced with attention to the needs of the context, the needs of the reader(s) and the needs of the developing text. Thus, for example, the previous sentence is written in a particular style because it is appearing in a collection likely to be read by academics and teachers; if I were giving it as a paper at a conference I would probably have couched it very differently, e.g. 'The most important thing about SFL is that it says that ...'. It is also oriented to the fact that you as reader are likely to want to know how systemic linguistics might help the development of writing skills, and so it starts with *the most important insight*, importance and relevance being obviously related. In addition it is formulated so that the sentence starts with mention of the model of SFL rather than, say, writing skills and this is because the previous sentence ended with mention of the model. Thus the choice of the first seven words of the second sentence of this paragraph can be shown to have been affected in the way indicated in Figure 8.1.

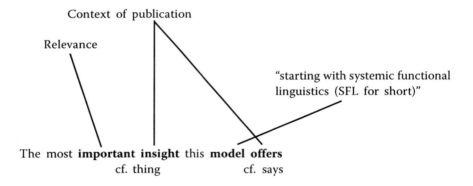

Figure 8.1 Influences on the beginning of a sentence

8.3 Theme as the starting point of a sentence

I am going to say nothing more about the effect of context on choice but want to say something about the other two factors. I noted above that my second sentence was affected by what I had said in the previous sentence. All sentences can be divided into two parts: the Theme and the Rheme (Halliday 1985). The Theme is the starting point of the sentence; it usually specifies what the sentence is about and is closely associated with given information. The Rheme is the heart of the message and is therefore normally associated with new information. The association with Given and New is rough and ready as Ndahiro (1998) shows, but it helps us get a handle on why there should be a division between Theme and Rheme in the first place. Linguists disagree about where the Theme ends and the Rheme begins, but in many ways the most informative divisions – and the easiest to operate – are those which occur at the point when the subject is reached or where the main verb of the sentence starts (positions of course that often result in different analyses) (Davies 1997; Berry 1996).

To show the effect of Theme and Rheme on the way we write, consider the following extract from the editorial (by Helen Wallace) in *BBC Music* (June 2001, page 3). I have numbered sentences for ease of reference. Where orthography and syntax do not coincide, I have indicated the second, separate 'sentence' with a letter:

(1)   [1] The words Wigmore Hall conjure up a very particular musical utopia. [2] In a city where only the gargantuan galleries of the Royal Albert Hall connect us to Victorian times, this little concert venue provides London with a last link to 19th-century Europe, and with a way of life that disappeared with the world wars.

[3] Only at Wigmore Hall, perhaps at a Lieder recital, do you encounter still the whiff of old Vienna, or the dry, sophisticated perfume of Paris, when the music of Poulenc, who was a Wigmore Hall devotee, is aired once again.

[4] For many, the experience of a Wigmore Hall recital is the most intense, essential way of encountering music: [4a] the intimate space and heavenly acoustics make possible a meeting of minds between audience, artist and composer impossible elsewhere. [5] But these enchanting evenings of chamber music, attended often by the elderly, many of whom have supported the Hall since coming to London as refugees, are far from museum pieces. [6] Listening to the performances on our Centenary cover CD, it is the current vitality of music making that strikes home.

Table 8.1 shows how the passage might be analysed in terms of Theme and Rheme, using the point immediately before the main verb as the boundary between the two. I have added implied information and indicated the relationship between the Themes and the previous text.

As can be seen, the writer has in this passage kept the topic of Wigmore Hall as Theme throughout the passage, sometimes by implication, sometimes explicitly. Other options available to writers are to draw the Theme from the previous Rheme or from a general overall Theme (Daneš 1974). Both options are in fact taken up elsewhere in the same editorial. The sentence following the passage quoted above is:

(2) [7] William Lyne has nurtured a generation of performers who can stand proudly beside those no longer with us.

The Themes of subsequent sentences all draw on the Rheme of this sentence (*a generation of performers* ...), with each new sentence referring to a different celebrated performer.

The point is that the Theme of a sentence typically does not come out of the blue (though as it happens *William Lyne* does in the sentence just quoted, showing that we are talking here about a strong tendency, not a rule) but reflects the way that the sentence draws upon the development

Table 8.1 A Theme-Rheme analysis of an extract from a BBC Music editorial

Theme	Rheme
[1] The words **Wigmore Hall**	conjure up a very particular musical utopia.
[2] In a city where only the gargantuan galleries of the Royal Albert Hall connect us to Victorian times, **this little concert venue**	provides London with a last link to 19th-century Europe, and with a way of life that disappeared with the world wars.
[3] Only at **Wigmore Hall**, perhaps at a Lieder recital, do you	encounter still the whiff of old Vienna, or the dry, sophisticated perfume of Paris, when the music of Poulenc, who was a Wigmore Hall devotee, is aired once again.
[4] For many, the experience of a **Wigmore Hall** recital	is the most intense, essential way of encountering music:
[4a] the intimate space and heavenly acoustics [of **Wigmore Hall**]	make possible a meeting of minds between audience, artist and composer impossible elsewhere.
[5] But these enchanting evenings of chamber music [at **Wigmore Hall**], attended often by the elderly, many of whom have supported **the Hall** since coming to London as refugees,	are far from museum pieces.
[6] Listening to the performances [at **Wigmore Hall**] on our Centenary cover CD, it	is the current vitality of music making that strikes home.

of the text so far. When writers ignore this, the effect can be confusing or obscure.

There are two possible reasons why a passage may be hard to read and may seem unclearly focused. The first is that the wrong lexical choices are made for Theme. This may seem a surprising claim as to why a piece of writing might seem unnatural but the evidence for it is good. Writers and readers have built-in expectations that some lexical items will appear in Theme and others will avoid it (for a number of instances as well as detailed discussion, see Hoey 2005); evidence can be drawn from corpora. I refer to the processes whereby these expectations are built up as processes of 'priming', and their effect is that, for particular users in a particular genre and/or domain, certain words or phrases are 'primed' for use as (part of) Theme (or otherwise) or primed to occur in Rheme. So, for example, in newspapers, the adjective *undercover*, and more specifically the phrase *undercover agent*, avoids Theme; the combination *word against* likewise always in my data occurs within the Rheme and usually close to the end of the sentence. On the other hand the word *consequence* is apparently primed for newspaper readers and writers for occurrence in Theme.

In principle, then, a passage might be so written that few or none of its Themes conformed to the likely primings of the readers. Such a passage would be hard to read and barely acceptable as English. Consider the following re-write of Extract (1) in which every Theme, apart from the first, has been chosen from lexis that most users of the language are likely to avoid using in Theme:

(3)   [1] The words Wigmore Hall conjure up a very particular musical utopia. [2] A last link to 19th century Europe and a way of life that disappeared with the world wars is provided for London in a city where only the gargantuan galleries of the Royal Albert Hall connect us to Victorian times.

[3] Still do you encounter only at Wigmore Hall, perhaps at a Lieder recital the whiff of old Vienna, or the dry, sophisticated perfume of Paris, when the music of Poulenc, who was a Wigmore Hall devotee, is aired once again.

[4] The most intense and essential way of encountering music is experienced for many at a Wigmore Hall recital: [4a] a meeting of minds between audience, artist and composer impossible elsewhere is made possible by the intimate space and heavenly acoustics. [5] Attended often by the elderly, many of whom have supported the Hall since coming to London as refugees, these enchanting evenings of chamber music are, however, far from museum pieces. [6] Striking home is the current vitality of music making, when listening to the performances on our Centenary cover CD.

The first Theme I altered in the passage was that for Sentence 2, where the new Theme begins with *A last link*, which is used as Theme relatively rarely in my 100 million words of Guardian data. (There were no instances of *a last link* in my data either in Theme or Rheme.) Out of 516 instances of *a link*, where *link* was head of its own nominal group, only 48 appear as part of Theme and of these only 25 appeared as part of the sentence Theme as opposed to occurring as Theme in a subordinate clause within non-sentence initial position. In my terms, then, *a link* is negatively primed for occurrence as Theme.

Still, which begins Sentence 3 of the rewritten passage, has a variety of uses. It can refer to continuation (as in *he still bobs up occasionally*), it can be used to intensify a comparative (*still more eccentric*), it can mark the relationship of the current utterance to previous utterances in speech or writing (*Still, the Eton mystique persists*), it can describe a state of quietness, it can refer to a photograph taken from a movie and it can refer to a vessel used for distilling whisky and the like. It is the first of these uses that we are concerned with here. In this use, *still* occurs quite commonly in Theme if we define Theme as I did earlier as everything prior to the main verb. However almost all its thematic occurrences are in post-Subject position and if Theme is defined as everything up to and including the Subject, then this use of *still* is extremely rare in Theme. (The third use of *still* seems never to occur in post-Subject position, on the other hand – an instance of the way polysemous items avoid each other's characteristic grammar; see Hoey 2005.) The truth is that the positional priming I am referring to is more subtle than the simple division into Theme and Rheme. The first use of *still* occurs 32 per cent of the time in post-Subject Theme, which is about average given that Themes are approximately half as long as Rhemes on average. However it is primed to avoid all other positions in Theme. In pre-Subject position, it occurs only 47 times in my data out of a sample of 2127 cases of the first sense of *still* – a mere 2 per cent of instances. This is one reason why its use in the rewritten text above seems so odd.

The other Themes in the rewritten version can be handled more briefly. To begin with the phrase *most intense*, this is typically primed on the basis of my data to avoid Theme. Defining Theme as before as everything up to the main verb, only 13 instances of *most intense* out of 97 (13 per cent) occur as sentence Theme (with a further four occurring as Theme of a non-initial clause) and only four of these occur (with *the*) in sentence-initial position. Similarly, *meeting of minds*, which begins 'sentence' 4a, only occurs as Theme three times out of 31 instances, with a further two occurring at the beginning of sentence fragments. As one might expect, *attended*, which begins sentence 5, is also strongly primed for most users to avoid sentence-initial position, with only three such cases found in a data set of 2,749 (0.1 per cent). There are only five instances of *striking home* in my data and none of them are thematised.

What I have been arguing is that thematic choice is governed in part by a knowledge of what is typically available as Theme and what is not; and, as my rewritten text shows, choosing Themes from lexis that is primed to avoid thematic position may result in a text of marginal acceptability or intelligibility. However, as is well recognised, a passage may be suspect without the explanation lying in the choice of lexis for the Theme. Table 8.1 shows the way that each sentence in the original text picks its Theme up from its predecessors. I mentioned above that there are two possible reasons why a passage might be hard to read – the second is of course that there may be no, or inadequate, thematic progression. As an example, consider now another rewritten version of the passage we have been considering. What I have aimed to do in this version is vary the Themes so that the text no longer always thematises some aspect of Wigmore Hall. I have tried to ensure that the sentences mean roughly the same as before, though probably no change can be made without some slight adjustment to the meaning of the text. Despite its having more or less the same content as the original passage, I think this version will be found lacking in some respects by many readers.

(4) [1] The words Wigmore Hall conjure up a very particular musical utopia. [2] London has only the gargantuan galleries of the Royal Albert Hall to connect us to Victorian times, [2a] but 19th century Europe is evoked by this little concert venue in London, as is a way of life that disappeared with the world wars.

[3] You can encounter still the whiff of old Vienna at Wigmore Hall, perhaps at a Lieder recital, or the dry, sophisticated perfume of Paris, when the music of Poulenc, who was a Wigmore Hall devotee, is aired once again.

[4] For many, the most intense, essential way of encountering music is the experience of a Wigmore Hall recital; [4a] a meeting of minds between audience, artist and composer impossible elsewhere is made possible by the intimate space and heavenly acoustics. [5] But there is no way that these enchanting evenings of chamber music, attended often by the elderly, many of whom have supported the Hall since coming to London as refugees, are museum pieces. [6] The performances on our Centenary cover CD show that it is the current vitality of music making in Wigmore Hall that strikes home.

In this version, the Themes all seem to arrive from nowhere. In sentence 2 *London* has neither been mentioned nor particularly implied in the previous sentence and much the same can be said of *19th century Europe*, though here at least there is the connection between *Victorian* and *19th century*. In sentence 3 the Theme *you* is largely empty of content but there has in any case been no reference to the potential user of Wigmore Hall before (unless *us* is counted). *The most intense, essential way of encountering music* – the Theme of Sentence 4 – has only been alluded to in the vaguest terms. The *meeting of minds* (4a) might be seen as growing out of ways of encountering music, but the connection is not as direct as it could be. But *there* (Sentence 5) makes no connections of any kind to earlier content, and *the performances on our Centenary cover* (Sentence 6) introduce a new topic.

Clause 4a retains its normally Theme-avoiding lexis, but all the other sentences now begin with Themes that are either positively primed for Theme function or have no negative priming. Sentence 4 might seem to be a second exception to this claim in that it retains as part of Theme the Theme-avoiding *the most intense*, but the effect of this is overridden by the movement of *For many* to sentence-initial position, since the phrase *for many*, (the comma is important) is strongly primed for occurrence in Theme. Excluding cases of *for many, many* (as in *for many, many years*) 38 per cent of cases of *for many* followed by a punctuation mark (i.e. , ; and .) occur sentence-initially, and a further 16 per cent occur clause-initially. The point I am making is of course that even where the Themes are constructed out of lexis with a positive priming for Theme, the passage in which these Themes occur will still feel odd if there is no thematic progression.

There is nothing wrong with the vocabulary or syntax of Extract (4), and any student who produced it would be entitled to some praise. But it does not function effectively as a text because the Themes, the starting points, of each of the sentences are ill-chosen or unmotivated. Quite often when a student's text seems awkward, it is the discontinuity of the Themes with the previous text that is partly to blame. Consider the following passage from one of my students:[1]

(5) [1] Teachers need to adjust their own talk intuitively to come within the capabilities of the particular child they are addressing, and to try to encourage a response from the child, using whatever means they can, in the form of gestures, facial expressions, articulating more carefully and careful selection of tone of voice. [2] It is the child's social and cognitive development that draws him/her into interaction with others. [3] And it is through interaction of this kind [sic] that will help the teacher to determine when each child is ready to take another step forward. [4] This

approach requires great sensitivity on the part of the teacher, [4a] and the child's attempts at communication should be rewarded with obvious pleasure, something that is lacking in the classrooms I visited.

The first thing to note about this passage is that this student has mastered the relationship between Theme and appropriate lexis. Each of her Themes is in conformity with our typical priming expectations. But her mastery is sentence-level only. Her Themes are lexically appropriate but textually inappropriate. If we analyse the passage in terms of Theme and Rheme, we have a very different picture (Table 8.2) from that noted for the original Wigmore Hall passage. (I should note here that Sentences 2 and 3 pose issues for Theme-Rheme that I am cavalierly ignoring.)

Two things stand out in the analysis as compared with the original analysis for the 'Wigmore Hall' passage (Table 8.1). First, notice how simple the Themes are. These sentences do not for the most part have a precise

Table 8.2 A Theme and Rheme analysis of a short extract from a piece of student's writing

Theme	Rheme
[1] Teachers	need to adjust their own talk intuitively to come within the capabilities of the particular child they are addressing, and to try to encourage a response from the child, using whatever means they can, in the form of gestures, facial expressions, articulating more carefully and careful selection of tone of voice.
[2] It	is the child's social and cognitive development that draws him/her into interaction with others.
[3] And it	is through interaction of this kind that will help the teacher to determine when each child is ready to take another step forward.
[4] This approach	requires great sensitivity on the part of the teacher,
[4a] and the child's attempts at communication	should be rewarded with obvious pleasure, something that is lacking in the classrooms I visited.

starting point. Second, their Themes, such as they are, do not link back in any clear way to earlier material in the passage. It is not entirely apparent what is intended by *this approach* and there has been no direct reference to *the child's attempt at communication*; the teacher's attempts have been in focus rather than the child's.

Now consider this rewritten version (Extract 6). I have altered the wording of the sentences as little as possible, so some infelicities remain. I have also reversed the order of the first two sentences. I have of course also ensured that my replacement Themes continue to make use of lexis that is positively (or at least not negatively) primed for being thematised.

(6)   [2] The teacher's ability to draw a child into interaction with others will be dependent on the latter's social and cognitive development. [1] Teachers need to adjust their own talk intuitively to come within the capabilities of the particular child they are addressing, and to try to encourage a response from the child, using whatever means they can, in the form of gestures, facial expressions, articulating more carefully and careful selection of tone of voice. [3] Through interaction of this kind the teacher will be helped to determine when each child is ready to take another step forward. [4] This approach however requires great sensitivity on the part of the teacher, [4a] and s/he should reward the child's attempts at communication with obvious pleasure, something that is lacking in the classrooms I visited.

An analysis of the revised version is given in Table 8.3.

Table 8.3 A Theme-Rheme analysis of the rewritten version of the student extract

Theme	Rheme
[2] The teacher's ability to draw a child into interaction with others	will be dependent on the latter's social and cognitive development.
[1] Teachers	need to adjust their own talk intuitively to come within the capabilities of the particular child they addressing, and to try to encourage a response from the child, using whatever means they can, in the form of gestures, facial expressions, articulating more carefully and careful selection of tone of voice.
[3[Through interaction of this kind the teacher	will be helped to determine when each child is ready to take another step forward.
[4] This approach however	requires great sensitivity on the part of the teacher,
[4a] and s/he	should reward the child's attempts at communication with obvious pleasure, something that is lacking in the classrooms I visited.

I leave you to judge whether the rewritten version is an improvement. The analysis shows that the Themes of the rewritten version are slightly longer and connect much more clearly with the immediate context. The reader of this version knows at the beginning of each sentence where the writer is coming from (in both the literal and idiomatic sense of that phrase). Word processors are a mixed blessing in that they allow writers to reorder or paste extra material into their text which may result in disjointedness if care is not taken to stitch the new or reordered material into the existing fabric of the text. Certainly writers can benefit from being advised to watch out for such disjointedness as it manifests itself in Themes that drop into the text from nowhere. As I said earlier, though, Themes are not required to link back and a learner writer needs to know that a sentence may begin with an entirely new Theme without being inappropriate. (See the sentence in the middle of this paragraph beginning *Word processors*.) Similarly, a sentence may use a Theme that makes use of lexis that characteristically avoids being thematised. It would, though, probably be unwise to do both at the same time.

8.4 Text as interaction

In the rewriting of my student's passage, I did not confine myself to reordering the words in the sentences; I also reordered the sentences themselves. My reasons for doing so are connected with the need for relevance referred to in section 2. Text linguistics lays great emphasis on the fact that writing is interactive and that the resultant text is not a product but a means whereby a reader can perform his or her part of the interaction. More specifically, every sentence a writer produces can be seen as an answer to a question that the reader may want answered. A sentence that seems to answer no question that the reader had in mind may be deemed irrelevant by that reader (though not necessarily, of course, by all readers), or at very least irrelevant for that reader's purposes.

The skilled writer is one who accurately anticipates the questions his or her readers will want answered and the order in which they will want them answered without compromising what s/he wants to say. This is of course a tall order, and there are some circumstances in which it becomes literally impossible, given space constraints. Thus a nuclear physicist wanting to communicate the latest work on sub-particle physics to a readership of sixth-form arts students will both have to compromise his/her message and leave important questions unanswered. All writing is to some degree a compromise of this kind, and it need not be so because of any difference of knowledge level or intelligence between writer and readers. It is sufficient that the reader's purpose may not require all that the writer is capable of offering. In my discussion of Theme above, for example, I seriously simplified my account of Theme and Rheme and the intellectual controversies that exist about the extent of Theme *vis-à-vis* Rheme, because I recognised that such an account would distract from the main argument of this chapter.

The traditional view of the relationship between writer and reader places the reader in subordinate position and assumes that the reading process is one of careful reconstruction of the writer's message, the purpose of the reader being in some sense subordinate to that of the writer. Such a view of their relationship is seriously misleading and derives, I suspect, from the Romantic tradition with its emphasis on the individual's self-expression. It may be appropriate as a description of the writer-reader relationship that pertains for literary writing, but relatively few of those needing help with their writing skills have literary aspirations. For all other kinds of writing, the relationship is better seen as one in which the reader has a purpose or set of purposes in reading and the writer's task is to allow those purposes to be fulfilled. In such a conception of the writer-reader relationship, the writer may be seen as being in some respects subordinate. Certainly a good writer is amongst other things one who begins by identifying accurately the likely purpose a reader will have in reading it.

The need of the writer to make his or her text relevant to the reader's purposes manifests itself in several ways. First, it will be reflected in the style of language adopted. The nuclear physicist writing for sixth-formers is likely to adopt an altogether different style from that s/he would adopt in writing an academic paper. This is not just a matter of technical vocabulary, though that certainly is a part, but also of grammatical and textual structure. Second, it will be reflected in the sequencing of the information in the emergent text. Certain pieces of information will not have their proper significance if told too early; other pieces may be unintelligible or open to misinterpretation if placed too early. I do not intend to say anything about the way style is affected by the needs and purposes of the reader but I want to say a little about the interactivity of text.

Winter (1969, 1982) was amongst the first to note that every sentence a writer produces can be seen as answering a question that has arisen as a result either of the preceding text or of the context and purpose of the text. Consider again Extract (1). It can be projected into dialogue as follows:

(7) Writer: [1] The words Wigmore Hall conjure up a very particular musical utopia.

Reader: What is the nature of this very particular musical utopia?

Writer: [2] In a city where only the gargantuan galleries of the Royal Albert Hall connect us to Victorian times, this little concert venue provides London with a last link to 19th-century Europe, and with a way of life that disappeared with the world wars.

Reader: In what way does it provide a link with 19th century Europe?

Writer: [3] Only at Wigmore Hall, perhaps at a Lieder recital, do you encounter still the whiff of old Vienna, or the dry, sophisticated perfume of Paris, when the music of Poulenc, who was a Wigmore Hall devotee, is aired once again.

Reader: What is the experience of such a recital like?

Writer: [4] For many, the experience of a Wigmore Hall recital is the most intense, essential way of encountering music:

Reader: Why should that be?

Writer: [4a] the intimate space and heavenly acoustics make possible a meeting of minds between audience, artist and composer impossible elsewhere.

Reader: If they link us with 19th century Vienna and Paris, aren't the concerts old-fashioned?

Writer: [5] These enchanting evenings of chamber music, attended often by the elderly, many of whom have supported the Hall since coming to London as refugees, are far from museum pieces.

Reader: Why not?

Writer: [6] Listening to the performances on our Centenary cover CD, it is the current vitality of music making that strikes home.

I hope you will agree that there is nothing particularly strained about this projected dialogue, though clearly it is not the only possible such projection and it is not being suggested that all readers formulate, still less articulate, questions as they read. Now compare this with a projected dialogue for the original version of my student's piece of writing:

(8) Writer: [1] Teachers need to adjust their own talk intuitively to come within the capabilities of the particular child they are addressing, and to try to encourage a response from the child, using whatever means they can, in the form of gestures, facial expressions, articulating more carefully and careful selection of tone of voice.

Reader: What draws a child into interaction with others?

Writer: [2] It is the child's social and cognitive development that draws him/her into interaction with others.

Reader: What will be the effect of interaction of this kind?

Writer: [3] It is through interaction of this kind [*sic*] that will help the teacher to determine when each child is ready to take another step forward.

Reader: What must the teacher have if s/he is to use this approach?

Writer: [4] This approach requires great sensitivity on the part of the teacher,

Reader: What form should this sensitivity take?

Writer: [4a] the child's attempts at communication should be rewarded with obvious pleasure, something that is lacking in the classrooms I visited.

I have indicated with dotted lines those places where the following sentence can apparently be elicited by asking a question that does not seem to follow from the previous sentence(s). Thus there is no apparent reason why a reader should suddenly wonder what draws a child into interaction with others when the topic of the previous sentence is the teacher and his/her actions; this is particularly so as the first sentence has indirectly answered the question (*gestures, facial expressions*, etc.). There is no dotted line between Sentence 2 and the question that follows, but there probably should be, since the most natural antecedent for *interaction of this kind* would be the interaction provoked by the teacher in Sentence 1 rather than the generalised *interaction* referred to in Sentence 2. Certainly *this approach* has no natural antecedent unless we interpret *interaction of this kind* as referring to the teacher's attempts at interaction with the child. It is possible for a question to draw on an earlier part of the text – this happens in the projected dialogue for the Wigmore Hall passage with the question that elicits Sentence 5 – but it is only possible if intervening sentences have been about something different. Here not only has the writer never left the topic of child interaction but her use of *this* with *approach* signals an immediate antecedent in the text when the only possible antecedent is not immediate. The only place where question and answer follow each other naturally is between 4 and 4a, which the writer punctuated as a single orthographic sentence.

Now consider how the rewritten version, given as Extract (6) above, projects into dialogue:

(9)   Writer: [2] The teacher's ability to draw a child into interaction with others will be dependent on the latter's social and cognitive development.

Reader: What does the teacher need to do to draw a child into interaction with others?

Writer: [1] Teachers need to adjust their own talk intuitively to come within the capabilities of the particular child they are addressing, and to try to encourage a response from the child, using whatever means they can, in the form of gestures, facial expressions, articulating more carefully and careful selection of tone of voice.

Reader: What will the teacher learn from doing this?

Writer: [3] Through interaction of this kind the teacher will be helped to determine when each child is ready to take another step forward.

Reader: What must the teacher have if s/he is to use this approach?

Writer: [4] This approach however requires great sensitivity on the part of the teacher;

Reader: What form should this sensitivity take?

Writer: [4a] the child's attempts at communication should be rewarded with obvious pleasure, something that is lacking in the classrooms I visited.

There is still much that might be changed, but the text now is capable of a natural projection into dialogue like that used for Extract (1) (the Wigmore Hall text). I suggest that often when a text gets confused or obscure it is because the writer has become more concerned with the need to get a key point in (or show off some hard-earned knowledge) than with the needs of the reader and the connectedness of the text as it develops. One strategy for showing a student where s/he has apparently gone wrong is to ask him or her what question s/he thinks she is answering at this point in the text and why this particular position has been chosen. As we saw with the 'child interaction' passage, sometimes it takes only minor rewriting to make a passage conform to both normal Theme practice and the interactive needs of a putative reader.

Two footnotes to this discussion. The first is that the biggest problem most students face is that there is no natural reader for their texts. They are writing for lecturers who have no needs to be met, no purposes that need to be fulfilled, except that of assessing the writers! The more natural we can make the writing task, the more real the readership is, the more likely it is that our students will see the point of formulating each sentence with awareness of its place in the developing text and of answering a reader's questions in the order the reader would want them answered. The second footnote is a simple one. The linguistic features I have been drawing attention to do not have the status of grammatical rules. Place must always be found for creative deviation from the norm. Looking at text in terms of Theme-Rheme, identifying the lexis associated with Theme and projecting the text into dialogue may indeed help a writer shake off the shackles of incoherence and lack of focus or direction. But the person who had shackles removed might justly be dispirited if s/he then found s/he was being measured up for a straitjacket ...

Notes

1. The student in question is academically advanced. Her text has been chosen not because she is a poor writer but because she indicates the kind of weakness that can occur even in a good writer.

References

Berry, M. (1996). What is Theme? A(nother) personal view. In *Meaning and Form: Systemic Functional Interpretations*, R. Fawcett, M. Berry, C. Butler and G. W. Huang (eds.), 1–64. Norwood, NJ: Ablex.

Daneš, F. (1974). Functional sentence perspective and the organisation of the text. In *Papers on Functional Sentence Perspective*, F. Daneš (ed.), 106–28. The Hague: Mouton.

Davies, F. (1997). Marked theme as a heuristic for analysing text-type, text and genre. In *Applied Languages: Theory and Practice in ESP*, J. Piqué and D. J. Viera (eds), 45–79. Valencia: Universitat de Valencia.

Halliday, M. A. K. (1985). *An Introduction to Functional Grammar*, London: Edward Arnold.

Hoey, M. (2001). *Textual Interaction: An Introduction to Written Discourse Analysis*. London: Routledge.

Hoey, M. (2005). *Lexical Priming: A New Theory of Words and Language*. London: Routledge.

Ndahiro, A. (1998). Theme, rheme, given and new in written discourse: evidence from annual business reports. Unpublished PhD thesis, University of Liverpool.

Winter, E. O. (1969). Grammatical question technique as a way of teaching science students to write progress reports: the use of the short text in teaching (mimeo). University of Trondheim.

Winter, E. O. (1982). *Towards a Contextual Grammar of English* London: George Allen & Unwin.

9 | Multimodal layout in school history books: the texturing of historical interpretation

Caroline Coffin and Beverly Derewianka
Open University and University of Wollongong

9.1 Introduction

Over the past few decades, the texture of school textbooks has changed from 'the densely printed page' (Kress 2004) to a complex interplay of multimodal elements. This has implications for how a reader accesses curricular content. In this chapter, we will investigate the multimodal layout of history textbooks. Our aim is to show the significance of multimodal texturing in making available to the reader particular 'reading pathways'. We argue that these pathways have implications for how historical information and perspectives are negotiated and made sense of.[1]

9.1.1 History in Schooling

The representation of curricular knowledge in textbooks is, in part, a reflection of the nature of the school subject as a knowledge system – how it manages and produces knowledge. Freebody *et al.* (2004, p. 20) draw a distinction between 'stipulative' knowledge systems such as the sciences, with their convergent solutions and well-defined parameters, and 'open-textured' systems such as history, with potentially multiple solutions. As Jenkins asserts, historical knowledge is always open to interpretation and re-interpretation depending on one's cultural/ ideological context, biases and agenda:

> The sifting out of that which is historically significant depends on us, so that what 'the past' means to us is always our task to 'figure out'; what we want our inheritance/history 'to be' is always waiting to be 'read' and written in the future like any other text: the past as history lies before us, not behind us. (Jenkins, 2003, p. 30)

It is, however, only in the last 40 years or so that history within secondary schooling has gradually shifted from being presented as a neutral subject founded on an immutable body of facts to a curriculum area in which students are actively encouraged to view the past as contested ground. That is, up until the 1970s, school history tended to be driven by a set of stable, chronological accounts of the past – the 'grand narratives' of nations, governments and international conflicts. However, since then, at least within the UK and Australia, there has been an increasing focus on the examination of different perspectives on events, and a recognition that history (even for school students) should be understood as a process of interpretation and reinterpretation. For this reason, history textbooks now include various types of documentary evidence such as personal letters, news reports, posters, maps, legal documents and cartoons.[2] Students are expected to interrogate, evaluate and draw on these sources in order to carry out a 'historical enquiry' and produce their own interpretation of past events. (See Coffin, 2006, for further discussion.)

This objective is illustrated in the following curriculum statement from the UK:

> Pupils should be taught to:
> a. identify, select and use a range of appropriate sources of information including oral accounts, documents, printed sources, the media, artefacts, pictures, photographs, music, museums, buildings and sites, and ICT-based sources as a basis for independent historical enquiries
> b. evaluate the sources used, select and record information relevant to the enquiry and reach conclusions. (National Curriculum Key Stage 3)

This is not to say that in the past history was always taught by all teachers as a factual record of events. Indeed, Osborne (2003) demonstrates how, even in the late nineteenth century and early 1900s, the use of primary sources was deemed by some teachers as central to students understanding the historical process. Sources served to open their eyes to 'the meaning of proof in history, to create an attitude of healthy scepticism and to put into their hands an instrument for getting at the truth' (Fling 1909 p. 207, quoted in Osborne 2003 p.5). While in the past, primary sources were often made available as collections separate to the textbook, today they are integrated into the body of the textbooks to the point where they often occupy a central rather than complementary or peripheral role. They are at the core of students' study rather than simply being an adjunct.

This shift is illustrated in Figure 9.1 which is a double page spread with a typical contemporary layout taken from the opening chapter of a UK text book, *GCSE Modern World History*.[3] The chapter is concerned with the causes of the First World War.

9.1.2 The contemporary history textbook

Modern history textbooks for secondary school students are characterised not only by the inclusion of multiple and varied original sources, but by the proliferation of other visual and verbal elements. Figure 9.1, for example, exemplifies how different types of charts, headings and fonts and prompt questions (e.g. *How did Germany react to Britain's concerns?*) are deployed. Colour is also an important element of these pages (though, unfortunately, this is not obvious in the black and white reproduction presented here). This trend in deploying multiple semiotic modes in history text books has many parallels with the construal of historical content in electronic hypermedia. Figure 9.2 represents a typical 'page' from a history website. The focus is World War I.

Figure 9.2 demonstrates how, typically, in a hypermedia environment, the reader is presented with a vast array of choices: links to examples of primary sources; references materials; various kinds of images and photos; animated maps of battle lines; video clips and audiofiles (e.g. interviews with veterans); projects and interactive tasks; links to other sites; links within the body of the text to additional information; and opportunities for both synchronous and asynchronous discussions.

In a hypermedia environment, a reader is invited to play a relatively active and determining role in the construction of meaning (Armani *et al.* 2002). This contrasts with the reading experience associated with traditional history textbooks and the traditional 'grand narratives' mentioned earlier. In these reading contexts, because the content is more strongly framed by the author, the reader is generally compelled to access the information in a linear fashion: as the text unfolds, the thematic choices regulate the flow of information in a particular way, typically guiding the reader towards a predetermined interpretation of past events.

It can be argued that the multimodal textbook chapter has the characteristics of both the traditional chapter and the hypermedia experience. Like the traditional chapter, it is constrained by the physical page, provoking, to some extent, a sequential reading path. However, the linearity of the densely printed page is disrupted by a variety of multimodal elements, resulting in a compositional organisation more akin to the hypermedia text. In the hypermedia ecology, such elements are generally

FOCUS TASK

1 Draw up a chart like this:

	Germany	Austria–Hungary	Italy
Britain			
France			
Russia			

2 Using the descriptions of the relationships between these countries on pages 5 and 6, complete the chart to show causes of tension between the countries. You may not be able to fill in all the spaces.
3 Which relationship is the greatest source of tension?
4 Explain how each of the following contributed to tensions between the European powers:
   a) colonies   b) people wanting independence   c) arms build-up.

2 Study the statistics in Source 8. Which country do you think is the strongest? Explain your choice.
3 Which alliance do you think is the strongest? Explain your choice.

SOURCE 8

		Britain	France	Russia	Germany	Austria–Hungary	Italy
Population (millions)		46	40	167	65	50	35
Steel production (millions of tons)		7.9	4	4	17	2.6	3.9
Merchant ships (millions of tons)		20	2	0.75	5	3	1.75
Foreign trade (£ million per year)		1	0.4	0.2	1	0.2	n/a
Number of soldiers available (in thousands), including reserve forces		711	1250	1200	2200	810	750
Warships (including under construction)		122	46	26	85	24	36
Submarines		64	73	29	23	6	12

Resources of the Great Powers in 1914.

The Balance of Power

Politicians at the time called this system of alliances the 'Balance of Power'. They believed that the size and power of the two alliances would prevent either side from starting a war.

SOURCE 9

4 Look at Source 9. Did the cartoonist think that the alliances helped to prevent war?
5 Do you think that the alliances made war more likely or less likely?

A modern redrawing of an American cartoon published in the *Brooklyn Eagle*, July 1914. The cartoon was called 'The Chain of Friendship'.

7

Figure 9.1 GCSE Modern World History

SOURCE 10

There is no comparison between the importance of the German navy to Germany, and the importance of our navy to us. Our navy is to us what their army is to them. To have a strong navy would increase Germany's prestige and influence, but it is not a matter of life and death to them as it is to us.

Sir Edward Grey, British Foreign Secretary, in a speech to Parliament in 1909.

SOURCE 11

You English are like mad bulls, you see red everywhere! What on earth has come over you, that you should heap on such suspicion? What can I do more? I have always stood up as a friend of England.

Kaiser Wilhelm, speaking in an interview with the *Daily Telegraph* in 1908. The Kaiser liked England and had friends there. He was a cousin of King George V of Britain.

The tension builds, 1900–1914

Anglo-German naval rivalry

One of the most significant causes of tension in Europe was the naval rivalry which developed after 1900. Ever since the Battle of Trafalgar in 1805, Britain had ruled the seas without any challenge. Its navy was the most powerful in the world. This situation began to change in 1898 when the new Kaiser, Wilhelm, announced his intention to build a powerful German navy.

Britain felt very threatened by this. Germany's navy was much smaller than Britain's but the British navy was spread all over the world, protecting the British Empire. Germany didn't have much of an empire. Why did it need a navy? What was Germany going to do with all of these warships concentrated in the North Sea?

Not surprisingly, Germany did not see things the same way. The Kaiser and his admirals felt that Germany needed a navy to protect its growing trade. They felt that the British were over-reacting to the German naval plans.

Britain was not convinced by what the Germans said. In fact, in 1906 Britain raised the stakes in the naval race by launching HMS *Dreadnought*, the first of a new class of warships. Germany responded by building its own 'Dreadnoughts'. The naval race was well and truly on and both Britain and Germany spent millions on their new ships.

SOURCE 12

Guns on rotating turrets can fire shells over 9 km in any direction

Fast modern turbine engines

Thick armour plating

A British 'Dreadnought', the HMS *Barham*, with the British fleet in Scapa Flow.

SOURCE 13

1906						
1907						
1908						
1909						
1910						
1911						
1912						
1913						
1914						

Britain — Total built by 1914: 29   Germany — Total built by 1914: 17

Number of 'Dreadnoughts' built by Britain and Germany, 1906–14.

1 Why was Britain concerned by Germany's naval plans?
2 How did Germany react to Britain's concerns?
3 Do you think that either country was acting unreasonably? Give your reasons.

8

Figure 9.1b

hidden in an invisible network-like structure, requiring the reader to make deliberate decisions in forging pathways, whereas, in the multimodal textbook chapter, all the elements are immediately available and fixed on the page in a particular configuration. This prompts the question – to what extent does the multimodal layout of history textbooks make available or constrain particular reading pathways?

It is commonly asserted that contemporary textbooks do not, in fact, set out to establish a reading path for the students. Kress (2004), for example,

Figure 9.2 A 'page' from a history website.

claims that in the traditional textbook, which represented a 'body of knowledge', the reader's task was to attempt to follow the pre-given ordering of the written text whereas in contemporary textbooks their task is 'to perform different semiotic work, namely to design the order of the text for themselves' (p. 4). According to this view, the textbook writer is the designer of an assemblage of materials, with the multimodal page presenting to the reader multiple entry points and hence multiple pathways.

Barthes (1972), in contrast, does not see the multimodal text as a 'free for all' where the reader's interest reigns supreme. He distinguishes between a 'relay' relationship between visual and verbal, where the text and image stand in a complementary relationship and the message is realised at a higher level, and an 'anchorage' relationship where the text directs the reader through the signifieds of the image/s towards a meaning chosen in advance. Similarly, Lemke (2003) proposes that the reading experience is influenced by what he refers to as multi-cursal parallelism, or functional meaning relations among elements that may constrain the sequence of viewing and interpreting even though they do not strictly sequence them.

The question of reading pathways being author or reader controlled connects to a more general issue concerning the effect that multimodal design has on coherence and readability. A recent detailed review of history textbooks in the USA, for example, found that they 'have abandoned narrative for a broken format of competing instructional activities' (Sewall 2004, p. 14) in an effort to avoid what editors perceive as 'text-heavy', 'information-loaded' and 'fact-based' content. In the competition for space between the visual and the verbal, Sewall argues that the verbal is reduced and compressed to the point where it becomes 'so telegraphic and so general as to make no sense' (p. 14), leaving teachers and students alike baffled and confused.

> Textbooks across the curriculum are being transformed into picture and activity books instead of clear, portable, simply designed, text-centred primers. Bright photographs, broken formats, and seductive colors overwhelm the text and confuse the page. Typeface is larger and looser, resulting in many fewer words and much more white space. The text disappears or gets lost. What text remains is dense and often unintelligible. (Sewall 2004, p.14)

Horn (1999), on the other hand, asserts that multimodal ensembles involve the co-deployment of multiple semiotic modes in such a way that they create a 'unified communication unit'. This is achieved through the tight coupling of words, images, and shapes:

> 'Tight coupling' means that you cannot remove the words or the images or the shapes from a piece of visual language without destroying or radically diminishing the meaning a reader can obtain from it. (Horn 1999, p. 27)

At the start of our investigation into the multimodal texturing of contemporary history text books, we formed the impression (in line with Sewall's findings) that they frequently contain a somewhat haphazard collage of disparate items. As readers from another generation, we felt disoriented, even after several attempts at trying to detect underlying organisational principles. We wondered how students would make sense of these texts. We felt that, rather than there being a coherent, privileged reading pathway achieved through tight coupling (as Horn suggests), reading this type of text book was more a matter of randomly dipping in and out of various components somewhat chaotically brought together.

In order to explore rather more systematically what kinds of texturing occur in history text books we therefore decided to conduct a comprehensive analysis of the various verbal and visual elements which regularly occur in multimodal layouts. In the following sections, we report on the analysis of one particular chapter from a secondary school history text book (the text book from which the extract in Figure 9.1 is taken) as a means of highlighting some of the key issues which have emerged in our studies of multimodal texturing. First, however, we introduce our tools of analysis.

9.2 A framework for the analysis of textbooks

In analysing multimodal texts, it would be possible to consider the construction of representational/ideational, interactive/interpersonal and compositional/textual meanings (see Kress and van Leeuwen 1996 for further details). Here we are interested only in the compositional/textual. At the same time, we are aware of the implications that the textual has – both for the interpersonal positioning of the reader and the (ideological) representation of the past. We made this point at the beginning of the chapter when we said that pathways have implications for how historical information and perspectives are negotiated and made sense of.

Within the textual, it is possible to look at the following features:

• the internal composition of each element or figure

- how the elements are positioned in the unfolding text

- the relationship between a visual element and its immediate verbal context

- how all the visual and verbal elements cohere to form an integrated macrotext.

Our focus is on the macrotext – what Royce (2002) refers to as 'intersemiotic complementarity', by which images and written language work in concert on the page. It is through the analysis of how the multimodal elements cohere across the page/s that we can investigate the extent to which particular reading paths are offered or constrained.

In analysing the composition of the macrotext, we will be examining in particular how compositional resources can function to integrate certain discourses. Building on Christie's analysis of classroom pedagogic discourse (Christie 2002), we have identified two overarching types of text book discourse or registers each with their own distinct pedagogic function. We refer to these as the 'regulative' and 'instructional'. Regulative discourse serves to set up the pedagogic goals and directions of a text book, chapter or section of a chapter. In the sample pages in Figure 9.1, examples would include the prompt questions such as: *2 Study the statistics in Source 8. Which country do you think is the strongest? Explain your choice.* Aside from the use of imperatives (*study, explain*) and interrogatives (*which country do you think is the strongest?*) to direct students' enquiry and processes of reasoning, regulative discourse uses explicit organising and ordering devices to guide the sequencing and pacing of students' investigation and learning. Such devices include the numbering of questions, sources (i.e. *2*, and *Source 8* in the example above) and steps in a task. Likewise, the use of font size in headings and subheadings layers and orders the hierarchy of information. In this way regulative discourse converges and fuses with (or in Christie's terms 'speaks through' and 'projects') the 'instructional' discourse which constitutes the core (i.e. historical) content of the chapter. In history text books the content provides, in line with curriculum objectives, alternative perspectives on past events. In the sample pages in Figure 9.1, instructional discourse includes the various sources, the authorial texts and the task content.

The main analytical tools we will draw on to examine the composition of the macro text will be those of information value, framing and salience, tools which have been developed by van Leeuwen and Kress (e.g. 1996). We would argue that such tools can provide the analyst with particularly powerful insights into the way in which composition and layout 'manage' and orchestrate the interaction between regulative and instructional discourse, as well as the degree to which the various elements of a multimodal text are brought together into a coherent whole. In turn, this enables the analyst to see how particular reading pathways are enhanced or constrained (and so position the target reader). Each of the analytical tools is introduced below.

9.2.1 Information value

Information value is concerned with where elements are placed. For example, where they are located on the horizontal axis (left to right) and on the vertical axis (top to bottom). Within (western) visual images and layouts, Kress and van Leeuwen (1996) contend that the left hand side tends to consist of items which are familiar and self-evident (and therefore referred to as 'given') whereas the right hand side is often used to display information that is problematic, contestable, at issue and needing special attention (referred to as 'new'). In relation to top and bottom zones, it is proposed that the informational values of 'ideal' and 'real' are attached. Ideal refers to the generalised, the essence of something (such as in advertisements the image of a perfect man or woman) whereas real refers to the specific or instance (such as a specific beauty product used by the ideal man/woman). Centre-margin arrangements are a further dimension of placement and information value but, given their absence in the text book data we have examined so far, they will not be a focus of our discussion in this chapter.

9.2.2 Framing

Framing refers to how the parts of a picture or layout are connected, disconnected or (through an absence of framing) are 'continuous'. Elements may be strongly or weakly framed so that they either stand out as distinct elements or blend into their surroundings. The more the elements of the multimodal text are connected, the more they are presented as one unit of information, as belonging together. Framing devices are many and varied. They include:

- frame lines (with different degrees of thickness contributing to stronger or weaker framing)

- empty space between elements

- discontinuities of colour or shape (e.g. transitions from one colour to another)

- vectors (for example, a photo may be tilted in a particular direction or there may be a repetition of colours or shapes).

9.2.3 Salience

Salience is concerned with the way in which elements are more or less emphasised and thus attract more or less attention. The concept accounts for why certain elements in a text layout may be more eye-catching and viewed as more important. Devices for achieving different degrees of salience or prominence include:

- placement in the visual field (e.g. top or bottom, centre or marginal)
- sharpness of focus
- degrees of light
- size
- contrast (tonal, colour, shading, saturation)
- perspective (foreground, background)
- use and size of font, use of italics, bold etc.

9.3 Analysis

9.3.1 Multimodal layout in a history text book

In this section we look in detail at the multimodal layout of the opening chapter in *Modern World History* (Walsh, 2001), from which we took the sample pages shown in Figure 9.1. We selected this particular text book both because of its representativeness with regard to the mix of authorial text and sources and because of its popularity in the UK – it is deemed (on the back cover) as 'the leading textbook for GCSE Modern World History courses'. The opening chapter which is concerned with the causes of the First World War is typical of the book as a whole – both in terms of the design and layout and in the use of different textual and visual elements. Subsequent chapters follow similar patterns in the mix of elements and their positioning, framing and salience.

The notion of 'regulative' and 'instructional' discourse provides a useful way of examining the degree to which a reading path appears to be set up by the text book author. We found that regulative discourse is consistently used to project and thus manage instructional discourse (the historical content) in a range of ways.

Regulative discourse

In this textbook chapter the regulative discourse includes:

- Focus text (this is not represented on the sample pages in Figure 9.1 but serves as an overall preview at the start of each chapter to guide the purpose of students' investigation e.g. telling students what they will find out, what they will investigate and the questions they will answer)

- Focus Tasks (in the sample pages, students are asked to create a chart to show tensions across the Triple Alliance)

- Prompts (students are directed to study a specified source or to pull together information from a variety of sources)

- Activities (these are not represented in the sample pages but typically include instructions to create diagrams or charts)

- Question numbers (as illustrated in the sample pages in Figure 9.1)

- Source number labels (8–13 in the sample pages in Figure 9.1)

- Headings and subheadings – ordering the hierarchy of information concerning the topic under discussion (e.g. 'The tension builds'; '1900–1914 Anglo-German rivalry')

Instructional discourse

Aside from that which is projected through the regulative discourse (see list above), the instructional discourse consists of the text and visual images produced by the text book writer (hereafter referred to as authorial text) and the primary and secondary sources. In Figure 9.1, the sample pages include the first four elements listed in bold below. The other types of authorial contributions and source material listed are used in the remainder of the book:

- **Tables of statistics (e.g. in the sample pages, Source 8 compares the resources of the Great Powers in 1914)**

- **Cartoons – both authentic and contemporary (in Figure 9.1, source 9 is a modern redrawing of an American cartoon)**

- **Photos (such as the British 'Dreadnought' in Figure 9.1)**

- **Extracts from speeches and written documents, letters, diaries etc. (sources 10 and 11 are both examples of speeches)**

- Maps

- Graphs

- Diagrams (e.g. a cross-section of a trench, weapons and equipment used)

- Paintings

- Poems

- Illustration and sketches

- Advertisements

- Posters

- Handbills

- Postcards

- Leaflets

- Murals

- Comic strips

- Film stills

- Flow charts

- Biographical profiles

- Time lines

- Banknotes

At the 'macro' level, the regulative operates in at least two ways to establish what appears to be a reading path through the chapter.

First, in identifying the overall structuring of the core instructional content of the chapter, we can single out the sequence of headings and subheadings (see Figure 9.3). The salience provided by the relative sizes and fonts helps to provide a regulative guide through the content, and as we shall discuss further on, constrain students' interpretation of the causes of the War.

Put starkly like this, with no intervening multimodal distractions, the organising principles of the content are clear. In the actual chapter, however, it is somewhat difficult to discern the macroflow of information as signalled by these headings. As can easily be seen by looking at Figure 9.1, the logical

---

The causes of the First World War
Murder in Sarajevo
The Alliances
The Central Powers or the Triple Alliance
Germany
Austria-Hungary
Italy
The Triple Entente
Britain
France
Russia
The Balance of Power
The tension builds, 1900-1914
Anglo-German naval rivalry
The arms race on land
Plans for war
Germany
Austria-Hungary
Russia
France
Britain
Morocco, 1905 and 1911
The Balkans: the spark that lit the bonfire
Did Germany cause the war?
The witnesses

Figure 9.3 Headings and sub-headings in the chapter

flow of the authorial text as established by the headings and subheadings is so disrupted by other elements as to be virtually invisible to the casual reader.

Second, we can look at how the more overtly regulative discourse (the focus tasks, activities and prompts) provide a scaffold for investigating the instructional content. Rather than students being left to their own devices to passively 'absorb' the content of the chapter (i.e. an explanation of the causes of the war), the author provides a purpose for reading by posing (in the opening section of the chapter) the question 'Who should bear the blame?'. This problematises the historical explanation and, by forcing the students to take up a position, shifts the text in the direction of an argument genre (see Coffin, 2004, 2006, for further discussion of historical explanation and historical argument and the pedagogic role and value of each). The question becomes the controlling idea for how the rest of the chapter should be read, generating a particular expectancy which is constantly reinforced throughout the chapter through the use of regulative discourse. The Focus element at the beginning of the chapter elaborates on the opening question ('you will make up your own mind about whether Germany caused the war or whether other countries should share the blame'). The Focus question is then reinforced at mid-point in the chapter (p. 7) and at the end of the chapter (pp. 12–13) with two Focus Tasks which require the students to revisit the surrounding text and consolidate their positions. At the local level, prompts in the margin ask the student to reflect on specific aspects of the issue. Armani *et al.* (2002) refer to this as a 'fil-rouge' map constructing the most economical, privileged pathway through the territory, evoking the implicit presence of the teacher.

As an illustration of the interaction between the regulative and the instructional discourse Figure 9.4 charts the provoked reading pathway in the two sample pages (from Figure 9.1). That is, the arrows show how students are directed to certain sources, instructed to answer certain questions and complete certain tasks. Similarly, the instructional content as constituted by the Headings is regulated through the choice of fonts: students are led to see 'tension' and 'Anglo-German naval rivalry' as salient factors. This level of 'guidance' is repeated throughout the chapter. For example, towards the end of the chapter (p. 11), students are referred back to page 2 and invited to reconsider their answer to question 2 below:

> Do you think that if the Archduke had not been shot, the war would not have started? Give your reasons. (These are only your first thoughts. You can revise your opinion later.)

As a result, it would appear that the interaction of the regulative and the instructional prescribes a relatively narrow pathway through the chapter with the likelihood that students will form a particular understanding of the causes of the First World War.

We will now move on to consider how information value, salience and framing contribute to (or detract from) progression along particular pathways.

Information value

The dominant pattern in terms of information value appears to be the 'left/right' axis. Each page is divided into two columns: a left-hand margin which takes up about a third of the page and the wider right hand column. The margin typically contains 'smaller' elements: prompts, photographs, biographies, cartoons, and so on. The right hand column contains the core authorial text as well as other elements such as sources, images and tasks.

It is difficult to discern a consistent 'given/new' organization corresponding to the left and right hand columns. Sources are found in both positions, as are various types of images. The only predictable pattern that the reader can rely on is the placement of prompts in the left hand

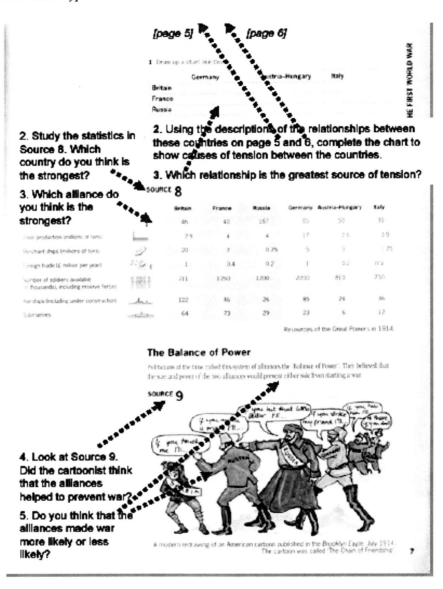

Figure 9.4 The interaction between the regulative and instructional

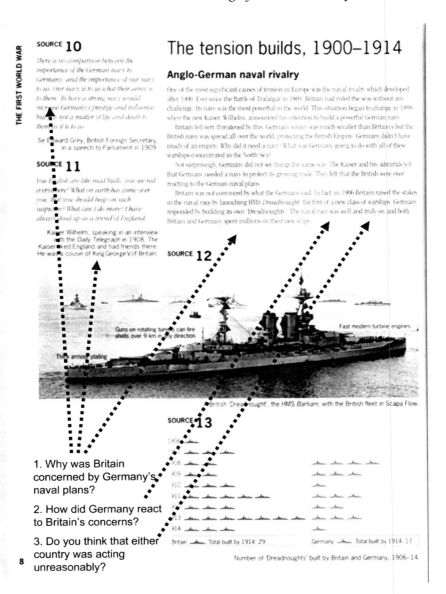

THE FIRST WORLD WAR

SOURCE **10**

There is no comparison between the importance of the German navy to Germany, and the importance of our navy to us. Our navy is to us what their army is to them. To have a strong navy would increase Germany's prestige and influence, but is not a matter of life and death to them as it is to us.

Sir Edward Grey, British Foreign Secretary, in a speech to Parliament in 1909

SOURCE **11**

You English are like mad bulls, you see red everywhere! What on earth has come over you, that you should heap on such suspicion? What can I do more? I have always stood up as a friend of England.

Kaiser Wilhelm, speaking in an interview with the *Daily Telegraph* in 1908. The Kaiser liked England and had friends there. He was a cousin of King George V of Britain.

The tension builds, 1900–1914

Anglo-German naval rivalry

One of the most significant causes of tension in Europe was the naval rivalry which developed after 1900. Ever since the Battle of Trafalgar in 1805, Britain had ruled the seas without any challenge. Its navy was the most powerful in the world. This situation began to change in 1898 when the new Kaiser, Wilhelm, announced his intention to build a powerful German navy.

Britain felt very threatened by this. Germany's navy was much smaller than Britain's but the British navy was spread all over the world, protecting the British Empire. Germany didn't have much of an empire. Why did it need a navy? What was Germany going to do with all of these warships concentrated in the North Sea?

Not surprisingly, Germany did not see things the same way. The Kaiser and his admirals felt that Germany needed a navy to protect its growing trade. They felt that the British were over-reacting to the German naval plans.

Britain was not convinced by what the Germans said. In fact, in 1906 Britain raised the stakes in the naval race by launching HMS *Dreadnought*, the first of a new class of warships. Germany responded by building its own 'Dreadnoughts'. The naval race was well and truly on and both Britain and Germany spent millions on their new ships.

SOURCE **12**

Guns on rotating turrets can fire shells over 9 km in any direction

Fast modern turbine engines

Thick armour plating

British 'Dreadnought', the HMS *Barham*, with the British fleet in Scapa Flow.

SOURCE **13**

1906
1908
1909
1910
1911
1912
1913
1914

Britain ▲ Total built by 1914: 29   Germany ▲ Total built by 1914: 17

Number of 'Dreadnoughts' built by Britain and Germany, 1906–14.

1. Why was Britain concerned by Germany's naval plans?

2. How did Germany react to Britain's concerns?

3. Do you think that either country was acting unreasonably?

8

Figure 9.4b

margin and the placement of core authorial text on the right hand side. In this way, the 'given' regulative marginal prompts can be seen as providing a context (e.g. purpose or focus for reading) for the 'new' instructional material on the right.

Framing

When considering the competition for page space, decisions need to be made regarding principles of intersemiotic compositional cooperation. What might need to be sacrificed to achieve compositional balance and flow? In the present case, for example, legibility is often a casualty, with the font size reduced in order to make space available for other elements (or for white space).

When we look at the degree to which the various elements are separated from each other (through, for example, the use of lines of discontinuity of colour), we notice no clear delineation between the left margin and main text. Elements from the right hand column often protrude into the left hand margin (for instance, the photo of the British 'dreadnought' or the key in Source 8). Perhaps most disorienting is the way in which the various elements in the right hand side merge with each other, interrupting in particular the flow of the core text. That is, the intervening elements which constantly disrupt the authorial text are not readily distinguished one from the other in terms of framing, so that the reader is constantly working to discern authorial text from source from activity etc.

It is not a complete mélange, however. Many of the elements are framed through shading/discontinuities of colour and are therefore boxed off one from the other. Focus questions, for example, are coloured in light orange, questions in light green, profiles in pale pink which disconnect them from the main black on white text which thus stands out as the dominant narrative.

Focus Tasks (as exemplified in the sample pages) are bounded by a thin coloured line, and Activities by a thin red line. This may give a subtle message to the reader that the pedagogic tasks are self-contained and cut off from the other elements.

Sources are marked off by lines above and below (as illustrated in Figure 9.1 with lines separating Source 10 and 11) but interestingly there are no lines separating them from the core authorial text (i.e. Anglo-German rivalry) to the right. Thus those placed in the margin are disconnected from each other but a little more linked to the main text. The absence of colour and black on white print in the display of sources also binds them more to the main text than the coloured focus and question boxes.

There is cohesion of design which helps separate the instructionally oriented discourse from the regulatively oriented discourse (e.g. green for questions, light orange for focus and focus tasks, black italics for sources). Elements are thus related by discourse type (i.e. instructional or regulative) though this does not necessarily mean that students will recognise the significance of such flagging.

Salience

As one might expect, the visual elements tend to be accorded much greater space relative to their content value than the verbal elements and are therefore more liable to attract attention. The cartoons and caricatures in particular are highly salient because of their colour (compared to the grey scale photos and the black and white text) and the degree of colour saturation as well as their 'attract' value – the promise (generally unfulfilled) of humour.

Of the verbal elements, most salient (and therefore likely to be read first) are those texts which are blocked and in colour and where the title is double underlined (e.g. the Focus Task in Figure 9.1). Elements with bulleted/starred text tend to stand out. Because the authorial text varies in terms of the size of the 'chunks' it often tends to lose its dominance as the main artery.

Combinations of verbal and visual draw attention to themselves when they are superimposed or there are stark contrasts (e.g. black and white boxes superimposed on a coloured map; a coloured image on a book cover (within a primary source) contrasting with the surrounding black and white verbal text). Least salient are elements such as the pale coloured Focus where 'focus' is in orange font on orange and therefore blends in and is lost. The visual salience of elements is sometimes at odds with their pedagogical salience. Prominent texts are not necessarily the most important in guiding students' learning/reading/interpretative pathway and size is not always an indication of pedagogical value. At the start of the chapter, for example, an overly large map of the route taken by Archduke Franz Ferdinand's car in Sarajevo overshadows the accompanying text which provides an all-too-brief timeline of critical events. On the other hand, elements that are important to the purpose of the chapter, such as Source 11 in Figure 9.1, but which are not visually salient, are at risk of being ignored and not integrated into the reading path. Kress (2003, p. 4) notes that making some elements salient (e.g. through size, colour, shape) and others less salient encourages a particular reading path. By the same token, increasing the salience of less relevant elements (such as Ferdinand's car route) can disrupt the reading path.

9.3.2 Language analysis

So far, we have drawn on the analytical tools of Information Value, Framing and Salience. To conclude the analysis, we would like to return to more traditional, language oriented tools of textual analysis as a means of extending the insights derived from the visually oriented analysis. These include the use of cohesive devices which connect preceding and subsequent pieces of text and the use of thematic structuring.

The question 'Who should bear the blame?' at the beginning of the chapter invites an anticipatory hypothesis on the part of the reader, reinforced and elaborated on by the prompts interspersed along the way. This is referred to in discourse pragmatics as a 'cataphoric structure':

> Cataphoric maps arouse curiosity and provide an overarching direction with some orientation landmarks. (Armani *et al.* 2002)

The Focus Task at the end of the chapter refers back to the opening question, with a slight rephrasing ('Was Germany to blame for the war?'), performing an anaphoric function and forcing the reader back into the overall thrust of the chapter.

In SFL terms (e.g. Martin 1992), we might see the above structuring in terms of the chapter title ('The Causes of the First World War') functioning prospectively as the instructional macro-Theme and the accompanying question ('Who should bear the blame?') as realising a regulative macro-Theme projecting instructional 'content' whereby students are prompted to reason and evaluate. They must decide on the most and least important causes of the war and develop a stance on moral responsibility. The final Focus Task would then function cumulatively as the macro-New.

9.4   Discussion

An overarching objective of the analysis was to show the significance of multimodal texturing in making available to the reader particular 'reading pathways' which in turn influence how historical information and perspectives are negotiated and made sense of. In other words, how does the multimodal arrangement of regulative and instructional discourse integrate meanings across modes into coherent wholes? More significantly, how far does the reader pathway set up by the text layout entail a particular integration of meanings, thus constraining the possible range of interpretative stances taken up by students? Specifically, we were interested in determining the extent to which the author's use, and layout, of the elements identified enable students to make up their own minds 'about whether Germany caused the war or whether other countries should share the blame'.

These questions go beyond issues of 'readability' and 'navigation' through a text. Rather they concern how the reader is positioned to interpret the text in a particular way because of how it is constructed. Lemke (2003) points out that it is no longer easy for the author to build extended arguments. Instead one tries to 'offer readers/users opportunities to make meanings of their own, come to their own conclusions, based on the web of related elements provided, which may be combined and sequenced, logically, temporally, or experientially in many different ways'. However, in the case of the present text, it would seem that the interpretive autonomy implied by the multimodal text may in fact be illusory, with the author orchestrating particular meanings and interpretations through their selection of elements and the nature of the regulative tasks.

Indeed, our analysis has shown that rather than the chapter being a jumble of loosely related multimodal elements, for the assiduous reader, the interaction of the regulative and the instructional prescribes a relatively narrow pathway through the chapter leading to a particular interpretation of the past. In fact, the chapter would appear to have the characteristics of an anchorage relationship (discussed earlier) whereby the text directs the reader through the signifieds of the image/s towards a meaning chosen in advance.

The observation that the textbook writer appears to deliberately create a particular reading path is confirmed by our discussions with authors of history textbooks. For example, Dave Martin (personal communication), the author of a range of books for secondary school students, states that it is common practice for text book authors to collaborate with layout editors in order to strategically place tasks and activities in relation to the body text and other elements so that the reader negotiates the material along a particular pathway. He recognises, however, that individual students and teachers will decide on different routes, which will not necessarily include looking at every element of the page/spread. Interestingly, in some recently published textbooks, the presence of an intended pathway is made overt. For example, the feature 'Your pathway' in Hodder Murray texts (such as the 'Essential' GCSE series) sets out to explicitly tell students what their pathway through the book is.

This is not to say that, based on the presence of a reading pathway (made explicit by the text book author or through analysis) we can ever predict an *actual* interpretation or understanding by an *actual* student reader.[4] However, our research suggests that it is more likely that readers will make certain meanings and not others based on the author's orchestration and textual integration (or not) of the meanings represented in the different elements. Nevertheless, without the benefit of user trials, such a suggestion remains tentative.

9.5 Conclusion

What implications might we draw from the above discussion?

At the design level, we could propose that authors and textbook publishers give more sensitive consideration to the structuring of multimodal chapters. Obviously design decisions are motivated not only by functional principles but by aesthetic, pragmatic and economic pressures, a point confirmed by our interactions with textbook writers. Martin (personal communication), for example, stresses that 'every illustration is expected to work for a living. They are not there to brighten up the book.' Other authors similarly have emphasised the financial constraints, having to justify the inclusion of every image in terms of its educational value – 'we need to be sure it is worth the expensive space it is occupying.' Although most authors claim a surprising degree of control in specifying the layout of the page, Martin also points to the compromises required when working as part of a production team:

> In layout discussions I could not have the illustration quite as big as I wanted, first due to space and then when I asked for the cropping of a blown up image that was not possible as the publisher had only paid for an illustration at a certain resolution.

While acknowledging the practical problems faced by designers, as discourse analysts we should be able to provide useful input with regard to the functional organization of the text. As Lemke (2003) recommends:

> We ought to be able to say when an actual genre is most likely to include an image, and what the function of that image will be in relation to textual meaning and the sequential development of the text as a whole. Functionally, we want to be able to specify how, typically, such visual-graphical elements contribute to ideational/(re)presentational meaning, interpersonal-orientational-attitudinal meaning, and organizational-textural-structural meaning.

In relation to textual meanings in particular, the analysis of the interaction between regulative and instructional discourses provided useful insight into how the author/designer intended the chapter to be approached. We then saw how the notions of information value, framing and salience allowed us to explore the extent to which the author's texturing of the chapter reinforced a particular reading path (and therefore impeded others). This suggests that text book authors may find the tools of analysis set out here a useful means of critically evaluating their deployment of multimodal resources.

In terms of pedagogy, an obvious implication highlighted by our analysis is the need for teacher scaffolding of the reading process. Even though it is commonly recognised that contemporary youth are a much more 'visual' generation, reading a multimodal textbook is not necessarily the same as playing computer games or skimming web pages. The multimodal textbook requires the reader to work hard at meaning making and students need to develop multimodal communicative competence (Royce 2002). In terms of reading process theory, the processes and strategies applicable to monomodal texts operate differently from those employed for integrated media (Healy and Dooley 2001). Not only do the readers have to make sense of conceptually demanding graphics such as maps, charts, diagrams, flowcharts, and so on, they need to understand the relationship between the various visual elements and between the visual and verbal. In addition, as we have demonstrated here, they need to perceive the chapter as an integrated whole – a single complex sign – and to ascertain the most pedagogically productive reading path. Reading needs to be seen in such circumstances as a social activity rather than a solitary act, with a knowledgeable teacher inducting the students into the reading practices required for successful comprehension. Unsworth (2001) suggests, in relation to information value for example, that teacher-supported interactive work with the text might be necessary in focusing students' attention on the 'left-hand side of the layout relating it to their experience and establishing a basis for progression to the right-hand side' (p. 105). At a broader level, he proposes a pedagogic framework to facilitate explicit teaching about how texts and images mean, involving steps such as 'orientation to the text', 'reading the text', 'working with the text' and 'reviewing' – providing opportunities at each stage to discuss the visual, the verbal and the interaction of the two modalities.

Notes

1. Foundational to much of the research currently being carried out into the reading of multimodal textbooks has been the work of Florence Davies (e.g. 1995, Johns and Davies 1983) on the macrostructure of science course books, including the interrelationships between text and visual elements. We acknowledge the profession's debt to her pioneering efforts in this area.
2. Evidence which is generated at (or close to) the time of a particular historical event is usually referred to as a primary source and distinguished from the texts or 'secondary sources' produced by a text book author or contemporary historians and commentators with some distance from events. Secondary sources may also include contributions to knowledge about a past age in the form of TV and stage drama, film, historical fiction, museum reconstructions, models, re-enactments, etc.

    It should be noted that, recently, in some history text books (e.g. Dawson, 2004) there has been a move to eliminate the distinction between primary and secondary sources on the basis that whether a source is primary or secondary depends on the question being asked.
3. The General Certificate in Secondary Education (GCSE) is a public exam taken in Year 11 (approximately age 16) in the English school system.
4. Nor, indeed, is it to say that it is pedagogically undesirable for teachers or authors to guide students towards a particular understanding of the past, as Frances Christie has pointed out to us. In some contexts and in some phases of pedagogic activity it may be preferable to teach things 'as they are' and in others to teach them 'as they might well be conceived'. This balance or tension between teaching for apprenticeship and teaching for 'independent thinking' is an important pedagogic issue.

References

Armani, J., Botturi, L. and Rocci, A. (2002). Maps as learning tools: The SWISSLING solution. Paper presented at the 4th International Conference on New Educational Environments, Lugano.

Barthes, R. (1972). *Image-Music-Text*. Glasgow: Fontana.

Christie, F. (2002). *Classroom Discourse Analysis. A Functional Perspective*. London/New York: Continuum Press.

Coffin, C. (2004). Learning to write history: the role of causality. *Written Communication* 21 (3): 261–89.

Coffin, C. (2006). *Historical Discourse: the language of time, cause and evaluation*. London: Continuum.

Davies, F. (1995). *Introducing Reading*. Harmondsworth: Penguin.

Dawson, I. (2004). *What is History?* London: John Murray.

Freebody, P., Hedberg, J., Guo Libo, and team (2004). Digital curricular literacies: Project 1. *CRPP Research Report Series*, Digital Curricular Literacies Team, Singapore: National Institute of Education.

Healy, A. and Dooley, K. (2001). Reading education, diverse audiences, new text typologies, new times. Paper presented at International Literacy Conference: *Literacy and Language in Global and Local Settings*, Cape Town, November 2001.

Horn, R. (1999). Information design: Emergence of a new profession. In *Information Design*, R. Jacobson (ed.), 15–33. Cambridge, MA: The MIT Press.

Jenkins, K. (2003). *Refiguring History*. London: Routledge.

Johns, T. and Davies, F. (1983). Text as a vehicle for information: The classroom use of written texts in teaching reading in a foreign language. *Reading in a Foreign Language*, 1 (1): 1–19.

Kress, G. (2003). *Literacy in the New Media Age*. New York: Routledge.

Kress, G. (2004). Reading images: Multimodality, representation and new media. Paper presented at Expert Forum for Knowledge Presentation Conference: *Preparing for the Future of Knowledge Presentation*, accessed 15 January 2006: http://www.knowledgepresentation.org/BuildingTheFuture/Kress2/Kress2.html

Kress, G. and van Leeuwen, T. (1996). *Reading Images: The Grammar of Visual Design*. London: Routledge.

Lemke, J. (2003). Multimedia genres and traversals. Paper presented at IPrA Invited Panel: *Approaches to Genre*, Toronto, Canada, accessed 20 January 2006: http://www-personal.umich.edu/~jaylemke/papers/IPrA%20Toronto%20Genres%20Paper.htm

Martin, J. R. (1992). *English Text: Systems and Structure*. Amsterdam: Benjamins.

National Curriculum Key Stage 3, accessed 27 Jan, 2006: http://www.nc.uk.net

Osborne, K. (2003). Voices from the past. Primary sources: A new old method of teaching history. *Canadian Social Studies* 37 (2).

Royce, T. (2002). Multimodality in the TESOL classroom: Exploring visual-verbal synergy. *TESOL Quarterly* 36 (2): 191–205.

Sewall, G. (2004) *World History Textbooks: A Review*. New York: American Textbook Council.

Unsworth, L. (2001) *Teaching Multiliteracies across the Curriculum*. Milton Keynes: Open University Press.

van Leeuwen, T. and Kress, G. (1996). Critical layout analysis. *Internationale Schulbuchforschung* 17: 25–43.

Walsh, B. (2001). *GCSE Modern World History*. London: John Murray.

10 Texturing interpersonal meanings in academic argument: pulses and prosodies of value

Susan Hood

University of Technology, Sydney

10.1 Introduction

There is a very extensive research literature on the organisational structuring of academic texts as genres, both from a pragmatic perspective (e.g. Swales 1990; Dudley-Evans 1994; Paltridge 1997; Hyland 2002), sometimes referred to as EAP genre theory (c.f. Hyon 1996), and from genre theory within Systemic Functional linguistics (SFL) (e.g. Drury 1991; Schleppegrell 2004; Coffin *et al.* 2005). Theoretical differences in the conception of genre translate into different practices in the analysis and justification of stages, but from both theoretical perspectives resultant descriptions have had an important impact on academic literacy programs. However, such descriptions do not in themselves exhaust the process of analysis in how meanings pattern and unfold in texts. From an SFL perspective, we can map the organisational structure of discourse in the space between genre and grammar, in the discourse semantic patterning of meanings in the phases of texts that make up the stages of genres (Martin 1992; Martin and Rose 2003). An analysis of such patterns enables a more detailed modelling and explanation of the structuring of discourse. It is from such a discourse semantic perspective that I approach the analysis of academic articles. In particular I focus on the textual organisation of meanings in the introductions to research articles, and in this endeavour I draw on a growing body of work, including for example, Whittaker (1995), Coffin and Hewings (2004), Hewings (2004), Lores (2004), Ravelli (2004), and Love (2005).

Textual meaning is described as the 'mode of meaning that relates to the construction of text [...], building up sequences of discourse, organizing the discursive flow, and creating cohesion and continuity' (Halliday and Matthiessen 2004: 30). Textual meaning is understood to be an enabling or facilitating function in relation to the other metafunctions (the ideational and the interpersonal). It functions to organise the message, where the notion of 'message' includes both the ideational and the interpersonal. To date, research on the texturing of academic texts has most often focused on the organisation of the message in ideational terms and has privileged the thematic structuring at clause level. Relatively less attention has been paid to the organisation of interpersonal meanings and to the role of higher-level Themes in forecasting the interpersonal dimension of the message at a discourse semantic level. There are important exceptions. Hunston's research on stance in academic writing (e.g. 1994, 2000), draws attention to the organisational function of evaluation that indicates significance; Thompson and Zhou (2000) focus on the dual role of disjuncts in text cohesion and interpersonal stance; Coffin and Hewings (2004) begin to apply Appraisal theory from the point of view of Engagement to consider the hyper-thematising of writer stance in pre-academic essays, and Martin (2004) suggests association of evaluation with higher order Themes and News across many different registers. In this chapter I focus on the textual organisation of interpersonal meanings, focusing on patterns of attitude at the level of whole texts and in phases of texts. Before I elaborate more fully on this research, I briefly establish the theoretical foundations of my analyses.

The textual structuring of meaning at a grammatical level is realised in Theme-Rheme and Given-New structures. Analyses of clause-level Theme in this chapter follow the position elaborated, for example, in Berry (1995), and adopted by Davies (1997), Forey (this volume) and Montemayor-Borsinger (this volume), whereby Theme in English is taken to include components of the clause up to and including the participant functioning as Subject (though see Thompson and Thompson, this volume, for arguments against this position). So where a circumstantial element occurs in initial position, this is considered to be a marked topical Theme, and the participant that functions as Subject would be an unmarked topical Theme. The Theme would therefore be as underlined in (1).

(1) <u>According to Marks and Flemming (1999), the ratio of early school leaving</u> is 3:2 (males:females)

Where there is a marked hypotactic clause in a clause complex, this is taken to be thematic to the independent clause, and to constitute a marked Theme. The Theme in that case would extend to include the subject of the independent clause, as underlined in (2).

(2)   ... <u>when controlling for this factor, the gender gap in early school leaving</u> is smaller

Following Coffin and Hewings (2004) projecting clauses are analysed in the same way as marked hypotactic clauses. They are also considered Theme, in this case to the independent projected clause. Coffin and Hewings (2004: 162) suggest that such clauses function as 'an interpersonal lens through which the projected clause is interpreted'. The underlined wording in (3) provides an example.

(3)   <u>The Australian Labor party [...] stated</u> 'now more than ever, young boys need contact with men who can offer positive role models ...'

Finally, in terms of existential Theme, *there* is taken to be thematic, as in (4), in line with analyses in Halliday (1994: 142).

(4)   <u>There</u> are markedly higher rates of suspension for boys.

With reference to Martin (1992) and Martin and Rose (2003), thematic structures are also analysed beyond the clause. Initial points of prominence in phases of text are referred to as hyper-Themes, and initial points of prominence in larger sections of text are referred to as macro-Themes. This order of thematic prominence will be discussed in more detail later in the chapter.

A second dimension of texturing is that of Given-New structures. Given information is that which it is assumed to be retrievable for the reader, and in unmarked clauses it is that which comes first. New information is described as the information that the reader is expected to 'attend to' (Halliday 1994: 298), or as the 'information which is being presented as "newsworthy"' (Fries 2002: 121). In spoken language New information is identified by the culmination of tonic prominence. In written language the marking of New is less clear, and is often identified as the information that comes last in the clause, in other words where the unmarked tonic prominence would be likely to occur if the text were spoken. Even so, there remain issues to do with the identification of New in written discourse. Fries (2002) suggests the need for a new term, 'N-Rheme', to reflect the close association of New with Rheme in written English text. For Fries, N-Rheme typically expresses the core of the newsworthy part of the clause, that is 'the part of the clause that the writer wants the reader to remember' (2002: 126; c.f. Banks 2004).

The identification of New as the information in final position also seems to become more complex when we focus on the location of explicitly evaluative terms. It may be, for example, that information that is not in clause-final position but that is explicitly evaluative can be considered as 'newsworthy' precisely because it is evaluative. That is, the evaluation presents the information as being newsworthy, and affords it tonic prominence. In the analyses in this study I identify the final element in the clause as New, but signal with a retrospective arrow, that the points of prominence in a wave structure are not categorically bounded in a strict sense (see, e.g., Figure 10.3). For the same reason Theme is represented with a prospective arrow. Analyses also identify points of prominence at the end of phases or sections of text, where there is a summative accumulation of newsworthy information. These are referred to as hyper-News (Martin 1992).

The aim of this chapter is to explore the textual patterning of interpersonal meanings, that is, the ways in which such meanings are organised across phases of discourse. The data include the introductory sections of a set of four recently published research articles in the disciplinary field of education. Additional data are drawn from the introductions to undergraduate research dissertations collected as part of a previous study of research writing (see Hood 2004, 2005). In each case, the introductory sections constitute examples of evaluative reports in which writers create their own research space. I investigate, first, the extent to which interpersonal meanings are encoded in hyper-Themes, and hyper-News in the texts. I then consider the extent to which interpersonal meanings encoded in higher-level themes can be said to be predictive for a phase of text, and the extent to which the interpersonal meanings encoded in higher level News can be said to be consolidating for a phase of text. Finally, I consider how interpersonal choices in hyper-Theme position and hyper-New position pattern out in terms of clause-level Theme and New structures.

I draw on Appraisal theory (Martin 2000; Martin and Rose 2003) to investigate interpersonal meanings encoded as ATTITUDE (Hood 2004, 2005; Martin and White 2005; Hood and Martin 2007). ATTITUDE is inscribed in texts in expressions that encode a positive or negative value that can be graded up or down, and can be categorised as either Affect (expressing value as feelings and emotions), Judgement (expressing evaluations of people and behaviour), or Appreciation (expressing evaluation of things and events). ATTITUDE can be inscribed but it can also be evoked or *flagged* by various means including resources of GRADUATION. It is not possible to elaborate in detail on the theory in this chapter, however, the dimension of GRADUATION is further explained in the context of analyses later in the chapter and is represented in the network diagram in Figure 10.2.

10.2 The positioning of ATTITUDE in higher–level theme

If these higher-level Themes function as points of departure for the message in phases of text, then expressions of ATTITUDE in such positions have the potential to be interpersonally predictive for their respective phases. The first question to address then is the extent to which expressions of ATTITUDE are located in macro-Themes and hyper-Themes. The higher-level Themes for Text 1 (the longest introduction) are presented in Figure 10.1. The title

Motivating boys and motivating girls: Does teacher gender really make a difference?

Introduction

Do boys fare **best** in classes taught by male teachers? Do girls fare **best** in classes taught by female teachers?

In recent years there has been considerable popular debate around these questions.

The present study seeks to address this debate by specifically examining the impact of student gender (...) as a function of teacher gender on academic motivation and engagement. Essentially it assesses two competing models.

Over the past two decades, there has been a great deal of research investigating student motivation and engagement.

Gender and educational outcomes

There are gender differences on **key** educational outcomes.

The interaction of student and teacher gender

There has been substantial anecdotal evidence pointing to the need for more male role models in boys' lives.

However in the same study, focus groups and interviews with boys themselves indicated no particular **preference** for male or female teachers on the topic of teaching and learning

Grade and gender

It appears that grade (year in school) is another **significant** factor in motivation and engagement.

The hierarchical nature of motivation and engagement

Duda (2001) **emphasised** the **need** to evaluate the combined effects and interactions of individual motivation and class-level motivation on a variety of outcome measures as well as the theoretical basis for pursuing such research.

Figure 10.1 Higher-level Themes and inscribed ATTITUDE (Text 1)

of the article (*Motivating boys ...*) is taken to be the highest level of macro-Theme, establishing the point of departure for the whole text. A second level of macro-Theme is reflected in the section heading (*Introduction*) together with the elaboration of that in the opening two clauses of that section (*Do boys ...? Do girls ...*). This is followed by a series of hyper-Themes (indented to the right) that function as points of departure for phases of the writer's message. Where headings appear, they are included as a component of a hyper-Theme and are underlined. Inscribed ATTITUDE is indicated in bold. The higher-level periodic structures of all four texts were analysed in this way and the discussion of findings refers to all the texts.

The analysis of inscribed ATTITUDE in macro- and hyper-Themes across all four texts reveals no apparent necessary co-patterning. There are some higher-level Themes that encode inscribed ATTITUDE, as indicated in bold in (5a-b):

(5a)   Do boys fare **best** [App: valuation] in classes taught by male teachers? Do girls fare **best** [App: valuation] in classes taught by female teachers?

(5b)   In a recent literature review, Hull and Schultz (2001) demonstrate how **generative** [App: valuation] this work has been, and they argue that it could be **usefully** [App: valuation] linked to school literacy

and at times expressions of ATTITUDE are amplified, as indicated in italics in (6a-b):

(6a)   The learning of Chinese characters is considered to be *the most **challenging** problem* faced by both first-language and second/foreign-language learners of Mandarin Chinese.

(6b)   In addition to these reasons for internationalisation in schools, ***complex** and **troubling** issues* in the world, ...

However, there are also many instances where there is no encoding of explicit ATTITUDE in higher-level Themes, as (7a-c):

(7a)   Much research on reading and writing in schools has focused and continues to focus on individual and cognitive skills and related interventions.

(7b)   The character script of the digraphia is used in all forms of written communication – ranging from official documents, literature and mass media to record-keeping in a family or a village.

(7c)   Over the past two decades, there has been a great deal of research investigating student motivation and engagement.

It was noted earlier, however, that ATTITUDE may be expressed in less direct ways, that is, it may be invoked rather than inscribed (Martin and Rose 2003; Martin and White 2005). One of the key means by which this indirect encoding of ATTITUDE is achieved in academic writing is through resources of GRADUATION (Hood 2004; Hood and Martin 2007). As Hood (2004) explains, when ideational meanings are graded, for example, when they are expressed as relatively more or less, this signifies a subjective position or stance in relation to that ideational meaning. There is an interpersonal or subjective dimension encoded in relation to the ideational. Figure 10.2 represents a network of options for grading ideational meanings, either as FORCE, which is to do with adjusting the intensity or quantity of a meaning, or as FOCUS, which is to do with adjusting the degree of authenticity or specificity of an entity or the fulfilment of a process.

If we take instances of GRADUATION into account in analysing attitudinal meaning, a clearer pattern of attitudinal expression begins to emerge, with instances of inscribed or invoked ATTITUDE in every higher-level Theme (with the exception of headings which are discussed below). The higher-level Themes that rely entirely on invoked ATTITUDE are shown in (8a-c). GRADUATION is indicated in italics and explained in square brackets.

(8a) *Much* [grad: +quantity] research on reading and writing in schools has focused and *continues to* [grad: −completion] focus on individual and cognitive skills and related interventions.

(8b) The character script of the digraphia is used in *all* [grad: +scope] forms of written communication – *ranging from* official documents, literature and mass media *to* [grad: +scope] record-keeping in a family or a village.

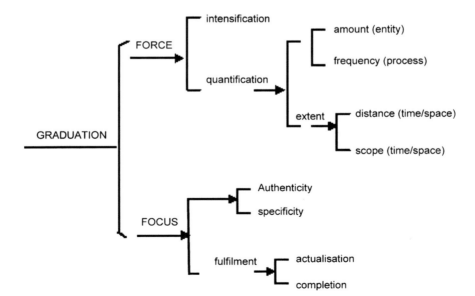

Figure 10.2 Network of options in GRADUATION

(8c) *Over the past two decades* [grad: + scope], there has been *a great deal of* [grad: +quantity] research investigating student motivation and engagement.

In some cases additional evaluative positions are indirectly encoded alongside explicit ATTITUDE, as in (9).

(9) In a *recent* [grad: –distance] literature review, Hull and Schultz (2001) demonstrate *how* **generative** this work has been, and they argue that it *could be* [grad: –actualisation] **usefully** linked to school literacy.

In summary, when resources of GRADUATION are taken into account, each higher-level Theme can be seen to select for attitudinal meaning, and thus has the potential to forecast meanings in both an ideational and an interpersonal sense.

10.2.1 Headings and evaluation

The issue of headings and evaluative meaning requires some further commentary at this point. Headings typically encode only ideational meaning and not interpersonal meaning. This is the case for the data in this study. In each case, however, a heading or sub-heading (underlined) is followed by a further hyper-thematic element that picks up the ideational content while adding an interpersonal dimension, as in (10), (11), and (12).

(10) Introduction

   While *many* [grad: quantity] of the *current* [grad: distance] *debates* [grad: fulfilment] about internationalism in Australia have focused on education at the higher education level, there has been *increasing* [grad: quantity] **interest** [appreciation] in the **issue** [appreciation] of internationalisation of the curriculum among educators at the secondary school level.

(11) The interaction of student and teacher gender

   There has been *substantial* [grad: quantity] anecdotal evidence *pointing to* [grad: fulfilment] the **need** for *more* [grad: quantity] male role models in boys' lives.

(12) Grade and gender

   It *appears* [grad: –fulfilment] that grade (year in school) is *another* [grad: +quantity] **significant** [+appreciation] factor in motivation and engagement.

The hyper-Theme in this study is taken to include both the orthographically marked signal of a new phase of the text, as well as the discursive marker.

10.3 The function of ATTITUDE in higher-level themes

At this point I want to explore in more detail the implications of the positioning of ATTITUDE in macro- and hyper-Themes. The questions to address here are whether and in what ways such thematically placed interpersonal meaning functions textually. As a first step, it is useful to consider what happens when there is no expression of ATTITUDE in this position of prominence in a phase of text. Here I draw on a sample phase of a research report produced by a novice academic writer (reported in Hood 2004). The hyper-Theme is identified as the underlined opening clauses in (13).

(13) <u>Roger, Bull and Smith (1988) studied interruption in another angle. They formed the Interruption Coding System (ICS) for the classifications of interruptions.</u> The subjects chosen for their two experiments were instructed to interrupt as often as possible and to monopolise the conversation as long as possible. Based on the results, Roger, Bull and Smith organised the coding system into a flow chart. They divided interruptions into single and complex ones according to the number of interruption attempts. For more than one attempt, the interruption was regarded as complex. If the interruptor could prevent the other from completing and ultimately completed his own utterance, the interruption was successful. Otherwise it was unsuccessful. If the interruption followed a clear offer of the floor by the interruptor, it was called snatch-back. The completion of an utterance by the interruptors and the occurrence of overlapping were also considered in the whole system. At last there were 14 categories of interruptions in total. They were [... list of categories ...]. These classifications were based on the structure of turn-taking. Compared with the work of West of Zimmerman, Roger, Bull and Smith did not relate interruptions with any social issue.

As Hood (2004) notes, the novice writer has devoted a considerable phase of text to a review of a particular research article (by Roger *et al.*) as a part of her introduction to her own study, yet it is not made clear to the reader whether they are expected to align with or distance themselves from this study. There is no indication of the preferred stance, until perhaps the culmination of the phase in (14), where there is an ambiguous suggestion of evaluation in hyper-New.

(14) Compared with the work of West of Zimmerman, Roger, Bull and Smith did *not* relate interruptions with *any* social issue.

The problem can be rectified with the inclusion of an expression of ATTITUDE in the hyper-Theme, as in (15),

(15) Roger, Bull and Smith (1988) **contributed** another angle to a study of interruption. They formed the Interruption Coding System (ICS) for the **detailed** classification of interruptions. ... (detailed description of methodology).

The initial indication of stance in the revised text radiates forward across the subsequent phase of discourse. The reader's alignment is managed from the beginning of the phase, enabling the remaining text, while overtly objective (ideational in orientation), to take on a radiated positive prosody. The inclusion of a concessive conjunction (boxed) then signals the shift in value in the hyper-New, as shown in (16).

(16) ... These classifications were based on the structure of turn-taking. However, compared with the work of West of Zimmerman, Roger, Bull and Smith did *not* relate interruptions with *any* [grad; quantity] social issue.

It is apparent in the examples above that just as the experiential content of the hyper-Theme encourages us to expect the development of the experimental dimension of the message, so from an interpersonal perspective, the encoding of ATTITUDE in hyper-Theme encourages us to read the subsequent text within a particular axiological frame. In the following section I explore the extent to which the higher-level Themes in the published texts can be said to be interpersonally predictive, and the means by which the initial encoding of ATTITUDE is reinforced or consolidated.

10.4 Strategies for predicting, reinforcing and consolidating attitudinal stance in phases of text

An analysis of the periodic patterning of ATTITUDE in the introductory sections of just four texts in one disciplinary field does not provide a basis for making definitive claims about ATTITUDE and periodicity in all academic writing. Nevertheless, it can indicate some tendencies, as well as variations. Here a close analysis of individual phases of text enables an exploration of writer strategies in texturing interpersonal meaning. For the purposes of this analysis, each phase is analysed for hyper-Theme and hyper-New (not always present), as well as clause level Theme and New. Recurring patterns in the data are discussed and illustrated below. Headings are underlined, explicit ATTITUDE is in bold and Graduation is in italics. Square brackets, as in [...], indicate an ellipsed topical Theme is the clause.

10.4.1 ATTITUDE in hyper-Theme reiterated in the subsequent text

First, it was found that the kind of ATTITUDE expressed in hyper-Theme, is reiterated elsewhere in the phase of text. These reiterations could be as inscriptions of ATTITUDE or as GRADUATION invoking ATTITUDE.

In Figure 10.3, for example, the lexical choice *key* in the hyper-Theme inscribes APPRECIATION of the importance or significance of certain outcomes. This kind of APPRECIATION is later reiterated explicitly in *needs to be noted*.

Hyper-Theme		
Gender and educational outcomes There are gender difference on **key** educational outcomes		
Theme ⟶		**New** ⟵
For the most part, these *difference*	are **not**	in boys' **favour**
Indeed, given this, the education of boys	has been	an issue of *ongoing debate* (Weaver-Hightower, 2003).
On average, *girl*	*outperform*	boys in a *greater number* of subjects
and there	are	*more* girls among the **higher achieving** students (Collins, Kenway, & McLeod, 2000)
More, females	*complete*	school (Department of Education and Youth Affairs, 2000).
According to Marks and Fleming (1999), the ratio of early school leaving	is	3:2 (males:females)
although it **needs to be noted** that *many* boys	leave	school to take apprenticeships
and when controlling for this factor, the gender *gap* in early school leaving	is	*Smaller.*
There	are	*markedly higher rates* of **suspension** for boys (Ainley & Lonsdale, 2000).
Boys	are	*more* **negative** about school
[boys]	see	homework as *less* **useful**
and [boys]	are	*less likely* to ask for help
and [boys]	are	*more* **reluctant** to do *extra* work
Moreover, teachers believe that boys	are	*less* **able** to **concentrate**
[boys]	are	*less* **determined** to *solve* **difficult problems**
and [boys]	are	*less* **productive**

Figure 10.3 Hyper-Theme predicting ATTITUDE in Text 1

The *key outcomes* are then elaborated throughout the phase as a series of abilities and attributes. The ATTITUDE encoded around these personal qualities is that of JUDGEMENT rather than APPRECIATION (higher achieving, suspension, extra work, concentrate, determined, productive). However, the semantic relationship between *outcomes* and personal qualities means that the positive and negative JUDGEMENT around the qualities also serves to reinforce the APPRECIATION of the *outcomes* as significant.

The grading of extent as *"difference"* in the hyper-Theme is also reiterated in many other instances in the phase, in *differences, out(perform), more, gap, more girls, 3:2; smaller; markedly higher; more, less, less, more, less, less, less,* building a prosody of significance across the phase.

A similar pattern of the reiteration of hyper-thematic values is seen in the phase from Text 3, presented in Figure 10.4.

The writer establishes an interpersonal point of departure for the phase in the amplified inscription *most* **challenging problem,** with significance also flagged in *both* [extent], and grading of Focus in *considered* [– fulfilment] establishes the issue as unresolved. These hyper-Thematic values are reiterated in instances of inscribed and invoked ATTITUDE across the

Hyper-Theme		
The learning of Chinese characters is *considered* to be *most* **challenging problem** faced by *both* first-language and second/foreign-language learners of Mandarin Chinese		
Theme———————————➤		
	◄———————————	**New**
The **complexity** and 'opaque sound-shape' of characters	are largely *assumed* to be responsible for	this **difficulty** (e.g. Liu, 1987; Zhang, 1992)
Since there	are	**no explicit** and **reliable** grapheme – phoneme correspondence rules,
Many assume that the learning of characters	is	*basically* a matter of memorisation, *especially* for the mastery of the *first few hundred* **simple** characters
There	are	*some* phonetic markers in the traditional character-based system,
but [whether it has the cognitive and pedagogic **economy** that is *often* attributed to alphabetic systems (*e.g. Goody, 1977*)]	is	*questionable.*
Furthermore which of its character *might* **enable** and which *might* **impede** its *large-scale* dissemination and access to writing across a *broad range* of dialectal groups	has been	a matter of *historical and contemporary debate.*
Columas (1989: 106), *for example,* maintained that '*until (relatively) recently,* **mastery** of the Chinese script	was	the prerogative of a *very small* **elite.**
With this **mastery** ...	*invariably* acquired	in conjunction with learning mandarin.

Figure 10.4 Hyper-Theme predicting ATTITUDE from Text 3

phase, propagating prosodies of significance and unresolvedness as summarised below:

- Significance: *most challenging problem, complexity, opaque, difficulty, no explicit and reliable, simple, economy, enable, impede, basically, especially, the first few hundred, often, large scale, historical and contemporary, a broad range, mastery, elite, mastery*

- (Un)resolvedness: *assumed, many assume, questionable, might, might, debate, invariably.*

A further example from Text 2 is presented in Figure 10.5. In hyper-Theme position, the writer flags significance through GRADUATION as amount (*many*), and as distance in time (*current*). This is reinforced in the inscriptions: *increasing interest* and *issue* and further flagged in *debates*, which implies an issue of interest. These hyper-thematic values of 'significant interest' are reiterated across the phase in the inscriptions: *grappling with the issue, concerned about the issues, deserve, encourage,* and *recognition.* There are also many other instances of invoked ATTITUDE in the phase in *inclusion of both* [extent], *more* [quantity], *international* [extent], *multiple nations* [extent], *transcend ... boundaries* [extent],

Hyper-Theme

While *many* of the *current debates* about internationalism in Australia have focused on education at the higher education level, there has been *increasing* **interest** in the **issue** of internationalisation of the curriculum among educators at the secondary school level.

Theme ⟶

⟵ New

More school	are **grappling**	With this **issue**
Since there	developing	policies and strategies
	to **encourage**	The *inclusion* of *both* international and intercultural dimensions in the curriculum
Increasing interdependence in the world, the realities of globalisation, and *global* flows of students, information and ideas	have meant	That [[many educators see the *need* to internationalise the curriculum]]
Australian schools	are	*Indeed more international* with students who feel that they belong to, are concerned with, or are **concerned about issues** [[that relate to *multiple* nation, and *transcend* national *boundaries*]]
Student in these schools	*required* and **deserve**	an *international* education
that	**encourages**	**Recognition** of and dialogue about *different* cultures

Hyper-New

A flow on from this should be **respect** and **tolerance** for *difference* in education settings

Figure 10.5 Forecasting and consolidating ATTITUDE in Text 2

international [extent], *different* [extent]. The resultant prosody is one of 'significant interest in difference'.

10.4.2 ATTITUDE in hyper-New typically consolidates ATTITUDE in the preceding phase

A second finding was that, where phases of text include a hyper-New, the ATTITUDE expressed in this position is a consolidation of ATTITUDE accumulated in the preceding phase of text. In Text 2 (Figure 10.4) the prosody of 'significant interest in difference' built up over the phase is then consolidated in the hyper-Theme in inscribed positive JUDGEMENT in **respect** and **tolerance**. The explicit ATTITUDE in hyper-New functions to consolidate the prosody instantiated throughout the phase.

The consolidation of ATTITUDE in hyper-New position is also evident in the phase from Text 1 represented in Figure 10.6. Inscribed ATTITUDE is

Hyper-Theme		
The hierarchical nature of motivation and engagement Duda (2001) **emphasised** the **need** to evaluate the combined effects and interactions of individual motivation and class-level motivation on a *variety* of outcome measures *as well as* the theoretical basis for pursuing such research.		
Theme———————————▶		
		New
She **lamented**, however, that this	is *rarely* pursued	in motivational research
Duda also *indicated* that *particularly strong* class level effects	*might override*	the effects of individual orientations
whereas individuals with the *particularly strong* motivation orientations	are *likely to be less* effected	by class-level motivation
Although there	is	A *relatively more* **consistent** line of research assessing the hierarchical nature of motivation and engagement
there	is	*relatively little* [[that examines the hierarchical nature of motivation and engagement and the **issue** of class-level motivation in the academic context]].
The *present* study	therefore, *not only* examines	the **issue** of student and teacher gender in motivation and engagement,
but *also* in the same analysis (it)	accounts for	The hierarchical structure of the data.
Hence the *relative* **contribution** of student and teacher gender	can be assessed after accounting for	*Variance* at the student, class, and school levels.
Hyper-New		
This constitutes a **powerful** analysis of the contribution of teacher and student gender to motivation and engagement.		

Figure 10.6 Forecasting and consolidating ATTITUDE in Text 1

encoded in several instances across the phase with the most amplified instance of ATTITUDE *powerful* in hyper-New position.

The ATTITUDE encoded in hyper-New (*powerful*) can be seen to consolidate in explicit form, the prosody of significance that is propagated across the phase largely through resources of GRADUATION, in for example, *rarely, particularly strong, override, likely to be less, relatively more, not only, also, relative,* and *variance.*

10.4.3 The distribution of inscribed ATTITUDE in clause level Themes and News

What is very evident in the examples analysed above is that there is no consistent pattern in the ways in which ATTITUDE is distributed across the phase in terms of alignment with either clause-level Theme or clause-level New. We find instead that the values encoded in hyper-Themes may be rearticulated in both Theme and New positions across the subsequent phase. In Figure 10.4, for example, the explicit APPRECIATION encoded in hyper-Theme in *most challenging problem* is reiterated in some clause-thematic choices, for example: *complexity; impede; enable; mastery,* and in some clause-level New choices as in: *difficulty; no explicit and reliable.* In Figure 10.5, there is a stronger alignment of explicit ATTITUDE with clause-level New. It is interesting to note that in this phase of text, the writer chooses to provide a consolidating hyper-New to conclude the phase. However, in another phase of text with a hyper-New (Figure 10.6) the same preference for ATTITUDE in clause new position is not found.

The distributive pattern evident in these data is consistent with expectations for the patterning of interpersonal meanings. It is anticipated that interpersonal meanings will not be categorically constrained, that is, they will not be restricted to a narrow range of grammatical systems and will not be confined to particular positions within the clause (Martin 1992). Rather, it is expected that interpersonal meanings will be encoded across multiple systems of grammar, and by such means have the potential to take up positions across the clause, propagating a prosody or spread of value.

10.5 Conclusion

Descriptions of the generic structure of texts provide important means for describing and explaining similarities and differences in the social practices of academic life. However the task of describing the organisation of meanings in discourse does not end there. While small in scale, this study serves to illustrate the contribution of a discourse semantic perspective to explaining, at a more detailed level, the ways in which academic writers organise meanings into phases of discourse. The particular focus of this study is the textual patterning of interpersonal meanings. The analyses suggest that ATTITUDE is an intrinsic aspect of the higher-level periodic (textual) patterning of academic discourse as represented in the introductions to research articles. When both inscribed ATTITUDE and GRADUATION evoking ATTITUDE are taken into account, all macro- and hyper-Themes in the published texts are shown to encode an attitudinal stance. It is evident that evaluation in higher-level Themes has a predictive function. It is an important means by which academic writers forecast values for the subsequent phase, and the absence of such a stance is shown to be problematic for the reader in terms of tracking the writer's management of reader alignment. Similarly where phases of text include a hyper-New, that final position of prominence in the phase also encodes evaluative meanings that consolidate values accumulated in the preceding phase. The values encoded in such positions of prominence establish periodic pulses of evaluation and play an important role in signalling evaluative stance. However, this alignment with higher-level periodicity is not maintained in terms of the periodic structure at clause level. The values in hyper-Theme are reinforced prosodically rather than periodically across the phase. They propagate in both instances of inscribed ATTITUDE and GRADUATION invoking ATTITUDE and may be encoded across the clause, including in both clause-level Theme and New. The multiple instances of attitudinal meaning function to spread values prosodically across the discourse, rather than organise them in points of prominence.

References

Banks, D. (2004). Degrees of newness. In *Text and Texture: Systemic Functional Viewpoints on the Nature and Structure of Text*. D. Banks (ed.), 109–24. Paris: L'Harmattan.

Berry, M. (1995). Thematic options and success in writing. In *Thematic Development in English Text*. M. Ghadessy (ed.), 55–84. London: Pinter.

Coffin, C. and Hewings, A. (2004). IELTS preparation for tertiary writing: distinctive interpersonal and textual strategies. In *Academic Writing in Context: Social-functional Perspectives on Theory and Practice*. L. Ravelli and R. Ellis (eds), 153–71. London: Continuum.

Coffin, C., Painter, C. and Hewings, A. (2005). Argumentation in a multiparty asynchronous computer mediated conference: a generic analysis. *Australian Review of Applied Linguistics*, Series S, No. 19, 41–63.

Davies. F. (1997). Marked Theme as a heuristic for analysing text-type, text and genre. In *Applied Languages: Theory and Practice in ESP.* J. Pique and D. Viera (eds), 45–71. Universitat de Valencia: Servei de Publications.

Dudley-Evans, T. (1994). Genre analysis: An approach to text analysis in ESP. In *Advances in Written Text Analysis.* M. Coulthard (ed.), 219–28. London: Routledge.

Drury, H. (1991). The use of systemic linguistics to describe student summaries at university level. In *Functional and Systemic Linguistics: Approaches and Uses.* E. Ventola (ed.), 431–56. Berlin: Mouton de Gruyter.

Fries, P. H. (2002). The flow of information in a written English text. In *Relations and Functions within and around Language.* P. H. Fries, M. Cummings, D. Lockwood and W. Spruiell (eds), 117–55. London: Continuum.

Halliday, M. A. K. (1994). *An Introduction to Functional Grammar* (2nd edition). London: Edward Arnold.

Halliday, M. A. K. and Matthiessen, C. M. I. M. (2004). *An Introduction to Functional Grammar* (3rd edition). London: Arnold.

Hewings, A. (2004). Developing discipline-specific writing: analysis of undergraduate geography essays. In *Analysing Academic Writing.* L. Ravelli and R. Ellis (eds), 131–52. London: Continuum.

Hood, S. (2004). Managing attitude in undergraduate academic writing: a focus on the introductions to research reports. In *Analysing Academic Writing.* L. Ravelli and R. Ellis (eds), 24–44. London: Continuum.

Hood, S. (2005). What is evaluated and how in academic research writing?: the co-patterning of attitude and field. *Australian Review of Applied Linguistics*, Series S, No. 19, 23–40.

Hood, S. and Martin, J.R. (2007). Invoking attitude: the play of graduation in appraising discourse. In *Continuing Discourse on Language, Vol 2.* R. Hasan, C. M. I. M. Matthiessen, and J. Webster (eds.). London: Equinox.

Hunston, S. (1994). Evaluation and organization in a sample of written academic discourse. In *Advances in Written Text Analysis.* M. Coulthard (ed.), 191-218. London; Routledge.

_____ (2000). Evaluation and the planes of discourse: status and value in persuasive texts. In *Evaluation in Text: Authorial Stance and the Construction of Discourse.* S. Hunston and G. Thompson (eds.), 176-207.Oxford: Oxford University Press.

Hyland, K. (2002). Genre: language, context and literacy. *Annual Review of Applied Linguistics, Vol. 22: Discourse and Dialogue,* 113-135.

Hyon, S. (1996). Genre in three traditions: implications for ESL. *TESOL Quarterly* 3: 693-722.

Lores, R. (2004). On RA abstracts: from rhetorical structure to thematic organisation. *English for Specific Purposes,* 23: 280-302.

Love, K. (2005). Framing in online school discussions: A new mode of educational inequity. *Australian Review of Applied Linguistics, Series S, No. 19*, 64-86.

Martin, J.R. (1992). *English Text*. Amsterdam: John Benjamins.

_____ (2000). Beyond exchange: APPRAISAL system in English. In *Evaluation in text: authorial stance and the construction of discourse*. S. Hunston and G. Thompson, (eds.), 142-175. Oxford: Oxford University Press.

Martin, J.R. (2004). Sense and Sensibility: Texturing Evaluation. In *Language Evaluation and Discourse: Functional Approaches*. J. Foley (ed.), 270–304. London: Continuum.

_____ and Rose, D. (2003). *Working with Discourse: Meaning beyond the Clause*. London: Continuum.

_____ and White, P.R.R. (2005). *The Language of Evaluation: Appraisal in English*. Hampshire: Palgrave Macmillan.

Paltridge, B. (1997). *Genre, Frames and Writing in Research Settings*. Amsterdam: Benjamins.

Ravelli, L.J. (2004). Familiar territory, shifting grounds: aspects of organization in written texts. In *Academic Writing in Context: Social-functional Perspectives on Theory and Practice*. L. Ravelli and R. Ellis (eds), 104–30. London: Continuum.

Schleppegrell, M. J. (2004). Technical writing in a second language: the role of grammatical metaphor. In *Academic Writing in Context: Social-functional Perspectives on Theory and Practice*. L. Ravelli and R. Ellis (eds), 172–89. London: Continuum.

Swales, J. M. (1990). *Genre Analysis*. Cambridge: Cambridge University Press.

Thompson, G and Zhou, J. (2000). Evaluation and organisation in text: the structuring role of evaluative disjuncts. In *Evaluation in Text: Authorial Stance and the Construction of Discourse*. S. Hunston and G. Thompson (eds), 121–41. Oxford: Oxford University Press.

Whittaker, R. (1995). Themes processes and the realisations of meanings in academic articles. In *Thematic Development in English Texts*. M. Ghadessy (ed.), 105–28. London: Pinter.

[A]Appendix

Source texts:

Liu Yongbing. (2005). A Pedagogy for Digraphia: An Analysis of the Impact of Pinyin on Literacy Teaching in China and its Implications for Curricular and Pedagogical Innovations in a Wider Community. *Language and Education* (5), 400–14.

Martin, A. and Marsh. H. (2005). Motivating boys and motivating girls: Does teacher gender really make a difference? *Australian Journal of Education* 49 (3) 320–34.

Tudball, L. (2005). Grappling with internationalisation of the curriculum at the secondary school level: Issues and tensions for educators. *Australian Journal of Education* 49 (1), 10–27.

Van Enk, A, D. Dagenais and K. Toohey. (2005). A socio-cultural perspective on school-based literacy research: some emerging considerations. *Language and Education* (5), 496–517.

11 | Cultural stereotype and modality: a study into modal use in Brazilian and Portuguese meetings

Tony Berber Sardinha and Leila Barbara
Catholic University of São Paulo

11.1 Introduction

The Postgraduate Program of Applied Linguistics (LAEL) at the Catholic University of São Paulo (PUCSP) has had a long relationship with Florence Davies. She introduced us to Systemic Functional Linguistics, when she came to talk to us about topics such as Theme and Rheme, organisation of texts, modality, cohesion and many others, back in the mid-1980s and into the early 1990s. She was instrumental in establishing an agreement for academic exchanges between the University of Liverpool and the Catholic University of São Paulo. She was also a co-founder of DIRECT, the bi-national project looking at business discourse, set up in 1990 between PUCSP and the University of Liverpool. DIRECT is still thriving, with over 20 members in various universities across Brazil and in Portugal. While the project's initial focus was on English and on business communication between Brazilians and English-speaking business partners, nowadays the project's aim has been widened to include Portuguese as the main focus, as well as Spanish, and it deals with the language of several types of work.

One of the main strands of research within DIRECT has been around issues related to interaction in business meetings using a broadly Systemic Functional Linguistics model. Over the course of the years, we have looked at many business meetings and identified some issues that seem important in business communication. One of them is the issue of stereotyping, that is a priori assumptions held by members of one discourse community about another discourse community, culture or even a whole country, some of which are rooted in prejudice. One of the stereotypes that hits close to home is that involving Brazilian and Portuguese people. In intercultural business contacts, Brazilians tend to regard the Portuguese as rude and straightforward. The Portuguese, in turn, tend to consider Brazilians circumlocutious and vague.

Stereotyping is subjective and is born out of the interpersonal meanings exchanged between speakers. In order to explore stereotyping from a linguistic perspective, we focus in this chapter on an analysis of modality, which allows us to 'uncover the interpersonal relationships that are being expressed in the text' (Eggins 1994: 197). In particular, modality is a crucial resource in the process of negotiation between interactants. We therefore concentrate on modality in order to find out if there is any connection between the use of modality by two groups of speakers of Portuguese (Brazilians and Europeans) and the perceived stereotypes of tentativeness and rudeness that are (unfortunately) associated with Brazilians and Portuguese, respectively. The specific issue that we address in this chapter is therefore cultural stereotyping and whether there are any clues in the choices of modal expressions as to why each group perceives the other as being rude or tentative (or evasive). Ultimately, we want to be able to extend our knowledge as to whether there may be any links between the cultural stereotypes in question and the way participants interact in meetings in general. We approach our data from a systemic angle and we also make use of Corpus Linguistics methodology, as it allows us to explore the probabilities exhibited in the data. As Halliday has pointed out:

> quantitative patterns revealed in the corpus – as relative frequencies of terms in grammatical systems – are the manifestation of fundamental grammatical properties. The grammar is an inherently probabilistic system. (Halliday 2002: 407)

What we are looking for is any evidence of different probabilities in the use of modality in the language of Portuguese and Brazilian meetings, which may reflect different interpersonal 'grammars' even though the two groups of speakers share a common 'language.'

The discourse of meetings has been investigated in a number of different ways. For example, Schwartzman (1989) discusses meetings in a range of settings, from business to communities. Bargiela-Chiappini and Harris (1997) provide several papers that focus on meetings in corporations. There has been an increased interest in meetings from an intercultural point of view, mainly following the predominance of English in business contexts. For example, Poncini (2002) investigates footing and frame relationships in meetings held in an Italian company with distributors from around the world. Bilbow (2002) looks at speech acts in meetings at a large airline corporation. Collins and Scott (1997) describe the lexical choices that give rise to 'lexical landscapes' (networks of shared lexical choices) in Brazilian and British meetings. However, as far as we are aware, there has been no focus on the specific issue of the manifestations and effects of stereotyping in business meetings. Our investigation owes a great deal to Florence Davies, in the way that she has inspired us to put the theory to the test, rather than simply to apply it.

11.2 Stereotyping and prejudice

A stereotype can be defined as 'an oversimplified mental image of ... some category of person, institution or event which is shared ... by large numbers of people... Stereotypes are commonly, but not necessarily, accompanied by prejudice' (Stallybrass 1977: 601, cited in Tajfel and Forgas 2000: 57). Stereotyping is thus a common form of social categorisation.

In a way, stereotyping is a natural, instinctive process: 'Because of their basic importance to our own survival and self-esteem we tend to develop a partisanship and ethnocentrism in respect to our in-groups' (Allport 2000: 37). What is most important to us in this chapter is the fact that, as Fishman pointed out as long ago as 1956, 'there is no completely non-verbal social stereotyping' (Fishman 1956: 48, cited in Stangor and Schaller 2000: 58).

There is a vast literature on stereotyping, its nature, roots and consequences, mostly in social psychology, where, for example, studies have looked at the ways in which prejudice is communicated from person to person, and the effect of different kinds of message on prejudice acceptance (Wigboldus *et al.* 2000). There is even an area of studies called 'Image Studies' (or Imagology), which is concerned with 'the critical and historical study of the purported "character" which societies and nations ascribe to each other and to themselves' (Images Information Web Site).[1]

The problem of stereotyping is a very difficult one to investigate, as it is immersed in subjectivity. As Leersen (2003: 1) warns, 'nobody is in a position to describe a cultural identity. What is described is always a cultural difference, a sense in which one nation is perceived to be "different from the rest". In our case, this problem is compounded because we are dealing with cultures which have had centuries of contact, and so mutual stereotyping began long ago, at the time the Portuguese first settled on Brazilian soil in the sixteenth century. During the last century, as new waves of immigrants arrived in Brazil, the Portuguese were seen not as the ruling class any more, but as labourers, who came to a new territory in search of a better quality of life. More recently, with Portugal joining the European Union, it was the Brazilians who fled to Portugal, also hoping for better times, as Brazil faced economic hardship and rising unemployment. This will have helped fuel stereotyping of the newly arrived immigrants.

Nowadays, Brazilian and Portuguese stereotypes are abundant in the modern media, such as the web. They become clear when we look at how each culture is normally talked about in clauses such as 'Brazilians are...' and 'the Portuguese are ...' ('Os brasileiros são ...' and 'Os portugueses são...') in web material. Risking a slight diversion, we ran web searches with Google™ for these phrases and then fed the results into KWIC Google, a concordancer and collocator for Google web search results.[2] The following are among the top collocates for each search, based on 100 hits:

Brazilians: rich, sympathetic, welcome, victim, racist, fools, smart, charity;

Portuguese: citizens, favorite, bad, incapable, smoke, stupid, critical, consumers.[3]

In the business context, the most abundant set of references on stereotyping comes not from studies of the practices of stereotyping as such, but from books dealing with cultural issues in a stereotypical manner. For example, Lewis (1996) describes several aspects of business management around the world, focusing on cross-cultural issues and on what business people ought to know in order to do business successfully. In the process, however, his commentary is imbued with all kinds of stereotypical descriptions of peoples and cultures. For instance, in the case of Britain, he depicts British managers as 'diplomatic, tactful, feudal, laid back, casual, reasonable, helpful' (p. 75). American managers, in turn, 'symbolize the vitality and audacity of the land of free enterprise', being 'assertive, aggressive, goal and action oriented, confident, vigorous, optimistic, ready for change' (p. 78). German business people live by a set of rules governed by 'Ordnung', 'where everything and everyone has a place in a grand design calculated to produce maximum efficiency' (p. 70). Many other cultures are assigned such hard and fast labels, including Spaniards, who are 'impulsive', Russians, who are 'soulful', and the Portuguese, who are characterised as being 'improvising'.

The Portuguese figure in Lewis's account in a number of places, including a whole section on how to negotiate with them. They are portrayed as being 'amongst the best negotiators in the world' (Lewis 1996: 227). They are also credited with having 'great oratorical skills', cheerful manners and a 'multi-active nature', whereby their negotiations are linked to other transactions in which they are involved (p. 227). Other characteristics claimed for Portuguese businessmen are being suspicious, quick, perceptive and opportunistic.

Brazilians do not receive a full chapter in Lewis (1996), but they are subsumed under the Latins, including Latin Europe and South America (p. 80), which means some of their features are seen as shared by the Portuguese and vice-versa. The chief characteristics of business people in Brazil supposedly include autocracy, 'where family money is often on the line' (p. 80). Lewis adds: 'There is a growing meritocracy in Brazil, Chile and in the big northern Italian industrial firms, but Latin employees in general indicate willing and trusting subservience to their "establishments"' (pp 80–1).

However, bias is not a privilege of Anglo-oriented authors such as Lewis. André (2000), a Portuguese columnist writing for a regional newspaper, illustrates the same phenomenon:

> The Portuguese are very individualistic, which makes them resist authority ... This tendency to place the human heart above the law is carried over into business, where it is necessary first of all to win the good will of the buyer, whereas in other countries what is important is to offer the biggest material advantage. They lack capitalist spirit.[5]

André's view on his own culture clearly contradicts that of Lewis, for whom the Portuguese are superb negotiators; but he is equally inclined to represent the qualities in terms of simple stereotypes.

Lewis and André can be seen as representing relatively 'lay' perspectives; but the tendency to take a culturally narrow view is not restricted to the non-academic world. As Bargiela-Chiappini and Harris (1997: 7) put it:

> ethnocentrism has been an all too common feature of some past research. Within the academic community, one need not go beyond linguistics and organisational communication to expose the 'Anglocentrism' that has characterized much research until fairly recently.

One of the early proposals that fits this description is perhaps Kaplan (1966), who proposed a series of patterns of paragraph organisation, which became known as Kaplan's doodles, because of their graphic representation. In his model, paragraphs written by native English speakers are considered linearly organised, and the corresponding doodle is a straight arrow. On the other hand, paragraphs produced by the Japanese, Chinese, Thai and Koreans ('Oriental'), for example, would display a circular pattern (thus being depicted as a spiral). For speakers of Latin languages ('Romance'), the pattern is digressive, and as a result, the corresponding doodle is a broken line. These patterns were proposed not just as a series of hypotheses on rhetorical organization, but as 'cultural thought patterns', in other words as the way different peoples of the world think. Such unconscious prioritising of one's own culture can clearly have serious implications, and indeed may trigger all sorts of stereotypes of other cultures.

However, stereotyping is a common feature of all kinds of culture, both at a macro and a micro level. In the Brazilian context, there are several current stereotypes regarding the way people from one part of the country see people from other parts. Likewise, Brazilians foster stereotypical judgements towards people from neighbouring countries such as Argentina and Paraguay. As business in the continent intensifies due to the South American Trade Agreement, stereotypical images tend to become more common, mainly in the local press; for instance, Argentinian negotiators are often reported in the Brazilian press as grumblers, crying and whining until their demands are met. We hope that, as the DIRECT project develops, we will be able to gather data to allow studies into these areas.

11.3 Modality

As noted above, our focus is on the linguistic reflexes of stereotyping; and one promising line of enquiry is the deployment of the resources of modality. Modality can be defined, in simple terms, as the intermediate positions or 'the space between yes and no' (Thompson 1996: 57; Eggins 1994: 179). It is a very important part of the way in which speakers convey interpersonal meanings. Modality enables speakers to express attitudes and judgements, including degrees of certainty, usuality, obligation and inclination.

Modality is realised by two main devices in the clause: through the use of a finite modal operator or through mood adjuncts (these can be combined in the clause). For example, the clause 'She teaches Latin' is not modalised, nor is 'she doesn't teach Latin'. But between these two poles of polarity, there is a wide modal space, which can result in several possible rewordings between the two ends of the scale: 'She might teach Latin' includes a modal (*might*), which indicates 'perhaps yes, perhaps no'; 'she usually teaches Latin' makes use of a mood adjunct (*usually*) indicating 'sometimes yes, sometimes no'; and so on (Thompson, 1996: 57). In Halliday's terms (e.g. Halliday and Matthiessen 2004: 620), these are implicit devices for expressing modality: that is, the modality is expressed within the clause that is modalised. There are, however, explicit ways of conveying modality, namely by means of metaphors of modality. For instance, in 'I think Henry James wrote *The Bostonians*', modality is realised by the clause 'I think'. This is considered a grammatical metaphor of modality – instead of using a finite modal operator (*may*) or an adjunct (*perhaps*) or both, the speaker chose to express this feature as a clause, with a subject and a finite of its own, and therefore with a mood and residue as well. As Eggins puts it, 'what would usually be realized as a *constituent* of the clause comes out as a clause on its own' (1994: 181).

There are two types of modality: modalisation and modulation. Modalisation enables speakers to express probability and usuality; modulation, on the other hand, concerns the way in which obligation and inclination are conveyed, allowing speakers to 'get people to do things for us, or of offering to do things for them' (Eggins 1994: 187).

Modality offers speakers ways of graduating the degree of probability and certainty with which they advance a proposition. Normally three levels of modal commitment are recognised: high, median and low, for both modality and modulation. To illustrate, in the clause 'I *shan't* be happy again' the modalisation is high; in 'they *should* be back now', it is median, and in 'I *may* be wrong', it is low. As far as modulation is concerned, a clause such as 'You *must* ask someone' has high modulation; 'You *ought* to invite her' is modulated at a median level; whereas 'You *can* help yourself to a drink' has low modulation. The levels of commitment are relevant to our study because they relate, amongst other things, to the degree of 'pressure' on the addressee to accept the validity of the proposition or to accede to the obligation being imposed.

Interestingly, even when choices of modality are at the high end of the continuum, the proposition is still charged with interpersonal meaning and is more tentative than it would be if it had no modality at all. Eggins (1994: 183) offers the following example: '"I'm absolutely convinced that Henry James certainly must most definitely have written *The Bostonians*" is still *less sure* than saying "Henry James wrote *The Bostonians*". This is relevant to the present study in that the choice to modalise the proposition in itself signals readiness to negotiate, regardless of the level of modality expressed. If Brazilians, according to the stereotype under investigation, do make consistent use of modality, then they may indeed be perceived as more vague and tentative by their Portuguese peers. The reverse also applies. By not selecting for modality, speakers may express less tentative meanings, but they also risk coming across as too assertive.

11.4 Data and methodology

In order to attempt to throw some light on to aspects of discourse that may create or reinforce stereotypical images of Brazilians and Portuguese in business settings, we resort to an investigation into modalisation and modulation choices in business meetings. Our working hypothesis is that there may be a linguistic basis to stereotypical images of the other nationality which may be partly reflected in the kinds of modality choices typically made by Brazilians and Portuguese. We decided that a set of data that would allow us to look into this issue would be meetings that did not involve intercultural contact, that is, which were held by Brazilians only, on the one hand, and by Portuguese only, on the other. In this manner, perhaps we would avoid the problems associated with one group having a higher status of some kind in the interaction, thereby biasing the use of modality in some way.

The size of our sub-corpora is given in Table 11.1.

Ours is a small corpus by contemporary standards for general corpora, but in terms of meetings language data, it is not modest, given the difficulties associated with collecting authentic spoken data. Most meetings are private, which restricts free access to the event. In addition, meetings are spoken, and so they need comprehensive recording of some sort; field notes are not enough to give an account of the complexity of the discourse taking place. Finally, being spoken data, they need transcribing to permit analysis; rendering speech in writing is a very time-consuming job, especially for events where there are several participants, whose turns often overlap, and so on. However, the results and discussion below must be treated with caution, particularly because the figures for the Portuguese data are low.

The meetings were held in different places in Brazil and in Portugal. The subject matter of the meetings varied, from planning of production or sales or other types of activities, within the company or between companies, between interactants of the same or different ranks, in public and in private companies, i.e. in the most varied contexts. The role of participants was distributed differently between the two groups of

Table 11.1 The two sub-corpora

	Brazilian	*Portuguese*
Meetings	10	2
Tokens	120,022	12,164
Types	8,316	1,881

meetings. In some Brazilian meetings, there was a boss and his/her subordinates. In the Portuguese events, on the other hand, participants were always of the same rank.

The data were analysed using WordSmith Tools (Scott 1998). Concordances were run for each modal form and were then inspected to make sure that the search words were in fact used as modals. This was needed because a single form may indicate different word classes, such as *poder*, which may mean the modal 'can' or the noun 'power'.

11.5 Analysis

First we looked at the overall frequency of modals in each sub-corpus. As Table 11.2 indicates, there is a higher percentage of modals in the Brazilian meetings than in the Portuguese ones. (Note that we counted modal *lemmata*, that is, the different conjugated forms of each modal were counted as one single lemma.) In addition, there are more modal types in the Brazilian meetings (13 versus 8). This is perhaps not surprising, given that the size of the Brazilian sub-corpus is much larger. What seems more revealing, though, is the extent to which modals are shared. Of the 21 modals that were employed, just nine are shared (43 per cent). That is, less than half of the modals are common to both sub-corpora, with the Brazilian meetings exhibiting a wider range of unique modals.

The modals that were shared in both sub-corpora are shown in Table 11.3.

According to the figures, there seems to be a stronger preference for *achar* in the Brazilian meetings, whereas in the Portuguese encounters there is a relatively higher incidence of *querer* and *gostar*. Note that *achar*, which is low modality, is the most frequent modalisation in Brazilian Portuguese (25 per cent as opposed to 13 per cent in European Portuguese),

Table 11.2 Frequency of modals in both sub-corpora

	Brazilian	*Portuguese*
Total running words	120,022	12,164
Frequency of all modals (lemmata)	2,244	134
% modals	1.87	1.10
Total modal forms	13	8
Unique modals	7	2
(% of total modal forms)	(54%)	(25%)

whereas the most frequent in EP are *ter que* and *querer,* both high value and modulation, making up 53 per cent of the total occurrences (as opposed to 33 per cent in BP). In addition, ignoring the distinction between modalisation and modulation, the low level modals *achar, gostar* and *poder* add up to 50 per cent in BP and 37 per cent in EP whereas the very high level ones add up to 24 per cent and 31 per cent respectively. These figures leave out *querer* which is high or low depending on person and finite. In BP, of 124 occurrences of first person with *querer,* the total for inclusive first person and the tentative first person (which can be seen as lower in modality) is 71 (almost 60 per cent of the total).

Also, there is a significant difference in the overall use of modals at different levels. Leaving out *poder* which is high, and subjunctive which relates to low modality, the difference is still so high that it confirms the tendency, as the figures in Table 11.4 show.

The six modals that are unique to the Brazilian sub-corpus are listed in Table 11.5, together with their frequencies. The most common one is *precisar* (need).

Table 11.3 Occurrences of the modals shared in both corpora

Modal	*Brazilian*		*Portuguese*	
	No.	*%**	*No.*	*%***
achar (think)	559	25	16	12
dever (must)	67	3	4	3
gostar (like)	21	1	7	5
poder (can)	495	22	27	20
querer (want)	273	12	35	26
ter que (have to)	470	21	37	28
Total modals	1,885		126	

* Percentages based on 2,224 occurrences
** Percentages based on 134 occurrences

Table 11.4 Frequency of high versus low modality

	Brazilian		*Portuguese*	
	No.	*%*	*No.*	*%*
Low	697	40	19	18
Median	233	13	12	11
High	810	47	76	71
Total	1,740		107	

Table 11.5 Occurrences of the modals found only in the Brazilian corpus

Modal	No.	%
precisar (need)	188	52
deixar (let)	62	17
parecer (seem)	54	15
pedir (ask)	24	7
acreditar (believe)	17	5
mandar (tell sb to)	9	3
pensar (think)	5	1
Total	359	

The modals that occurred in the Portuguese meetings only appear in Table 11.6.

The difference in the incidence of modals in BP and EP cannot be underestimated as the incidence is roughly two in BP to one in EB. Despite the differences in the use of modals, the sense of needing to do something comes out strongly in both sub-corpora. Whereas the Brazilians prefer *precisa* (present + 3rd p. + need), the Portuguese employ *era para* (past + 3rd p.+ be supposed to).

Now, if we look at these data not in terms of the individual lexical items but in terms of the type of modality that is expressed (i.e. modalisation or modulation), we begin to see potentially significant differences across the two sub-corpora, as Table 11.7 suggests.

Table 11.6 Occurrences of the modals found only in the Portuguese corpus

Modal	No.	%
ser para (be supposed to)	5	63
dar para (can)	3	38
Total	8	

Table 11.7 Occurrences of types of modality

	Brazilian		Portuguese	
	No.	%	No.	%
modalisation	637	40	16	17
modulation	947	60	77	83
	1584*		93*	

* These totals do not match the total number of modals reported above because two modals, namely *poder* (can) and *dever* (must), serve a dual function (i.e. modalisation or modulation), and were not tallied here.

As can be seen from Table 11.7, there is a higher occurrence of modalisation in the Brazilian meetings, whereas in the Portuguese meetings modulation is far more frequent.

The modals used for modalisation are shown in Table 11.8.

Again, in the Brazilian meetings there is a greater choice of modals to express modalisation. Three of the four lexical modals are unique to the Brazilian meetings; there were seven different modals altogether in the Brazilian interactions, and so this means that about half (3/7) of those unique modals were used to express modalisation. In the case of the Portuguese meetings, there were two unique modals, but neither of them was employed to express modalisation.

The breakdown for modulation appears in Table 11.9. Here roughly the same pattern holds for the Brazilian meetings, that is, about half (4/7) of the unique modals were used to express modulation. However, with respect to the Portuguese meetings, both modals that appear in the Portuguese data only were used in order to express modulation.

Table 11.8 Expressions of modalisation in the two sub-corpora

	Brazilian		Portuguese	
	No.	%	*No.*	%
achar	559	88	16	100
acredito	17	3	0	0
parece	54	8	0	0
pensar	7	1	0	0
Totals	637		16	

Table 11.9 Expressions of modulation in the two sub-corpora

	Brazilian		Portuguese	
	No.	%	*No.*	%
ser para (be supposed to)	0	0	5	6
gostar (would like to)	21	2	7	8
dar (can)	0	0	3	3
deixar (let)	62	6	0	0
mandar (tell to)	9	1	0	0
pedir (ask)	24	2	0	0
precisar (need)	188	18	0	0
querer (want)	273	26	35	40
ter que (have to)	470	45	37	43
Totals	1,047		87	

When we translate these figures into a probability table, the result is as in Table 11.10. As Table 11.10 shows, in Brazilian meetings, there is a probability of 1.87 per cent that a word that is uttered is a modal, and 98.13 per cent that it is not. In the Portuguese meetings, the probabilities are 1.1 per cent and 98.9 per cent. At a more delicate level, when a word is uttered in the meetings, there is a 0.75 per cent chance that it will be an instance of modalisation in the Brazilian meetings, and only 0.19 per cent in the Portuguese ones; and there is a 1.12 per cent chance of modulation in the Brazilian meetings as opposed to 0.91 per cent in the Portuguese ones.[5]

When these probabilities are translated into how many modals are used in each case, the differences become more striking. In the Brazilian meetings, one in about every 54 words is a modal, whereas in the Portuguese encounters, it is just one in about 91 words. With respect to the type of modal, participants use modalisation on average every 133 words if they are Brazilian, but every 533 words if they are Portuguese (four times less often); and they use modulation every 89 words on average if they are Brazilian, but every 109 words if they are Portuguese. In general, the odds are in favour of *not* using modals (98 per cent chance of not using), and this represents the greatest similarity between the two groups. But when speakers do choose to use them, the probabilities work out differently for each group.

We can now provide a summary of our findings.

1. There are different probabilities attached to modal use for each group.

2. Modality, as restricted to modals or grammatical metaphors, is used in different degrees by participants in the meetings on both sides of the Atlantic. The Brazilians tended to use more modals,

Table 11.10 Probability of use of modals

	Use	Probability	Or every ... words	Type	Probability	Or every ... words
Brazilian	Yes	1.87%	53.49	modalisation	0.75%	133.71
				modulation	1.12%	89.14
	No	98.13%	1.02			
Portuguese	Yes	1.10%	90.78	modalisation	0.19%	533.98
				modulation	0.91%	109.37
	No	98.90%	1.01			

that is, both more tokens and types. On average, the Brazilians used one modal every 64 words, whereas the Portuguese used one modal every 97 words.

3. Modality is expressed in different ways. More than half of the modals were unique, with the Brazilian meetings encompassing a greater variety of modals.

4. Modality is used for different purposes. Whereas Brazilians used modality mostly to express modalisation, the Portuguese employed it in order to express modulation. Modals that were unique to the Brazilian meetings were used roughly in the same amount to express modalisation as modulation. The unique modals in the Portuguese meetings were both used to express modulation.

11.6 Final remarks

There are several limitations to our study. An important one has to do with the design of our corpus. The two sub-corpora were considerably different in size and composition, although they were controlled for register and genre. Subject matter varied across the two sub-corpora and indeed from meeting from meeting. This will have had an impact on the choice of modals and that may explain to a certain degree the difference in modal use detected in the corpus. While the influence of topic cannot be ignored, it cannot account for the whole of the variation in modality in our data. In fact, none of the three metafunctions was controlled for in the data, simply because it is nearly impossible (to say the least) to aspire to create a corpus of meetings that were controlled for any one of the metafunctions.

We started off looking for possible clues in the use of modal resources as to why Brazilians typically come across to the Portuguese as evasive, and conversely, why their Portuguese counterparts normally seem to sound as if they were rude. These two traits form part of larger national stereotypes regarding these two cultures. Our hunch was that there might be something in the modality choices that could account at least in part for that, since stereotyping is an interpersonal, social phenomenon, and modality is intimately involved in social negotiation.

Despite the limitations mentioned above, our findings seem to provide some evidence as to why people from these two cultures perceive the other in a prejudiced way. Since the Brazilians employ a wide range of modality choices as well as a higher number of occurrences of modalised utterances, they might come across to a Portuguese business meeting participant as less assertive, more cautious and more tentative than 'normal' (i.e. by Portuguese standards of 'normality'). The Portuguese, on the other hand, utilise not only a narrower range of modals but fewer of those as well, and thus might appear to a Brazilian participant at a meeting to be more assertive, more straightforward and more forceful than 'normal' (by Brazilian standards). Of course, we must stress that these are just possible interpretations, since we have no direct data from business participants to find out how they really felt toward their counterparts at meetings (not to mention the fact that when people are asked to give their intuitions on such matters the resulting data might not be as reliable as we would hope). But because we have heard these stereotypes so often, we believe that it is at least plausible that there is some connection between the modal choices and the perception of others in business encounters.

We must emphasise that our findings must not be taken as a justification of discriminatory practices. The differences we have detected in modal usage do not automatically translate into being rude or being tentative, much less into a national characteristic of rudeness or tentativeness, not least because it is unlikely that speakers are aware of how different their discourse is in comparison with the other group with respect to modal use. Nevertheless, as Halliday (2002: 407) argues:

> any kind of principled sampling is likely to bring out proportionalities that have remained entirely beneath one's conscious awareness. I would contend that it is precisely the most unconscious patterns in the grammar – the cryptogrammatic ones – that are the most powerful in their constitutive effect, in construing experience and in enacting the social process, and hence in the construction of our ideological makeup.

In addition, the use of modality is, of course, only part of the picture: other choices, in language and other forms of behaviour, will certainly play their part in how interactants are perceived by their interlocutors. In the final analysis it all depends on how one group interprets the other's discourse anyway, be it on the basis of the presence, absence, excess or lack of some linguistic feature, or indeed on none of these. Stereotypes such as the ones we have focused on are built around a complex set of processes, not on a one-to-one relationship between choices in the linguistic system and social categorisation.

Understanding stereotyping is an important part of coming to grips with business language. There is a vast literature on cultural characteristics in the business market, mostly geared towards executives who need to do business with different cultures, which tends to increase as a result of globalisation. A striking feature of much of that literature is the absence of research and, one might add, the total lack of reference to any linguistic study, let alone of a systemic functional nature. We would argue that this state of affairs ought to change: in other words, linguists must not shy away from these situations; they must reclaim their role as experts in language in use, especially in situations where a linguist's help is needed, such as in understanding why there is stereotyping and perhaps prejudice in business encounters. Systemic Functional Linguistics provides us with the theoretical and analytical tools to bring to the surface aspects of discourse that are significant to the questions at hand. There has, to the best of our knowledge, been no strictly functional linguistic literature on cultural stereotyping. Even so, through such categories as modalisation and modulation, and the choices made by participants in the modality system, we have been able to focus attention on one piece of the stereotyping puzzle.

José Saramago, the Portuguese author who won the Nobel literature prize, urged Brazilians to stop prejudice against their fellow Portuguese:

> Let us put an end to certain preconceptions, that the Portuguese are rude, smelly, have mustaches ... [...] Clearly we in Portugal also tell jokes about Brazilians. But what is that all about? [...] Whatever it is, it can't be anything positive. (Saramago, 1998)[6]

We subscribe to Saramago's plea, but we would add that, without a proper recognition of the way stereotyping works in and through language, there is little hope that this will change simply because some people dislike it.

Acknowledgements

The authors wish to thank CNPq (Conselho Nacional de Desenvolvimento Científico e Tecnológico) for the financial support under grant #500945/ 2003-9 (Leila Barbara) and grant #350455/2003-1 (Tony Berber Sardinha). An initial version of this chapter was presented by Leila Barbara at the first DICOEN (Lisbon 2001).

Notes

1. http://cf.hum.uva.nl/images/info/
2. http://lael.pucsp.br/corpora

3. Frequencies appear in brackets:
   'Os brasileiros são ...' (4) ricos, (3) solidários, (3) benvindos, (2) vítimas, (2) racista, (2) otários, (2) inteligentes, (2) doação.
   'Os portugueses são ...' (5) cidadãos, (3) favoritos, (2) mal, (2) incapazes, (2) fumam, (2) estúpidos, (2) críticos, (2) consumidores.
4. In the original: 'O português é fortemente individualista, o que o faz recusar qualquer tipo de autoridade ... Esta tendência para colocar a simpatia humana acima da lei [...] transmite-se até aos negócios, onde é necessário primeiro ganhar simpatia do comprador, enquanto que noutros países o importante é oferecer maiores vantagens materiais. Falta de espirito capitalista.' (Our translation)
5. This contrasts with the figures presented above for modalisation and modulation, where it was shown that the modulation choices for the Brazilians accounted for 60 per cent of the total, whereas for the Portuguese it was higher, at 83 per cent. But those statistics refer to the percentages within each group (e.g. Brazilian modulation: 947/1584 = 60 per cent, Portuguese modulation: 77/93 = 83 per cent), whereas now they refer to the percentages of the initial probability (e.g. Brazilian modulation: 60 per cent of 1.87 per cent = 1.12 per cent, Portuguese modulation: 83 per cent of 1.10 per cent = 0.91 per cent).
6. In the original: 'Acabemos com certos preconceitos, de que o português é bruto, cheira mal, usa bigodes ... [...] Evidentemente que nós, em Portugal, também contamos anedotas de brasileiro. Mas tudo isso o que é? [...] Seja o que for, positivo não é.' (Our translation)

References

Allport, G. W. (2000). The nature of prejudice. In C. Stangor (ed.) *Stereotypes and Prejudice: Essential Readings*. London: Psychology Press/Taylor and Francis, pp. 20–48.

André, R. (2000). Opinião: Criatividade à Portuguesa ou o modo de ser Português. *Jornal de Monchique*, XVI, 200.

Bargiela Chiappini, F. and Harris, S. J. (eds). (1997). *Managing Language – The Discourse of Corporate Meetings*. Amsterdam/Philadelphia, PA: John Benjamins.

Bargiella-Chiappini, F. and Nickerson, C. (1999). Business writing as social action. In *Writing Business: Genres, Media and Discourse*, F. Bargiela-Chiapini and C. Nickerson (eds), 1–32. New York: Longman.

Bilbow, G. T. (2002). Commissive speech act use in intercultural business meetings. *IRAL* 40: 287–303.

Collins, H. and Scott, M. (1997). Lexical landscaping in business meetings. In *The Languages of Business – An International Perspective*, F. Bargiela-Chiappini and S. Harris (eds), 183–210. Edinburgh: Edinburgh University Press.

Eggins, S. (1994). *An Introduction to Systemic Functional Linguistics*. London: Pinter.

Fishman, J. A. (1956). An examination of the process and function of social stereotyping. *Journal of Social Psychology*, 43: 27–64.

Halliday, M. A. K. (2002). On grammar and grammatics. In *Collected Works of M. A. K. Halliday: 1. On Grammar*, J. Webster (ed.), 384–418. London/New York: Continuum.

Halliday, M. A. K. and Matthiessen, C. M. I. M. (2004). *Introduction to Functional Grammar* (3rd edition). London: Arnold.

Kaplan, R. B. (1966). Cultural thought patterns in intercultural education. *Language Learning*, 16: 1–20.

Leersen, J. (2003). National identity and national stereotype. Online text on the Images Website at http://cf.hum.uva.nl/images/info/leers.html

Lewis, R. D. (1996). *When Cultures Collide – Managing Successfully across Cultures*. London: Nicholas Brealey Publishing.

Poncini, G. (2002). Investigating discourse at business meetings with multicultural participation. *Iral*, 40: 345–73.

Saramago, J. (1998). Entrevista. *Playboy*, October. São Paulo: Abril.

Schwartzman, H. B. (1989). *The Meeting: Gatherings in Organizations and Communities*. New York/London: Plenum Press.

Scott, M. (1998). *WordSmith Tools Version 3*. Oxford: Oxford University Press.

Stallybrass, O. (1977). Stereotype. In *The Fontana Dictionary of Modern Thought*, A. Bullock and O. Stallybrass (eds). London: Fontana/Collins.

Stangor, C. (ed.) (2000). *Stereotypes and Prejudice: Essential Readings*. London: Psychology Press/Taylor and Francis.

Stangor, C. and Schaller, M. (2000). Stereotypes as individual and collective representations. In C. Stangor (ed.) *Stereotypes and Prejudice: Essential Readings*. London: Psychology Press/Taylor and Francis, pp. 64–81.

Tajfel, H. and Forgas, J. P. (2000). Social categorization: Cognition, values and groups. In C. Stangor (ed.) *Stereotypes and Prejudice: Essential Readings*. London: Psychology Press/Taylor and Francis, pp. 49–63.

Thompson, G. (1996). *Introducing Functional Grammar*. London: Arnold.

Wigboldus, D. H. J., Semin, G. R., and Spears, R. (2000). How do we communicate stereotypes? Linguistic bases and inferential consequences. *Journal of Personality and Social Psychology*, 78: 5–18.

Boomer dreaming: the texture of re-colonisation in a lifestyle magazine

J R Martin

University of Sydney

12.1 Tackling a text

I am often asked by students and colleagues about how to analyse a text, given the extravagant model of language and attendant modalities of communication currently evolving as systemic functional semiotics (hereafter SFS). There is of course no simple answer to this question, not one at least that my students and colleagues imagine existing when they ask. That said, the question as to what SFS affords and how to deploy its various hierarchies and complementarities is a reasonable one, which I will try and address here with reference to an article from a lifestyle magazine (Figure 12.1). In part of course this response will be a personal one, based on 40 years or so of text analysis,[1] which began under the tutelage of Michael Gregory and Waldemar Gutwinski at Glendon College in 1967/8. But there are perhaps some general heuristic principles to propose as well, which I will highlight as they emerge from the discussion below. The basic resources employed in this analysis are drawn from Halliday and Matthiessen (1994) (grammar), Kress and van Leeuwen (1996) (image), Martin (1992) and Martin and Rose (2007) (discourse semantics), Martin and Rose (2008) (genre) and Martin and White (2005) (appraisal).

12.2 Preparing

The textual instance we have chosen here is presented as Figure 12.1. As can be seen it is a multimodal text, comprising verbiage and image, from the **insideinformation** section of a glossy lifestyle magazine which is included monthly in the *Sydney Morning Herald* broadsheet newspaper.

Big waves and Bondi Beach have always gone together, writes Peter FitzSimons, but no one had ever seen the ocean rise up with a strength such as this …

placeintime
bondi beach

And so there they lie, happily sweltering in the summer sun on Australia's most famous beach, just as they have for so many generations past. It is such a wonderfully peaceful scene – of people and nature as a happy whole – that it is simply unimaginable that in a few seconds nature could ever rear up and savage the lot of them.

Ah, but those 35,000 Sydneysiders who were lying in those very spots on the afternoon of February 6, 1938, surely felt equally at peace.

The day was, in the vernacular of the time, a 'stinker', and some thought it was in fact a record turnout on the beach, with the numbers perhaps swelled by the fact that those bronzed boys of the Bondi Surf Bathers' Life Saving Club had turned up in force to have one of their popular surf competitions.

At three o'clock there was still not the slightest clue that this afternoon would forever be known as 'Black Sunday' in the annals of Sydney. Then it happened. With a roar like a Bondi tram running amok, an enormous wave suddenly rolled over the thousands in the surf, including those many standing on the large sandbank just out from the shore – knocking them all over as it went. And then another wave hit, and then another.

Three huge waves, just like that, piggy-backed their way further and further up the beach and grabbed everything they could along the way – from babies to toddlers to adolescents to beach umbrellas, to old blokes and young sheilas alike, and then made a mad dash for the open sea

again, carrying all before it and sweeping everyone off the sandbank and into the deep channel next to it in the process.

In no more than 20 seconds, that peaceful scene had been tragically transformed into utter chaos. Now, the boiling surf, with yet more large waves continuing to roll over, was filled with distressed folk waving for help.

In their long and glorious history, this still stands as the finest hour of the Australian surf lifesaving movement. For, ignoring their own possible peril, the Bondi boys now charged into the surf, some attached to one of the seven reels available, some relying only on their own strength. As one, they began pulling the people out.

On the shore, many survivors were resuscitated, as the Bondi clubhouse was turned into a kind of emergency clearing house, and ambulances from all over Sydney town descended and carried the victims away.

Finally, just half an hour after the waves hit, the water was cleared of bobbing heads and waving arms, and it was time to take stock: 250 people had needed the lifesavers to pull them out, of whom 210 were OK once back on land. Thirty-five needed mouth to mouth to be restored to consciousness, while five people perished.

With thanks to Waverley Library and reader Diane Touzell, whose grandfather, Bill Jenkins, was one of the lifesavers.

Do you have a historical anecdote about a place in Sydney? Write to Peter FitzSimons at pfitzsimons@smh.com.au

Figure 12.1 Boomer dreaming text – 'placeintime bondi beach'

As a first step we might consider the layout of the text – its multimodal *graphology* if you will. To the left we have two photos, Bondi beach below, and Peter FitzSimons above; then to the right we have a *kicker* (a sub-heading), with the main text below. And below the main text we have two separated paragraphs, one thanking a reader for drawing Fitzsimons' attention to the 'Black Sunday' rescue, followed by another in bold soliciting further suggestions for his regular **placeintime** column. This general layout is outlined in Figure 12.2, including placement of the photographer's byline (Photography **Marco Del Grande**) and the column's heading (**placeintime** bondi beach) to the left of FitzSimons' photograph.

As we can see the layout distinguishes between verbiage and image, and within verbiage between kicker (above, larger font) and two columns of main text (several *lines* below, smaller font, first line in left column in bold), and within the main text between the *story* proper and the thanks (skipping a line) and between the thanks and the solicitation (skipping another line and changing to back to bold). In addition the graphology gives us words, sentences and paragraphs, and some intermediate units between word and sentence separated by dash, comma and colon. From a grammatical perspective the verbiage can be usefully organised into ranking clauses, with embedded clauses enclosed between double square brackets, using double slashes for clause boundaries and triple slashes for clause complex (i.e. sentence) boundaries – as for the kicker below.

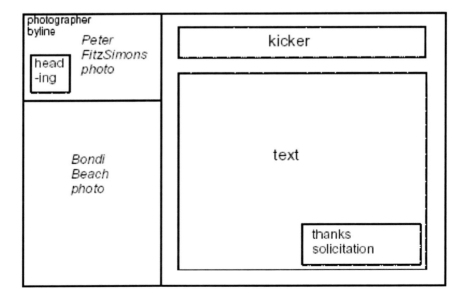

Figure 12. 2 General layout of '**placeintime** bondi beach' column

Big waves and Bondi Beach have always gone together, //
writes Peter FitzSimons, //
but no one had ever seen [[the ocean rise up with a strength such as this]]
... ///

Within clause complexes, paratactically related clauses can be organised one under another on separate lines, with hypotactic dependent clauses indented one tab; by convention, any included dependent clauses are enclosed in double angle brackets (i.e. <<...>>) and reproduced on the line below the clause they interrupt. Non-finite clauses have been specially highlighted below by placing their Predicators in italics. Paragraph boundaries (◀) are also marked.

And so there they lie, //
    happily *sweltering* in the summer sun on Australia's most famous beach,
    //
        just as they have for so many generations past. ///
        It is such a wonderfully peaceful scene – of people and nature as
        a happy whole – [[that it is simply unimaginable [[that nature could
        ever rear up // and savage the lot of them]]]]. ///

◀

Ah, but those 35,000 Sydneysiders [[who were lying in those very spots on the afternoon of February 6, 1938]], surely felt equally at peace. ///

◀

The day was, in the vernacular of the time, a 'stinker', //
and some thought//
    it was in fact a record turnout on the beach, //
        with the numbers perhaps *swelled* by the fact [[that those bronzed
        boys of the Bondi Surf Bathers' Life Saving Club had turned up in
        force// to *have* one of their popular surf competitions.]] ///

◀

At three o'clock there was still not the slightest clue [[that this afternoon would forever be known as 'Black Sunday' in the annals of Sydney.]] ///
Then it happened. ///
With a roar like a Bondi tram running amok, an enormous wave suddenly rolled over the thousands in the surf, including those many [[*standing* on the large sandbank just out from the shore]] //
    – *knocking* them all over //
        as it went. ///
And then another wave hit, //
and then another. ///

◀

The huge waves, just like that, piggy-backed their way further and further up the beach //
and grabbed everything [[they could]] along the way – from babies to toddlers to adolescents to beach umbrellas, to old blokes and young sheilas alike, //
and then made a mad dash for the open sea again, //
    carrying all before it //
    and *sweeping* everyone off the sandbank and into the deep channel next to it in the process. ///

❡

In no more than 20 seconds, that peaceful scene had been tragically transformed into utter chaos. ///
Now, the boiling surf, <<...>>, was filled with distressed folk //
    <<with yet more large waves *continuing* to roll over>>, //
    waving for help. ///

❡

In their long and glorious history, this still stands as the finest hour of the Australian lifesaving movement. ///
For,<<...>>, the Bondi boys now charged into the surf, //
    <<*ignoring* their own possible peril>>, //
    some *attached* to one of the seven reels available, //
    some *relying* only on their own strength. //
As one, they began pulling the people out. ///

❡

On the shore, many survivors were resuscitated, //
    as the Bondi clubhouse was turned into a kind of emergency clearing house, //
    and ambulances from all over Sydney town descended //
    and carried the victims away. //

❡

Finally, just half an hour after the waves hit,[2]
the water was cleared of bobbing heads and waving arms, //
and it was time to take stock: //
250 people had needed the lifesavers to pull them out, //
    of whom 210 were OK once back on land. ///

❡

Thirty-five needed mouth to mouth //
    to be *restored* to consciousness, //
    while five people perished. ///

The final two paragraphs of verbiage parse as follows:

> With thanks to Waverly Library and reader Diane Touzell, //
> whose grandfather, Bill Jenkins, was one of the lifesavers. ///

> Do you have a historical anecdote about a place in Sydney? ///
> Write to Peter FitzSimons at pfitzsimons@smh.com.au ///

Generically speaking, the FitzSimons' photo is a *portrait* and the beach photo a *landscape*. The main text, as we shall see, is arguably a narrative (referred to as a *historical anecdote* by FitzSimons in his own journalistic terms), with a recognisable Orientation Complication Evaluation Resolution Coda structure (see below); the narrative has been adapted to the column by adding a Kicker, Thanks and Solicitation stage, and by beginning with an intermodal phase relating the story to the Bondi Beach image (putting time in place as it were).

12.3 Tools

As a theory, SFS has been designed to afford more insight than we need for any one purpose (Halliday and Matthiessen 1999). In general terms it currently comprises five hierarchies and four complementarities. The hierarchies are delicacy, rank, realisation, instantiation and individuation:

- **delicacy** (classification – *general to specific*)

- **rank** (composition – *whole to part*)

- **realisation** (stratification – *abstract to concrete*)

- **instantiation** (metastability – *system to instance*)

- **individuation** (coding orientation – *reservoir to repertoire*)

Of these we can set aside instantiation and individuation because we are dealing with a single text. To explore instantiation we would need a corpus of comparable texts about the history of places, with a view to exploring text type, register and genre. To explore individuation we would need a corpus of comparable texts by Peter FitzSimons and his peers, with a view to exploring individuality, communality and style. We can however deal in the instance with realisation, rank and delicacy. As far as realisation is concerned, we can shunt among graphology, lexicogrammar, discourse semantics, register and genre. With rank, we can shunt among smaller and larger units on any of these strata. Through delicacy we can focus on general or specific classifications of any of these units.

Considered in relation to one another, these five hierarchies are of course themselves complementarities, to which we can add genesis, modality,[3] metafunction and axis:

- **genesis** (logogenesis/ontogenesis/phylogenesis)

- **modality** (verbiage/image etc. ...)

- **metafunction** (ideational/interpersonal/textual)

- **axis** (system/structure)

As far as genesis is concerned we can only deal with logogenesis here, since we do not have the corpus of texts we need to focus on FitzSimons' development as a writer nor on the evolution of this genre. For modality we'll have to deal with both verbiage and image, including the imagically enhanced graphology of the verbal text. A full metafunctional spectrum of meaning is of course available for analysis, which taking axis into account we can approach from both the perspectives of system and structure. This means that alongside kinds of meaning we can take into account their complementary patterns of realisation in particulate, prosodic and periodic patterns of realisation. Once again, because we are dealing with a single text, we have little to say about systemic agnation, and whether to model it typologically as networks or topologically as multidimensional clines. We can however try and deal with the text both synoptically as a finished product, and dynamically as a contingent ongoing recontextualisation of meaning as it unfolds.

Now what? My general strategy, as far as I am able to bring it to consciousness, is to take one hierarchy, realisation, and one complementarity, metafunction, and shunt around. As far as realisation is concerned, exploration involves bobbing up and down between genre and language, often within metafunctions, sometimes between. As far as metafunction is concerned, this means hopping back and forth between ideational, interpersonal and textual meaning, at different levels of abstraction. Overall my perspective is top down, so whatever I am working on I try to look up (the realisation hierarchy to higher levels of abstraction) and across (the metafunction complementarity to textual meaning).

An outline of the regions of meaning I typically canvass is presented in Table 12.1. The key is to move around, and not get stuck at any one spot – e.g. the graphological word as, in so much corpus based computationally facilitated analysis, or the clause, as in studies exclusively informed by Halliday's functional grammar and its off-shoots (ignoring phonology/

Table **12.1** A function/stratum matrix for text analysis

Metafunction stratum	Ideational	Interpersonal	Textual
Genre	Orbital/serial structure	Prosodic structure	Periodic structure
Register	Field – activity sequences, participant taxonomies	Tenor – power, solidarity	Mode – action/ reflection, monologue/dialogue
Discourse semantics	Ideation, external conjunction	Appraisal, negotiation	Identification, internal conjunction, information flow
Lexicogrammar	Transitivity; nominal group classification, description, enumeration	Mood, modality, polarity, comment, vocation; nominal group attitude, person	Theme and information; tense and deixis; ellipsis and substitution
Graphology/ phonology	Tone sequence	Formatting, emoticons, colour; tone, voice quality, phonaesthesia	Punctuation, layout; tonality, tonicity

graphology, lexis, discourse semantics, register and genre in the strange expectation that the meaning of a text will emerge from summary tables of its transitivity, mood and theme selections).

12.4 Exploring

Some people, a number of my colleagues in linguistics, sociology and cultural studies among them, have the gift of appreciating what matters in a text just by reading it, without apparently undertaking any detailed analysis. Sadly I am not one of them. I have to muck about, scratching away, pursuing dead ends, following up leads and so on. My toe-hold is the *unit* analysis outlined in Section 12.1 – the layout of the text (if written), its clause complex structure and its genre. On first reading this text I thought it was a story of some kind, probably a historical recount; teaching it to my media discourse students, they suggested it was in fact a narrative.[4] Judging from the solicitation stage, using his folk-rhetoric,

FitzSimon's thinks of his **placeintime** articles as *historical anecdotes*. Let's pursue this here.

If we say story, what are we predicting to confirm our view? Ideationally speaking the text should reconstrue a series of successive events, involving key participants, and set in a particular place and time (in this case Bondi Beach, 6 February 1938, 3 p.m.). From the point of view of field then, what activity sequences and participant taxonomies does our text instantiate?

As far as activity sequencing is concerned, what is about to happen is foreshadowed as unimaginable (using '^' to signal temporal successive and '&' simultaneity; explicit temporal conjunction underlined):

> nature could ever rear up
> ^ and savage the lot of them

What did in fact happen then unfolds in phases as follows – first the crowd builds up:

> The day was, in the vernacular of the time, a 'stinker',
> & ... those bronzed boys of the Bondi Surf Bathers' Life Saving Club had turned up in force to have one of their popular surf competitions.
> ^ and ... it was ...a record turnout on the beach ...

Then the waves hit:

> With a roar like a Bondi tram running amok, an enormous wave suddenly rolled over the thousands in the surf, including those many standing on the large sandbank just out from the shore
> & – knocking them all over
> & as it went.
> ^ And <u>then</u> another wave hit,
> ^ and <u>then</u> another.
> ^ The huge waves, just like that, piggy-backed their way further and further up the beach
> & and grabbed everything they could along the way – from babies to toddlers to adolescents to beach umbrellas, to old blokes and young sheilas alike,
> ^ and <u>then</u> made a mad dash for the open sea again,
> & carrying all before it
> & and sweeping everyone off the sandbank and into the deep channel next to it in the process.
> ^ <u>Now</u>, the boiling surf, <<...>>, was filled with distressed folk waving for help.
>
> & <<<u>with</u> yet more large waves continuing to roll over>>

The Bondi boys leap to the rescue:

^ ...ignoring their own possible peril,
& the Bondi boys <u>now</u> charged into the surf,
& some attached to one of the seven reels available,
& some relying only on their own strength.
^ As one, they began pulling the people out.

Survivors and victims are dealt with on shore:

^ On the shore, many survivors were resuscitated,
& <u>as</u> the Bondi clubhouse was turned into a kind of emergency clearing house,
& and ambulances from all over Sydney town descended
^ and carried the victims away

And finally, people take stock:

^<u>Finally</u>, just half an hour <u>after</u> the waves hit,
^the water was cleared of bobbing heads and waving arms,
& and it was time to take stock: ...

As we might expect, successive (*then, now, finally, after*) and simultaneous (*as, with*) temporal conjunctions are used to coordinate events; and there are many implicit temporal links with events connected *neutrally* by simple juxtaposition, the conjunction *and* or the dependency of non-finite clauses on finite ones. The text, as do stories in general, thus takes advantage of field based understandings, in this case of what happens when big waves hit a beach and a rescue operation gets underway – a reasonable expectation in an article composed for beach-savvy Sydneysiders.

Once the disaster gets going, each phase (waves, rescue, resuscitation, aftermath) is introduced with a marked theme:

With a roar like a Bondi tram running amok, an enormous wave suddenly rolled over the thousands in the surf, including those many standing on the large sandbank just out from the shore ...

For, **ignoring their own possible peril**, the Bondi boys now charged into the surf ...

On the shore, many survivors were resuscitated, ...

Finally, **just half an hour after the waves hit**, the water was cleared of bobbing heads and waving arms ...

And within phases, unmarked Themes[5] sustain their angle on the field (waves, Bondi Boys, rescue, survivors & victims). For this analysis elliptical Subjects in branched paratactic and in non-finite clauses have been lexically rendered to reinforce the thematic perspective of each phase.

With a roar like a Bondi tram running amok, **an enormous wave** suddenly rolled over the ... thousands in the surf, including those many standing on the large sandbank just out ... from the shore
– (**wave**) knocking them all over
as **it** [=wave] went.
And then **another wave** hit,
and then **another** (**wave**).
The huge waves, just like that, piggy-backed their way further and further up the beach
and (**waves**) grabbed everything they could along the way ...
and then (**waves**) made a mad dash for the open sea again,
(**waves**) carrying all before it
and (**waves**) sweeping everyone off the sandbank and into the deep channel ...
Now, **the boiling surf**, <<...>> was filled with distressed folk waving for help.
<<with yet more large waves continuing to roll over,>>

For, <<ignoring their own possible peril>>, **the Bondi boys** now charged into the surf,
some (**Bondi boys**) attached to one of the seven reels available,
some (**Bondi boys**) relying only on their own strength.
As one, **they** [=Bondi boys] began pulling the people out.

On the shore, **many survivors** were resuscitated,
as **the Bondi clubhouse** was turned into a kind of emergency clearing house,
and **ambulances** from all over Sydney town descended
and (**ambulances**) carried the victims away.

Finally, just half an hour after the waves hit, **the water** was cleared of bobbing heads and waving arms,
and **it** was time to take stock:
250 people had needed the lifesavers to pull them out,
of whom [=people] 210 were OK
once (**people**) back on land.
Thirty-five (**people**) needed mouth to mouth
(**thirty-five people**) to be restored to consciousness,
while **five people** perished.

Looking back across the interplay of non-finite clauses, ellipsis and conjunction one might argue that the interactive effect is to accelerate activity in relation to both the speed of the waves' incursion and the urgency of the lifesavers' rescue.

At this point we might also ask how higher levels of Theme and New scaffold the phases just outlined (Martin 1993). Both the waves and rescue phases have clear hyper-Themes, predicting what will come (note in passing the use of cataphoric text reference, *it* and *this* as boxed below, enabling these higher level Themes); in addition the wave phase is followed by a hyper-New, consolidating the effect of what went on.

> [hyper-Theme] At three o'clock there was still not the slightest clue that this afternoon would forever be known as 'Black Sunday' in the annals of Sydney. Then $\boxed{\text{it}}$ happened.

With a roar like a Bondi tram running amok, an enormous wave suddenly rolled over the thousands in the surf, including those many standing on the large sandbank just out from the shore – knocking them all over as it went. And then another wave hit, and then another.

> > The huge waves, just like $\boxed{\text{that,}}$ piggy-backed their way further and further up the beach and grabbed everything they could along the way – from babies to toddlers to adolescents to beach umbrellas, to old blokes and young sheilas alike, and then made a mad dash for the open sea again, carrying all before it and sweeping everyone off the sandbank and into the deep channel next to it in $\boxed{\text{the process.}}$
> >
> > [hyper-New] In no more than 20 seconds, that peaceful scene had been tragically transformed into utter chaos.
> >
> > [hyper-Theme] In their long and glorious history, $\boxed{\text{this}}$ still stands as the finest hour of the Australian lifesaving movement.

For, ignoring their own possible peril, the Bondi boys now charged into the surf, some attached to one of the seven reels available, some relying only on their own strength. As one, they began pulling the people out.

> On the shore, many survivors were resuscitated, as the Bondi clubhouse was turned into a kind of emergency clearing house, and ambulances from all over Sydney town descended and carried the victims away.

Further text reference (*that* and *the process*) in the wave phase, reinforced by a paragraph break, arguably splits the wave phase into two sub-phases – waves hitting people in the surf, then waves hitting people on the beach. But this break is not scaffolded by a shift in unmarked Themes, the use of a marked Theme, or the presence of a hyper-Theme or hyper-New; to have done so would perhaps have broken the momentum of the waves' 'attack'.

The activity sequence's final phase, taking stock, itself functions as a hyper-Theme for the body count.

> [hyper-Theme] Finally, just half an hour after the waves hit, the water was cleared of bobbing heads and waving arms, and it was time to take stock:
> > 250 people had needed the lifesavers to pull them out, of whom 210 were OK once back on land.
> > Thirty-five needed mouth to mouth to be restored to consciousness, while five people perished.

At a higher level of periodicity, the Kicker functions as a macro-Theme for the text as a whole, with its long wave length reinforced graphologically through its superordinate position and large bold font (and it deploys text reference, *this*, to confirm the text below as its domain):

> [macro-Theme] **Big waves and Bondi Beach have always gone together, writes Peter FitzSimons, but no one had ever seen the ocean rise up with a strength such as** this ...

So far we have taken genre as starting point, considered what a story genre might implicate for field, followed up the notion of activity sequencing, explored this through conjunction, and reconsidered our phasing from the perspective of theme – thus moving from genre via register to discourse semantics, and shunting between ideational and textual meaning once there. Moving back up to field, what can we say about participants as the drama unfolds?

From the perspective of composition, FitzSimons locates his story in Australia, of which Sydney is a part, of which Bondi is a part, including the Bondi Clubhouse and the Bondi tram. Moving to Bondi Beach, we have the beach proper (with beach umbrellas and life saving reels), and the water (including surf and waves, a sandbank and a deep channel, and the open sea); and overhead we have the sun.

From the perspective of classification, we find people, more specifically Sydneysiders, involving babies, toddlers, adolescents, young sheilas, old blokes and lifesavers; the lifesavers are opposed to distressed folk (including their bobbing heads and waving arms); and the distressed folk are divided into survivors and victims. In this text the Bondi Boys are also part of a composition hierarchy as members of the Bondi Surf Bathers' Life Saving Club, which is part of the Australian lifesaving movement.

The text has just two other lexical strings with more than two links, one having to do with time, and the other with peace and chaos:

Afternoon of 6 February 1938	peaceful
day	peace
the time	peaceful
three o'clock	chaos
afternoon	
Black Sunday	
20 seconds	

I will not take the step of rendering these ideational relations more explicitly as diagrams here (as lexical strings, or field taxonomies), after Martin (1992). We've done enough to see that we're talking about participants involved in a day at a Sydney beach.

As far as participant identification is concerned, the participants are organised into four main chains. Two[6] are concerned with people, first those in the photo, then those on the beach in 1935:

they (people on beach in image)
(they)
them

those 35,000 Sydneysiders who were lying on those very spots
the numbers
the thousands in the surf
those many standing on the large sandbank just out from the shore
them.

But the main protagonists are the *waves* and the *Bondi Boys*, which include several links even without rendering elided Subjects in branched and non-finite clauses and filling in any *agentless* passives. The wave chain involves comparative reference (e.g. *another wave*) and bridging (from *the waves* to *the boiling surf*).

an enormous wave
it
another (wave)
another (wave)
The huge waves
they
it
– the boiling surf
yet more large waves
the surf
the waves
the water

The Bondi Boys chain also provides bridging for the Australian Lifesaving Movement and the Bondi Clubhouse.

those bronzed boys of the Bondi Surf Bathers' Life Saving Club
their popular surf competitions
– the Australian lifesaving movement
their own possible peril
the Bondi boys
some (of them)
some (of them)
their own strength

they
– the Bondi clubhouse
the lifesavers

The wave chain operates exclusively in the wave phase, whereas the Bondi Boys are introduced early in the story, before undertaking the rescue proper and are mentioned again later on (when taking stock).

An agency analysis, focusing on effective material processes confirms the active role taken by the waves and Bondi Boys. As Table 12.2 displays, what gets affected in the story are people; and what affects them is nature (waves) and fellow man (Bondi Boys). The main participants in other words don't act on one another; this is not a struggle between man and nature. Rather nature savages people, and then other people rescue them. In effect we have two protagonists, not a direct showdown with nature (antagonist) overcome by Bondi Boys (protagonist).

So this time round we have shunted from field to discourse semantics (ideational classification and composition), glanced sideways at identification (textual meaning) and slid down to ergativity (ideational clause grammar). This concludes our brief tour of what is going on.

Now what? Back up to genre. As story analysts have repeatedly confirmed, what is going on has to be evaluated – a story has to make a point (Bamberg 1997, Labov and Waletzky 1967, Toolan 1988). This means looking at tenor, the rhetoric of solidarity in particular, and asking how FitzSimons aligns his readers in relation to their feelings about what went on. To

Table 12.2 Agentive *man* and *nature* on 'Black Sunday'

Agent	Process (material)	Medium
nature	savage	the lot of them [people]
the fact that ... surf comp ...	swelled	the numbers [people]
[an enormous wave]	knocking over	them all [people]
[the huge waves]	grabbed	everything ... babies to ...
[the huge waves]	carrying	all ["]
[the huge waves]	sweeping	everyone
[the huge waves]	had been transformed	that peaceful scene
they [the Bondi boys]	began pulling	people
[the Bondi boys]	were resuscitated	many survivors
[ambulances]	carried	the victims
[the Bondi boys]	cleared	the water
the lifesavers	pull out	them [250 people]
the lifesavers	to be restored	[thirty-five people]

follow this up let's turn to appraisal now, returning to begin to our analysis of periodicity.

The article's macro-Theme judges the wave's strength as the most powerful ever seen.

> Big waves and Bondi Beach have always gone together, writes Peter FitzSimons, but no one had ever seen the ocean rise up with a **strength** such as this ...

The hyper-Themes for the waves and rescue phases on the other hand focus on appreciation, of the tragic day (**Black Sunday**), and of the Australian lifesaving movement (long and **glorious** history, the **finest** hour).

> At three o'clock there was still not the slightest clue that this afternoon would forever be known as 'Black Sunday' in the annals of Sydney. Then it happened.

> In their long and glorious history, this still stands as the finest hour of the Australian lifesaving movement.

These appreciations of the lifesaving movement can of course be taken as tokens of judgement (of the Bondi Boys' strength and courage). But it is significant that the text uses almost no inscribed judgement to evaluate the lifesavers (referring just once to their *strength*), and employs just four instances of inscribed affect (*happily, happy,*[7] *felt equally at peace, distressed*). The main type of evaluation inscribed through the text is in fact appreciation.

> Australia's **most famous** beach
> **such a wonderfully peaceful** scene
> The day was, in the vernacular of the time, a **stinker**,
> a **record** turnout on the beach
> one of their **popular** surf competitions.
> **Black Sunday**
> that **peaceful** scene
> **tragically** transformed
> **utter chaos**.
> long and **glorious** history,
> the **finest** hour of the Australian lifesaving movement.
> ignoring their own possible **peril**.

For FitzSimons then it is the significance of the moment that matters, not directly the character of the lifesavers. His stance is more that of a historian than narrator, which perhaps goes some way to explaining the tension between my initial reading of the text as historical recount and my students' protest that it is in fact a narrative (of which more below). Note at this point that the text's final hyper-Theme has no inscribed attitude, and the clauses which elaborate it have just one candidate for inscribed judgement (*OK*). So for the story's final three paragraphs FitzSimons switches to what Coffin (as reported in Martin 2003) calls recorder voice, reporting what happened without explicit evaluation and pretty much letting the facts speak baldly for themselves.

> Finally, just half an hour after the waves hit, the water was cleared of bobbing heads and waving arms, and it was time to take stock:
>
>> 250 people had needed the lifesavers to pull them out, of whom 210 were OK once back on land. Thirty-five needed mouth to mouth to be restored to consciousness, while five people perished.

Contrast this with the text's only hyper-New, which explicitly evaluates the effect of the wave phase.

> In no more than 20 seconds, that **peaceful** scene had been **tragically** transformed into **utter chaos**.

This is not the whole story of course, as far as appraisal is concerned. Fitzsimons' text, even this last section, uses a great deal of graduation, especially force, by way of amplifying his message (Hood and Martin 2005). His final three paragraphs for example use quantity to maximise the relief effort and minimise casualties.

> On the shore, **many** survivors were resuscitated, as the Bondi clubhouse was turned into a kind of emergency clearing house, and ambulances from **all** over Sydney town descended and carried the victims away.

> Finally, just **half** an hour after the waves hit, the water was cleared of bobbing heads and waving arms, and it was time to take stock: **250** people had needed the lifesavers to pull them out, of whom **210** were OK once back on land.

> **Thirty-five** needed mouth to mouth to be restored to consciousness, while **five** people perished.

There are a number of grammatically intensified items:

> **most** famous, **so** many, **such** a wonderful peaceful scene, **simply** unimaginable, the slight**est** clue, **just** out, **mad** dash, **utter** chaos, fin**est** hour

And there is a great deal of lexicalised intensification, with force incorporated in the choice of lexical item:

sweltering, unimaginable, rear up, savage, stinker, swelled, slightest, enormous, rolled, knocking, huge, grabbed, dash, sweeping, boiling, roll, chaos, filled, ignoring, peril, charged, descended perished

And the quantification we illustrated for the final three paragraphs permeates the text as a whole, in relation to numbers of people:

> so many generations, 35,000 Sydneysiders, a record turnout, the numbers swelled, turned up in force, the thousands, those many, all, everyone, yet more large waves, many survivors, 250 (had needed the lifesavers), 210 (were OK once back on land), 35 (needed mouth to mouth), five people (perished)

And also in relation to extent in time and space:

> no more than 20 seconds, just half an hour after, long (history); always, ever, forever, suddenly, still; continuing to roll; further and further, all over Sydney

Iteration is also used rhetorically to maximise events, especially the waves' attack:

> an enormous wave suddenly rolled over the thousands in the surf ...
> And then another wave hit,
> and then another.
> from babies
> to toddlers
> to adolescents
> to beach umbrellas,
> to old blokes and young sheilas alike

Reviewing the interaction of appraisal and periodicity then, FitzSimons' strategy is to situate his key appreciations in hyper-Themes and hyper-New, and to propagate them throughout their respective domain with force. For the waves phase, both intensification (italics) and maximising quantification (underlined) are used as peace turns to chaos:

> At three o'clock there was still not the *slightest* clue that this afternoon would <u>forever</u> be known as 'Black Sunday' in the annals of Sydney.

> > Then it happened. *With a roar like a Bondi tram running amok*, an <u>enormous</u> wave <u>suddenly</u> *rolled* over the <u>thousands</u> in the surf, including those <u>many</u> standing on the <u>large</u> sandbank *just* out from the shore – knocking them <u>all</u> over as it went. And then another wave hit, and then another. [taxis]

> > The *huge* waves, just like that, *piggy-backed* their way <u>further and further</u> up the beach and *grabbed* <u>everything</u> they could along the

> way – from babies to toddlers to adolescents to beach umbrellas, to old blokes and young sheilas alike, and then made a *mad dash* for the open sea again, carrying all before it and *sweeping* everyone off the sandbank and into the deep channel next to it in the process.

> In no more than 20 seconds, that peaceful scene had been tragically transformed into *utter* chaos.

For the rescue and taking stock phases, quantification is the main strategy deployed to sustain the Bondi Boys' finest hour, a prosody which arguably extends over both these phases (with the periodicity adjusted accordingly below).

> In their long and glorious history, this still stands as the *finest* hour of the Australian lifesaving movement.

>> For, ignoring their own possible peril, the Bondi boys now *charged* into the surf, some attached to one of the seven reels available, some relying only on their own strength. As one, they began pulling the people out.

>> On the shore, many survivors were resuscitated, as the Bondi clubhouse was turned into a kind of emergency clearing house, and ambulances from all over Sydney town *descended* and carried the victims away.

>> Finally, just half an hour after the waves hit, the water was cleared of bobbing heads and waving arms, and it was time to take stock:

>>> 250 people had needed the lifesavers to pull them out, of whom 210 were OK once back on land.

>>> Thirty-five needed mouth to mouth to be restored to consciousness, while five people *perished*.

To summarise then, FitzSimons foregrounds appreciation over judgement and affect, and makes liberal use of force to dramatise events. So the text is about the kind of day it was, not in the first instance about how people reacted emotionally or how well or badly they behaved. The point of the story thus seems to involve the historical significance of the day – its value as a piece of history. And this stance is foregrounded in trite phrasing verging on lexicalisation as far as history making is concerned.

> And so there they lie, happily sweltering in the summer sun on Australia's most famous beach, just as they have for so many generations past.

> Ah, but those 35,000 Sydneysiders who were lying in those very spots on the afternoon of February 6, 1938, surely felt equally at peace.

> The day was, in the vernacular of the time, a *stinker*,

At three o'clock there was still not the slightest clue that this afternoon would forever be known as 'Black Sunday' in the annals of Sydney.

In their long and glorious history, this still stands as the finest hour of the Australian lifesaving movement. For ...

Even the connectives (*And so ..., Ah but ..., For ...*) seem to flag a long term elegiac view, particularly FitzSimons' sigh of resignation (*Ah*) as he moves from his intermodal present to the past tense of his tale.

At this point let's move inter-modally, and consider the way in which the two images position us in relation to the alignments just considered. As noted above there are two pictures, positioned as Given to the left of the verbiage (New). FitzSimons' portrait above the landscape is Ideal with the beach photo below as Real. The beach landscape is itself polarised into Ideal (sky) and Real (land and sea), and FitzSimons is positioned to the right of the top image in New position. In short then horizontally speaking we have the familiar beach and columnist as Given and the story as news; vertically FitzSimons is an oracular Ideal to the landscape's Real, and the sky is Ideal in relation to the people on the beach as Real. These information values are outlined in Figure 12.3.

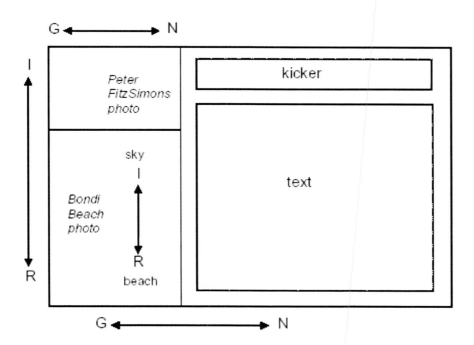

Figure 12.3 Information values – Ideal vs. Real, Given vs. New

As far as representational meaning is concerned the FitzSimons portrait is analytic. He is bald, with a full beard, closely trimmed, and an open necked shirt; there is no circumstantiation. If we needed reminding, the portrait confirms that this is in fact the Peter FitzSimons, a well known sports journalist and pay TV commentator, who played rugby for Australia in his sporting prime.[8]

The beach landscape conversely has little attribution, since individual participants are barely distinguishable; but there is rich circumstantiation for the sky (with feathery clouds), the sea (small surf and a few bathers), the beach (with many sunbathers) and the buildings on the border between land and sky. The orientation of the people and blankets on the beach along with the north of the beach and suburbs compose release vectors (lower left to upper right); these are counter-balanced by hold vectors (lower right to upper left) construed by the sea and feathery clouds in the sky. From a narrative perspective, the vectors thus oppose man and nature, more specifically people's urge to get into the water contained by the sea's incursion into the curving sand.

Interpersonally, FitzSimons' portrait is a close shot (head and shoulders), front on, level with the viewer and involving eye contact and a smile – rendering him a trusty friend. The landscape on the other hand is a long shot, from an oblique angle, positioning viewers well above the beach and involving no eye contact or affect – a very distancing effect.

Blue colour cohesion resonates across the landscape sky and the portrait (loud saturated blue in the landscape, more muted in the portrait). Intermodally, the blue of the portrait is picked up typographically by Peter FitzSimons' name in the Kicker; and the green of the sea is similarly replayed on the word *in* in the *placeintime* title of the column on the portrait. The general ambient effect is a cool Ideal in relation to the lightness of the sand on the beach (the Real).

Imagically speaking then the overall effect is cool, calm and distanced, with FitzSimons himself as a warm engaging guide. This foregrounds the order restored over the calamity described, and reinforces the historically distanced stance FitzSimons constructs for us in the verbal text through appraisal resources. The order construed by the images can also be read as counterpointing the waves unsuspected eruption in the verbal text, a point we'll return to when considering narrative structure below.

Intermodally then the texts position readers to look back from a safe distance on what went on. The early affect (*happily, happy, felt ... at peace*) invites us to empathise positively with the people on the beach. But then we are repositioned to back off, historically, to oversee the tragedy and its glorious redemption as the events of the day unfold. The overall effect is one of balance – there's no stopping accidents at the beach but there are lifesavers on hand to see us through. The yin of mateship complemented by the yang of nature. Nostalgia. Heritage. Our place, contextualised by time.

Pursuing tenor then we've considered appraisal (attitude and graduation in particular) in relation to periodicity, and then moved from verbiage to image to follow up the interpersonal alignment FitzSimons has naturalised for readers. At this point we are in a position to argue that what we are looking at is a story in the service of history. But exactly which story genre is it, and precisely what kind of history are we making here?

12.5 Consolidating – register and genre

Whatever kind of story we determine FitzSimons' Black Sunday *historical anecdote* is, we first have to keep in mind that it has been recontextualised as a magazine article. So we have a Kicker function, which we don't associate with story genres outside of media discourse. The glossy lifestyle magazine in addition affords the images which make this text a multimodal one. But the images don't simply accompany the verbal text, with perhaps with a short mediating caption as in much of the magazine. Rather FitzSimons' additionally recontextualises his story by devoting an initial phase of texture to the photo of Bondi Beach. He describes and appraises the scene, using nominal and verbal deixis which aligns FitzSimons and his readership as observing what is going on together (intermodal deixis underlined below).

> And so there they lie, happily sweltering in <u>the summer sun</u> on <u>Australia's most famous beach</u>, just as <u>they</u> have for so many generations past. <u>It</u> is such a wonderfully peaceful scene – of people and nature as a happy whole – that it is simply unimaginable that nature could ever rear up and savage the lot of <u>them</u>.

Maintaining place, we then shift back in time, as his story gets underway.

> Ah, but those 35,000 Sydneysiders who were lying in <u>those very spots</u> on the afternoon of February 6, 1938, surely felt equally at peace.

This explicitly intermodal phase is an important one for FitzSimons' *placeintime* column, which is designed to draw readers' attention to the historical significance of more and less familiar Sydney landmarks (e.g. The Harbour Bridge, The GPO Clock Tower, Canada Bay, Coogee Beach in other issues). It recurs often enough in these columns to warrant reification as a generic stage, which I'll refer to as Localisation here.

Localisation

And so there they lie, happily sweltering in the summer sun on Australia's most famous beach, just as they have for so many generations past. It is such a wonderfully peaceful scene – of people and nature as a happy whole – that it is simply unimaginable that nature could ever rear up and savage the lot of them.

Following Localisation we have a fairly canonical Orientation stage, introducing the story's key participants, setting them in time and place, and foreshadowing what's to come.

Orientation

Ah, but those 35,000 Sydneysiders who were lying in those very spots on the afternoon of February 6, 1938, surely felt equally at peace. The day was, in the vernacular of the time, a 'stinker', and some thought it was in fact a record turnout on the beach, with the numbers perhaps swelled by the fact that those bronzed boys of the Bondi Surf Bathers' Life Saving Club had turned up in force to have one of their popular surf competitions. At three o'clock there was still not the slightest clue that this afternoon would forever be known as 'Black Sunday' in the annals of Sydney.

The time line which we analysed above then kicks in, materialising the waves' incursion.

Complication

Then it happened. With a roar like a Bondi tram running amok, an enormous wave suddenly rolled over the thousands in the surf, including those many standing on the large sandbank just out from the shore – knocking them all over as it went. And then another wave hit, and then another. The huge waves, just like that, piggy-backed their way further and further up the beach and grabbed everything they could along the way – from babies to toddlers to adolescents to beach umbrellas, to old blokes and young sheilas alike, and then made a mad dash for the open sea again, carrying all before it and sweeping everyone off the sandbank and into the deep channel next to it in the process. In no more than 20 seconds, that peaceful scene had been tragically transformed into utter chaos. Now, the boiling surf, with yet more large waves continuing to roll over, was filled with distressed folk waving for help.

This is followed by a canonical pause in activity as FitzSimons delivers his lofty Churchillian appraisal of the 'Battle of Bondi'.

Evaluation

In their long and glorious history, this still stands as the finest hour of the Australian lifesaving movement.

Returning to the time line, material activity resumes as equilibrium is restored.

Resolution

> For, ignoring their own possible peril, the Bondi boys now charged into the surf, some attached to one of the seven reels available, some relying only on their own strength. As one, they began pulling the people out. On the shore, many survivors were resuscitated, as the Bondi clubhouse was turned into a kind of emergency clearing house, and ambulances from all over Sydney town descended and carried the victims away. Finally, just half an hour after the waves hit, the water was cleared of bobbing heads and waving arms, …

FitzSimons then segues to his Coda stage – a statistical retrospective on the waves' toll. Note the use of past in past tense to back up in time (*had needed*).

Coda

> … and it was time to take stock: 250 people had needed the lifesavers to pull them out, of whom 210 were OK once back on land. Thirty-five needed mouth to mouth to be restored to consciousness, while five people perished.

Once the Localisation stage has been proposed then, we are left with a prototypical Orientation Complication Evaluation Resolution Coda structure. This is then recontextualised with the interactive Thanks and Solicitation stages which construct FitzSimons' readership as past and potentially future participants in his authoring process.

Alongside this particulate reading of the genre, we should also note the interaction of periodicity and foreshadowing, since the article announces no less than five times about what is to come, and four of these 'warnings' are positioned as higher level Themes (cf. the discussion of comparable momentum induced by interpersonal meaning and hyper-Themes in *Nathaniel's Nutmeg*, a history of the spice trade in South-east Asia, Martin 2004b):

> Big waves and Bondi Beach have always gone together, writes Peter FitzSimons, but no one had ever seen the ocean rise up with a strength such as this …

> It is such a wonderfully peaceful scene – of people and nature as a happy whole – that it is simply unimaginable that nature could ever rear up and savage the lot of them.[9]

At three o'clock there was still not the slightest clue that this afternoon would forever be known as 'Black Sunday' in the annals of Sydney. Then it happened.

In their long and glorious history, this still stands as the finest hour of the Australian lifesaving movement.

Finally, just half an hour after the waves hit, the water was cleared of bobbing heads and waving arms, and it was time to take stock:

And from a prosodic perspective this foreshadowing interacts with the dramatisation of events as FitzSimons sets up the tension between peace and chaos in his intermodal Localisation, amplifies the tragedy, extols salvation and then calms things down again by digitalising the aftermath. The role of inscribed attitude and force in constructing this drama is summarised below.

> • TENSION ... [negative intensification amongst *positive attitude*]
> *happily* sweltering *most famous* so many *such a wonderfully peaceful happy* simply unimaginable ever rear up savage the lot of Ah 35,000 *felt equally at peace* 'stinker' *record* swelled in force *popular*

> • TERROR ... [intensification amplifying *negative appreciation* in hyper-Theme/New]
> At three o'clock there was still not the slightest clue that this afternoon would forever be known as *'Black Sunday'* in the annals of Sydney. Then it happened.

>> With a roar like a Bondi tram running amok enormous suddenly rolled thousands many large just all huge piggy-backed further and further grabbed everything mad dash knocking all sweeping everyone

> In no more than 20 seconds, that *peaceful* scene had been *tragically* transformed into *utter chaos.* Now, the boiling surf, with yet more large waves continuing to roll over, was filled with *distressed* folk waving for help.

> • SALVATION ... [*inscribed appreciation* invoking positive judgement]
> In their long and *glorious* history, this still stands as the *finest* hour of the Australian lifesaving movement.

>> ignoring *peril* charged *strength* many all over

> • STATISTICS ... [enumerated body count]
> Finally, just half an hour after the waves hit, the water was cleared of bobbing heads and waving arms, and it was time to take stock:

>> 250 210 *OK* Thirty-five *five* perished.

The dynamic wax and wane of this prosodic evaluation might be symbolised as follows:

ten/sion ⇒ **terror!** ⇒ **salv**ation ⇒ statistics

The overall effect is one of disorder threatened, fear realised and order restored. A crescendo diminuendo texture symbolising the ideational content of the story.

> Big waves and Bondi Beach have always gone together, writes Peter FitzSimons, but no one had ever seen the ocean rise up with a strength such as this ...
>
> ...
>
> > It is such a wonderfully peaceful scene – of people and nature as a happy whole – that it is simply unimaginable that nature could ever rear up and savage the lot of them.
> >
> > ...
> >
> > At three o'clock there was still not the slightest clue that this afternoon would forever be known as 'Black Sunday' in the annals of Sydney. Then it happened.
> >
> > ...
> >
> > In no more than 20 seconds, that peaceful scene had been tragically transformed into utter chaos. Now, the boiling surf, with yet more large waves continuing to roll over, was filled with distressed folk waving for help.
>
> In their long and glorious history, this still stands as the finest hour of the Australian lifesaving movement. ...

> Finally, just half an hour after the waves hit, the water was cleared of bobbing heads and waving arms, and it was time to take stock:
>
> ...

As far as I can see the analyses presented here confirm my students' argument that we are dealing with narrative not historical recount.[10] But I could perhaps save a modicum of face by suggesting that it is narrative in the service of history (in other words, I got the field right if not the genre) – for various reasons.

For example, the foreshadowing just reviewed depends on hindsight. It functions to evaluate what went on and is far too ideationally explicit to create the suspense we value in discourse which deploys narrative for entertainment. The foregrounding of appreciation over affect and judgement is another historicizing feature. The text is not explicit about victims' emotions, nor are the rescuers idolised as heroes; rather what happened is appreciated as a remarkable event where it is evaluated, and eventually rendered as statistics in a Coda (where we might have been expected FitzSimons to lush on about the glory of the Bondi Boys).

Reinforcing this interpersonal distancing is the selection of heterglossing engagement resources leading up the waves' incursion. In the role of historian, FitzSimons in effect 'references' his 'sources', making room for several voices other than his own in the text (as underlined below).

> And so there they lie, happily sweltering in the summer sun on Australia's most famous beach, just as they have for so many generations past. It is such a wonderfully peaceful scene – of people and nature as a happy whole – that <u>it is simply unimaginable</u> that nature could ever rear up and savage the lot of them.
>
> Ah, but those 35,000 Sydneysiders who were lying in those very spots on the afternoon of February 6, 1938, <u>surely</u> felt equally at peace.
>
> The day was, <u>in the vernacular of the time</u>, a '<u>stinker</u>', and <u>some thought</u> it was in fact a record turnout on the beach, with the numbers <u>perhaps</u> swelled by <u>the fact</u> that those bronzed boys of the Bondi Surf Bathers' Life Saving Club had turned up in force to have one of their popular surf competitions.
>
> At three o'clock <u>there was still not the slightest clue</u> that this afternoon would forever be known as 'Black Sunday' in the annals of Sydney. Then it happened.

He then switches to a more canonical monoglossing narrator voice for the Complication and Resolution proper.[11] The main engagement resource used here is concession (italics), reinforcing the insurgency as more sudden and relentless than could ever have been expected.

> With a roar like a Bondi tram running amok, an enormous wave *suddenly* rolled over the thousands in the surf, including those many standing on the large sandbank just out from the shore – knocking them all over as it went. And then another wave hit, and then another.
>
> The huge waves, *just like that*, piggy-backed their way further and further up the beach and grabbed everything they could along the way – from babies to toddlers to adolescents to beach umbrellas, to old blokes and young sheilas alike, and then made a mad dash for the open sea again, carrying all before it and sweeping everyone off the sandbank and into the deep channel next to it in the process.
>
> In no more than 20 seconds, that peaceful scene had been tragically transformed into utter chaos. Now, the boiling surf, with *yet more* large waves continuing to roll over, was filled with distressed folk waving for help.

In their long and glorious history, this *still* stands as the finest hour of the Australian lifesaving movement. For, ignoring their own possible peril, the Bondi boys now charged into the surf, some attached to one of the seven reels available, some relying *only* on their own strength. As one, they began pulling the people out.

On the shore, many survivors were resuscitated, as the Bondi clubhouse was turned into a kind of emergency clearing house, and ambulances from all over Sydney town descended and carried the victims away.

Then in closing FitzSimons' implicitly references sources once again (*time to take stock*), and switches from amplified gradable resources of attitude to digitalised enumeration. The voice of scholarly historical researcher takes over from that of the narrative commentator once again.

Finally, just half an hour after the waves hit, the water was cleared of bobbing heads and waving arms, and it was time to take stock: 250 people had needed the lifesavers to pull them out, of whom 210 were OK once back on land.

Thirty-five needed mouth to mouth to be restored to consciousness, while five people perished.

On top of all this of course we have the ways in which the narrative is contextualised as part of this lifestyle magazine. It is after all a special **placeintime** column, and its Solicitation stage explicitly invites *historical anecdotes* about places in Sydney. And many readers will also be aware that FitzSimons is a political biographer as well as journalist, and so would be used to dealing with historical time. In addition the Kicker arguably construes what happened as news rather than entertainment by focusing on nature (the waves) rather than heroes (the Bondi Boys) – not surprisingly from a newsworthiness perspective since the waves' incursion is far and away the loudest part of FitzSimons' *news*.

As noted above the Localisation stage crystallising in this column has the function of relating past events to a contemporary photograph, infusing place with time. And this intermodality regularly affords an image which distances viewers from a place (and even more so from any people in it), a viewing position reinforcing the interpersonal distancing just reviewed, the ideational dating to a far away time (not to mention his archaic namely of Sydney as *Sydney town*) (6 February 1938).

My generic misreading can perhaps be taken as salutary then, flagging the common sense tendency to categorise texts by field rather than by genre, as we do in video shops and bookstores (crime, western, fantasy, science fiction, gardening, travel, etc.). It shows why I need text analysis to find out what is going on. It also shows perhaps why I insist on a discourse analytical perspective, taking co-text into account for each analysis

– by continually gazing up the realisation hierarchy to deeper strata, and by looking across metafunctional complementarity from ideational and interpersonal to textual meaning. I do this because I theorise genres as multimodal configurations of meaning and cultures as systems of genres. In a model of this kind there's no getting away from shunting around amongst the hierarchies and complementaries system functional semiotics has designed.

12.6 Motivation

Clearly text analysis takes a lot of time, where it takes responsibility for a range of semiotic resources construing meaning. In working on this chapter I undertook more analyses than I've presented here; and it is difficult to push this process to its limits. Whatever I write about the Black Sunday article, I cannot presume to have exhausted the meaning of the discourse. This raises the issue of what is worth analysing, once we move beyond a tactical exercise like this one – which has been designed to exemplify my practice. Or more pointedly, why did I choose this text? Why bother?

My answer is this. Currently Australia in general, and large urban centres like Sydney in particular, is suffering from a savage epidemic of affluenza. Materially speaking we want more, and we want more and more false hope of getting more. In order to achieve this we until recently consistently returned to power a government intent on redistributing wealth from not so well off people to very well off ones and intent on steadily withdrawing federal financial support for public health, education, legal services, welfare and so on – resulting in a more and more stratified society in which users pay for what they can afford and the rest go without. This has resulted in a redistribution of hope from the many to the few, underpinning what Hage (2003) describes as a rising tide of paranoid nationalism – as people worry more and more about what they don't have and who they imagine has taken it away or will take it away from them. John Howard's neo-conservative government ruthlessly promoted this politics of division and fear for electoral gain.

It is in this political context that middle class broadsheet newspaper readers in Sydney receive their monthly lifestyle magazine. The glossy ads therein promote a lifestyle which only upper middle class people could enjoy (luxury cars, cutting edge information technology, expensive perfume, classy furniture, exotic holidays, etc. for a minority of the readership one would have to say – but the rest of us can dream, can't we?). As far as content is concerned, the leisure activities described are very fashionable ones (letting us in the right restaurants, bars, theatre, music, travel, designer clothing and so on) – things that only well-heeled upwardly mobile professionals and established mortgage-free middle class baby boomers can consume. The magazine obviously aims at a privileged highly educated group of Sydneysiders by any measure, whose lifestyle had been significantly enhanced by Howard's neo-con regime.

By the same token, this is the very group that had the most misgivings about the Howard government's approach to reconciliation with Indigenous Australians, its assimilationist interpretation of multiculturalism, and its grossly inhumane treatment of Australia's tiny trickle of refugees. As Hage (2003) argues, this affluent group can after all afford to be concerned, since they have more than their fair share of hope to flourish with in years to come (and the promise of more and more). But as Peter Read explores the issue, do we really belong here? 'How can we non-Indigenous Australians justify our continuous presence and our love for this country while the Indigenous people remain disposed and their history unacknowledged?' (Read 2000: 1). One way to achieve this I would argue is be re-colonising the terrain – by taking a step beyond simply stealing land away from Indigenous people for material gain, and embedding our own past in the landscape (what John Howard referred to as moving away from the 'black arm-band' view of Australian history). I read FitzSimons' column as re-colonisation of this kind; month by month he builds our baby boomer's dreaming, infusing what is now our place with our time. All with the purpose of making us feel more at home in the place we want to call home, enhancing our sense of 'belonging' in Read's sense of the term. How such a bourgeois dreaming evolves alongside or in place of Australia's much longer long history of Indigenous dreaming is something that is left unreconciled.

In short then, for me, behind analysis there has to be a politics. Otherwise I am unmotivated, wasting my time. Fortunately for me I see ideology everywhere, however innocent a discourse may want to appear. Politics is nowhere more important than when we are co-operating as linguists across disciplines – when we need a common purpose to negotiate meaning across our various divides. But this takes me towards another transdisciplinary exercise, which there is no room for here.

So … shunt up, shunt down, shunt around. Not perhaps the kind of answer that people want to hear, especially those depending on a single analysis (e.g. lexicogrammar) or a single tool (e.g. computationally automated corpus description). But the only way to discourse analyse a text, to my mind.

Notes

1. For examples see Martin (1986, 1996, 1999, 2004a); Martin and Peters (1985).
2. Taken here as a dependent clause, with *just half an hour* grading *after*; this could be alternatively read as a prepositional phrase with *[[after the waves hit]]* postmodifying *hour*.
3. Used here in the sense of channel of communication (not to be confused with Halliday's use of the term for intermediate degrees of polarity).
4. My thanks to Ken Tann in particular for this observation.
5. For this analysis I've analysed the first ideational function following a marked Theme as unmarked Theme (*contra* Thompson and Thompson, this volume), on the grounds that marked and unmarked Theme play such different functions in discourse, as this text confirms – unmarked Themes to sustain our angle on the field, marked Themes to shift our gaze.
6. Once the waves have hit, the people caught in the surf are dispersed as far as participant identification is concerned; we find non-specific *distressed folk waving for help* picked up as *them*; then non-specific *many survivors* bridging to *the victims*; then non-specific *250 people* pronominalised as *them* (narrowed grammatically as *of whom*).
7. FitzSimons in fact writes of *people and nature as a happy whole*, with *happy* arguably inscribing appreciation here.
8. FitzSimons is also the biographer of the federal opposition Labor leader Kim Beazley.
9. As part of the intermodal Localisation this foreshadowing cannot function textually as a higher level theme (compare a formulation such as *Then the unimaginable happened*, which could function in such terms, but not in this stage in the text).
10. Because of the story's Complication Resolution structure FitzSimons' term 'historical anecdote' cannot be adopted, since in SFL narratology anecdotes end with a remarkable event inviting an emotional response from listeners (Martin and Plum 1997).
11. There is one modality, *possible*; but this could be read as heteroglossing on behalf of the Bondi Boys, who knew what they were letting themselves in for, rather than on behalf of FitzSimons' own authority as historian and narrator.

References

Bamberg, G.W. (ed.) (1997). *Oral Versions of Personal Experience: Three Decades of Narrative Analysis.* Special Issue of *Journal of Narrative and Life History* 7: 1–4.

Christie, F. and Martin, J. R. (eds) (1997). *Genre and Institutions: Social Processes in the Workplace and School.* Open Linguistics Series. London: Pinter.

Coffin, C. (1997). Constructing and giving value to the past: an investigation into secondary school history. In F. Christie and J. R. Martin (eds), *Genre and Institutions: Social Processes in the Workplace and School.* Open Linguistics Series. London: Pinter, 196–230.

Eggins, S. and Slade, D. (1997). *Analysing Casual Conversation.* London: Cassell.

FitzSimons, P. (2005). placeintime: bondi beach. *The Sydney Magazine,* 23 February.

Hage, G. (2003). *Against Paranoid Nationalism: Searching for Hope in a Shrinking World.* Sydney: Pluto Press.

Halliday, M. A. K. and Matthiessen, C. M. I. M. (1999). *Construing Experience through Language: A Language-based Approach to Cognition.* London: Cassell.

Halliday, M. A. K. and Matthiessen, C. M. I. M. (2004). *An Introduction to Functional Grammar* (3rd edition). London: Arnold.

Hasan, R. (1984). The nursery tale as a genre. *Nottingham Linguistic Circular* 13 (Special Issue on Systemic Linguistics). 71–102.

Hasan, R. and Williams, G. (eds.) (1996). *Literacy in Society.* London: Longman (Language and Social Life).

Hood, S. and Martin, J. R. (2007). Invoking attitude: the play of graduation in appraising discourse. In *Continuing Discourse on Language* Vol. 2, R. Hasan, C. M. I. M. Matthiessen and J. Webster (eds.). London: Equinox, 739–64. [Spanish translation *Revista Signos*].

Jordens, C. and Little, M. (2004). 'In this scenario, I do this, for these reasons': narrative, genre and ethical reasoning in the clinic. *Social Science and Medicine* 58: 1635–45.

Kress, G. and van Leeuwen, T. (1996). *Reading Images: The Grammar of Visual Design.* London: Routledge.

Labov, W. and Waletzky, J. (1967). Narrative analysis: oral versions of personal experience. In *Essays on the Verbal and Visual Arts* (Proceedings of the 1966 Spring Meeting of the American Ethnological Society), J. Helm (ed.). Seattle, WA: University of Washington Press, 12-44. [republished in G. W. Bamberg (ed.). 3–38]

Martin, J. R. (1986). Grammaticalising ecology: the politics of baby seals and kangaroos. In *Semiotics, Ideology, Language,* T. Threadgold, E. A. Grosz, G. Kress and M. A. K. Halliday (eds). Sydney: Sydney Association for Studies in Society and Culture (Sydney Studies in Society and Culture 3). 225–68.

Martin, J. R. (1992) *English Text: System and Structure.* Amsterdam: Benjamins.

Martin, J. R. (1993). Life as a noun. In *Writing Science: Literacy as Discursive Power,* M. A. K. Halliday and J. R. Martin. London: Falmer (Critical Perspectives on Literacy and Education) 1993. 221–67. [Norwegian translation in *Å Skape Mening Med Språk: en samling artikler av M. A. K. Halliday, R. Hasan og J. R. Martin* (presentery og redigert av K. L. Berge, P. Coppock and E. Maagerø) Oslo: Landslaget for norskundervisning (LNU) og Cappelen Akademisk Forlag. 1998.]

Martin, J. R. (1995). Interpersonal meaning, persuasion and public discourse: packing semiotic punch. *Australian Journal of Linguistics* 15 (1): 33–67.

Martin, J. R. (1996). Evaluating disruption: symbolising theme in junior secondary narrative. in R. Hasan and G. Williams (eds.) *Literacy in Society*. London: Longman (Language and Social Life). 124–71.

Martin, J. R. (1999). Grace: the logogenesis of freedom. *Discourse Studies* 1 (1): 31–58.

Martin, J. R. (2001). Fair trade: negotiating meaning in multimodal texts. In *The Semiotics of Writing: Transdisciplinary Perspectives on the Technology of Writing*, P. Coppock (ed.). Brepols (Semiotic and Cognitive Studies X). 311–38.

Martin, J. R. (2008). Making history: grammar for explanation. In J. R. Martin and R. Wodak (eds) *Re/reading the Past: Critical and Functional Perspectives on Discourses of History*. Amsterdam: Benjamins. 19–57.

Martin, J. R. (2004a). Mourning – how we get aligned. *Discourse and Society* 15.2/3 (Special Issue on 'Discourse around 9/11'). 321–44.

Martin, J. R. (2004b). Sense and sensibility: texturing evaluation. In *Language, Education and Discourse: Functional Approaches*, J. Foley (ed.). London: Continuum. 270–304.

Martin, J. R. and Peters, P. (1985). On the analysis of exposition. In *Discourse on Discourse: Workshop Reports from the Macquarie Workshop on Discourse Analysis*, R. Hasan (ed.). Applied Linguistics Association of Australia (Occasional Papers 7) 1985. 61–92.

Martin, J. R. and Plum, G. (1997). Construing experience: some story genres. In G. W. Bamberg (ed.) *Oral Versions of Personal Experience: Three Decades of Narrative Analysis.* Special Issue of *Journal of Narrative and Life History* 7: 299–308.

Martin, J. R. and Rose, D. (2003). *Working with Discourse: Meaning beyond the Clause*. London: Continuum.

Martin, J. R. and Rose, D. (2008). *Genre Relations: Mapping Culture.* London: Equinox.

Martin, J. R. and White, P. R. R. (2005). *The Language of Evaluation: Appraisal in English.* London: Palgrave.

Martin, J. R. and Wodak, R. (eds.) (2004). *Re/reading the Past: Critical and Functional Perspectives on Discourses of History.* Amsterdam: Benjamins.

Read, P. (2000). *Belonging: Australians, Place and Aboriginal Ownership.* Cambridge: Cambridge University Press.

Toolan, M. J. (1988). *Narrative: A Critical Linguistic Introduction.* London: Routledge (Interface Series).

Index of Terms

abstraction 72, 75, 78, 84, 87,
110–11, 258
academic discourse 214–31
activity sequence 260, 263
Actor 15–16, 19, 97
adjective 179
adjunct 22, 29, 31, 66, 71, 166,
192, 239, 240
    attitudinal adjunct 85
    Circumstantial Adjunct 13, 30,
        32, 51, 54, 57, 66, 115, 156,
        163
    comment Adjunct 46
    conjunctive Adjunct 116, 120,
        122, 130, 147
      desirability adjunct 86
    initial Adjunct 46
    interpersonal adjunct 36
    Modal Adjunct 167, 46, 86,
        87, 115, 116, 117, 129, 239
    style adjunct 85, 86, 87
    thematic adjunct 86
    thematic interpersonal Adjunct
      35
adversarial interview 126, 137–38
advertisement 33, 34, 199, 202
agent 77–8, 81, 85, 88, 133, 179,
265–7
Allport, G. 236, 250
alternative 53, 70, 82, 152, 167,
198
ancillary 136
André, R. 236, 250
Appraisal Theory 215, 217, 248-71,
273
    Affect 217, 267, 271–3, 278
    Appreciation 217, 224–5, 228
    Attitude 5, 15, 18, 74, 87, 131,
      166, 168, 192, 215, 217–29,

      239, 259, 269, 273, 276,
      279
    concession 279
    Engagement 95, 151–2, 154,
      166, 215, 219, 221, 278–9
    Focus 220, 225
    Force 220, 268
    Graduation 5, 217, 220-221,
      224, 226, 228, 268, 273
    heterogloss 278
    inscribed attitude 267, 268
    judgement 36, 96, 103, 145,
      217, 225, 227, 238, 267–8,
      271, 277–8
    monogloss 279
    solidarity 266, 279
argument 3–4,14, 17, 49, 52, 54,
57–8, 62, 66, 73, 84, 87, 98–9,
112, 121–2, 139, 146, 189, 203,
208, 214–32, 278
Armani, J. 193, 205, 210, 214
attitudinal 49, 85–6, 212, 222–3,
231
authorial voice 166
axis 256

Bäcklund, I. 9, 42
Bamberg, G. 266, 282, 283, 284
Banks, D. 42, 44, 218, 231
Bargiela-Chappini, F. 170, 235, 238,
250
Barthes, R. 197, 214
Bazerman, C. 87, 89, 90
Becher, T. 89, 90
Berry, M. 9, 42, 57, 67, 122, 123,
152, 170, 177, 190, 217, 231
Bilbow, G. 235, 250
Bloch, B. 40, 42
Bloor, T. 70, 73, 91